Women in Prehistory

Oklahoma Series in Classical Culture

A Cycladic figurine of
the Neolithic period,
from Naxos. Oxford,
Ashmolean Museum.

WOMEN
IN
Prehistory

by
Margaret Ehrenberg

University of Oklahoma Press
Norman and London

ACKNOWLEDGEMENTS

I would like to express my gratitude to all the friends and
colleagues, whether specifically acknowledged or not, who
have helped me throughout the evolution of this book; no one
but myself is responsible for any errors which remain. In
particular I wish to thank the following: Tom Forrest of the
University of North Carolina at Charlotte, whose Sociology of
Sex Roles course, which I attended in 1984 while on a teaching
exchange, inspired my interest in the archaeology of women
and gender roles; my archaeological colleagues who offered
advice and comments from their different perspectives –
Jennifer Price of the University of Leeds, Janet Levy of the
University of North Carolina at Charlotte, and especially
Catherine Johns of the British Museum, without whose
encouragement I would not have begun to write the book; a
number of specialists in various fields from whom I sought
advice on their particular interests, including Harold
Mattingly, formerly of the University of Leeds, on the classical
texts referring to Iron Age Europe, Lesley Fitton of the British
Museum, on the Minoans, and Andrew Sherratt of the
Ashmolean Museum, Oxford, on the Later Neolithic and other
aspects; Erica Mattingly, Sue Hardman and particularly Ingrid
Lawrie for reading, checking and questioning the manuscript
in various draft stages; the individuals and museums who have
provided photographs; the Audio-Visual Service and the Inter-
Library Loan Service, University of Leeds; and finally Teresa
Francis of British Museum Publications, for her help and
patience.

$27.85 HW 5-23-90 (P.W.)

Contents

Introduction   *page* 7

1 The Search for Prehistoric Woman   10
Anthropological evidence   15
The behaviour of other animals and primates   20
Later documentary sources   21
Archaeological evidence   23

2 The Earliest Communities   38
The role of women in human evolution   41
Women in modern and Palaeolithic foraging societies   50
Matriarchy, patriarchy or equality   63
Mother goddesses or Venus figurines?   66

3 The First Farmers   77
The discovery of agriculture   77
The expansion of agricultural communities   90
The secondary products revolution   99

4 The Bronze Age   108
Was Minoan Crete a matriarchy?   109
Burials, grave goods and wealth in north-west Europe   118
A trade in women?   136
Rock art in the Alps and Scandinavia   139

continued

Contents *continued*

5 The Celtic Iron Age *page* 142

Domestic organisation in Iron Age Britain 143

Decoration on Hallstatt pottery and bronze vessels 147

Literary sources 151

Prophets and priestesses 157

Descent and marriage patterns 157

Women in war 162

Tribal chiefs and commanders in battle 164

6 Conclusions 171

Glossary 175

Notes 177

Bibliography 182

Index 188

Introduction

This book has been written for two distinct, though I hope increasingly overlapping, groups of readers. As an archaeologist I am writing for everyone interested in women's past; as a feminist I am writing for archaeologists, especially those who do not seem to have contemplated that 'Stone Age Woman' lived alongside 'Stone Age Man'.

I have reconsidered a range of archaeological evidence in order to see what light it can throw on the lives, social roles and status of women in prehistoric Europe, and have two aims in presenting it here. Firstly, I hope to explain something of how archaeology works to readers whose primary interest is in women of other times and places. Many recent studies of women's history and of the origins of their present roles and status in the Western world begin with a consideration of the distant or prehistoric past, but all too often their authors lack specialised knowledge of the nature, limitations and potential use of archaeological evidence. This is not their fault, but that of archaeologists who, with rare exceptions, have not tackled the issues raised by feminist scholars which lie within their domain. I also hope to convey something of the fascination and the challenge of interpreting archaeological evidence in these terms. It is therefore essential to begin by describing the methods, scope and limitations of archaeology where they are relevant to various themes which will be explored. Many people think of archaeology as consisting solely of digging holes in the ground, perhaps searching for buried treasure; others may have visited an excavation but remain unaware of how interpretations are reached from the evidence uncovered there. In order to show how archaeology can shed light on the lives of women in prehistory, it will be necessary to explain many aspects of modern archaeological methodology, including, for example, aspects of environmental archaeology and palaeo-osteology. As these techniques are relevant to almost all fields of archaeology, their consideration should be of interest to everyone wishing to understand the way in which prehistorians and archaeologists work.

But this book is also intended for fellow prehistorians and archaeologists who have not yet considered the application of feminist theory to archaeology. Why do prehistorians need to know about women in the past? Within the context of the topics studied under the general heading of theoretical archaeology, the lack of research into women's roles and status appears as almost an accidental oversight, except when it is seen as part of the general invisibility of women in nearly all academic disciplines. In the last decade archaeologists have not hesitated to examine topics such as power and belief systems, which to a previous generation of scholars would not have seemed either possible or proper subjects for archaeological investigation. No archaeologist would pretend that it is easy to study these areas, in which emphasis is placed on constructing theoretical models which can be tested against archaeological evidence. These models often have their roots in a range of related disciplines, such as anthropology, sociology and geography. On the other hand, some of the best recent archaeological work, on topics such as diet and exchange, involves the detailed examination of evidence from new excavations, or the reworking of previously discovered material, and often uses techniques borrowed from the physical and biological sciences. From one or both of these roots any and every aspect of prehistoric life and behaviour is being studied, working hypotheses constructed and proof sought, even if not always satisfactorily discovered. The one omission, it seems (with a few important exceptions, which will be drawn together here) is the nature of gender roles and relations, a topic of key importance to life today. To begin with the supposition that this topic may have been important in the past, and is therefore worthy of study, is surely not unreasonable. Progress in working other, previously intractable, areas suggests it should be possible.

It took me a long time to appreciate the need to work on the topic of women in prehistory. My own initial academic training was in a very traditional archaeology department, where great emphasis was placed on rigorous evaluation of evidence and a full awareness of the limits of archaeological inference; theory and the then 'new archaeology' were viewed with some suspicion. If I had asked, as a student, what women were doing while Neolithic Man was busy making flint arrowheads or Iron Age Man building elaborate hillforts, my question would have been considered impertinent or frivolous. Certainly I should have been told that such a question was not susceptible of archaeological investigation. Although I was always interested in theoretical archaeology and concerned with the position of women in our own society, it was a long time before I realised that the study of women in past societies, and in particular in prehistory, was, or could be, a subject for serious academic study. I did not see that the logical extension of the growing field of women's history into my own specialism of prehistory could produce women's prehistory, nor that my increasingly careful use of non-sexist language when referring to people in prehistory was insufficient to balance the decades of research biased towards probable male activities in the past.

In 1984 I exchanged my teaching post in the archaeology department of an English university for a similar post in the United States, where archaeology was taught within the department of Sociology and Anthropology, and I was there required to teach introductory anthropology. At the same time, I attended a class called 'The Sociology of Sex Roles'. This, combined with my anthropology teaching and discussions with my new colleagues, made me aware of the widespread interest in women in other cultures, past and present. In the United States these subjects were gradually becoming academically respectable, though this had not been without a good deal of tension and fighting by pioneering women in each field, mainly in the 1970s. Women had lost tenure at their universities because their books had not been judged, by their male colleagues, to be on subjects as worthy of study as other traditional male-orientated fields.[1] Reading in these fields, and thinking about my own discipline, I recalled few instances of discussion about women in the European literature on prehistory with which I was familiar, and no specific studies. Even in America, a few articles on human evolution and a smattering of articles on other aspects seemed to be the limit of interest in women in the archaeological record. Since then a number of articles have started to rectify that situation.

On my return to Britain I became increasingly interested in the possibilities of studying the roles and position of women from the archaeological record, and more specifically in European prehistory. This book, then, is an attempt to pursue some of these possibilities. The range of topics which could be covered by the title is vast, so it has been necessary to be selective, in order even to attempt to do justice to those areas and problems which I have chosen to consider. Its geographical scope has been limited to the Old World. However, the section on methodology is applicable to any part of the world at any period, and the survey which follows it extends where necessary beyond Europe, in particular in the discussions of the Palaeolithic (Chapter 2) and the origins of agriculture (Chapter 3).

The choice of topics was not without problems. I have not attempted to deal with every reference to women in the vast archaeological literature, and have refrained from commenting on the many sexist assumptions which it contains. Criticism of some equally dubious feminist literature, which is based on ignorant and undiscriminating use of archaeological evidence, is likewise outside the scope of my discussion. Nor have I mentioned many themes found in general text-books on European prehistory. This is not because I think they are unimportant, or that it would not be possible to draw some inferences about women in those areas: on the contrary, I hope other archaeologists may be stimulated by this volume to assess the contribution made by women to the site or culture they are studying. Although I have arranged my topics chronologically, and have sought to deal with some of the main issues of European prehistory, I have felt that it was more useful to treat some areas in depth than to attempt a more comprehensive, but necessarily more superficial, coverage.

I The Search for Prehistoric Woman

Prehistory holds a key to many of the questions uppermost in the minds of women interested in their present status in society, its origins and its future. Students of women's history can analyse the roles and position of women over the last few centuries from written accounts. We learn from these that the lives of most of our recent ancestors were not very different from our own, despite the growing appreciation of notable exceptions, the details of whose lives have been effectively suppressed by our patriarchal society.[1] But has it always been like this? And how can we know? The prehistoric period is by definition the time before the advent of written records, or history, which in north-west Europe more or less equates with the growth of the Roman empire, and we must rely mainly on the evidence of archaeology – the study of physical remains which were left for the most part incidentally, and which have survived through two millennia or more.

Although archaeology has its limitations, it also has important advantages over written records as a source of information about the past. If properly studied, most aspects of life may, directly or indirectly, be found to leave some slight physical traces. Archaeological evidence has been described as 'unconscious', in the sense that the people who made the objects, built the structures and discarded the rubbish which make it up, did so without the conscious knowledge that anyone in the future would 'read' or study it.[2] Thus archaeology should provide information about the behaviour of the whole of the society being studied, without any external sexual bias. This contrasts, for example, with the deliberate suppression of much literature written by women, because it was deemed unimportant in a male-dominated society. However, this does not mean that biases which existed within a society need go unnoticed. The choice of design of artefacts, buildings and other evidence of the culture will accord with what is deemed appropriate by that society or sub-group. So, to take a simple example, if women and men wear different clothes, this is a decision made by the society, albeit at a subconscious level, and suggests that women and men are perceived as different sub-groups.

Another problem faced by women's historians is that most early written records were written by men and about unusual events rather than about everyday lifestyles, and they usually refer to the lives of a small number of wealthy or exceptional people, few of whom were women. The everyday lives of the majority of women were never considered worth describing. By contrast, this is not so true of much archaeological evidence. The settlement sites with their houses and the evidence they provide for the society's economy may represent a complete cross-section of a community, and certainly reflect everyday life, rather than the one-off events described in most later written records. A whole community may be buried in a particular cemetery, and the everyday tools used by the group may survive. It is true that in some communities certain special people may have had more material possessions, or lived in houses built more substantially than those of poorer people. These are more likely to be discovered by archaeological excavation. Wealthier people may be buried with more elaborate grave goods, perhaps in more lasting graves. But the contrast between evidence for the rich and the poor, between special events and everyday life, is not nearly as marked as with historical evidence, and in many cases we are able to study the lives of the majority of a population. So, unlike the history of kings and queens, archaeology tells the prehistory of all women and men.

The degree of social and political power held by women in prehistoric societies is a subject to which little attention has as yet been paid by archaeologists, although archaeological evidence may be able to provide indications of wealth and status, and hence of the degree of social stratification within a society. The origin of social hierarchies is a key topic within current archaeology, and, together with analysis of the position of women within the system, it also plays a major part in feminist theories. This is clearly a complex issue: why do societies allow some individuals to become more influential, or hold more status than others? How is status gained? Does it come from the possession of individual wealth, or from skill in a particular field? Need everyone of high status in a society have acquired it in the same way? For example, could some individuals acquire status from skill in food production, others from trading, or perhaps ritual or religious specialisation? And what about bringing up children? Why, in modern Western societies, are women usually of lower status than men of the same social background? What is the social relationship between a rich woman and a poor man, and between a rich woman and a rich man? These are crucial questions, since, as we shall see, the existence of a few powerful women, perhaps as leaders of a society, does not necessarily mean that women in general had status above men in general. But these questions presuppose a class-based society. Were there ever any societies which were classless, where everyone had equal access to food and material possessions, and where everyone, woman or man, was considered to be of equal importance? Archaeology can, I think, help to answer these questions, as we shall see in the following chapters.

One aspect of this issue which needs to be addressed here is the much-debated question of the existence of matriarchal societies, where women

held as much power as men do within patriarchal societies. Although there seem to be few, if any, examples of true matriarchies now or in the recent past, the possibility that they existed in the prehistoric period must be carefully considered. By the time of the earliest written records of classical Europe – the advent of history – patriarchal societies held sway. A burning question for many women is whether it has always been like that. So when or where did male-dominated societies originate? And how and why did men begin to dominate women? Have women always been consigned to the domestic role? Was 'housework' always the lowest-status occupation? In the nineteenth century, the influential writers Bachofen, Morgan and Engels put forward the theory that matriarchal societies existed in the earliest phases of prehistory, and that these were later overturned by the patriarchal societies which were universal by the time of written records. This model was based partly on classical mythology, partly on nineteenth-century anthropology: no archaeological data were then, or subsequently, seriously examined for substantiating evidence. Not surprisingly, in view of its potential importance to women's status, and to support arguments surrounding ideas for contemporary and future society, many feminists have sought to re-examine this theory of matriarchy, and some anthropologists have joined in the debate. Archaeologists have not, so far, become involved, and yet if questions such as this can be resolved at all, the answers must surely lie within the scope of their discipline.

So how can prehistorians try to answer these and numerous other questions about life and society in the distant past? Archaeological evidence comes mainly from careful excavation of the surviving remains of settlements, burials and other sites where people have spent some time and disturbed the ground or left debris. But it is a long step from a house being occupied to its providing archaeological evidence of the way of life of its occupants. For instance, why was the house abandoned? If it burnt down, was flooded or inundated with sand, the possessions of the owners may have been left inside. But usually when people move house, they take their portable property with them. We cannot normally expect them to leave anything other than unwanted debris. Over the course of years and centuries most of this debris will decay, especially organic materials such as wooden furniture, tools and utensils, cloth and basketry, and most food remains. Even these will usually be subject to disturbance, for example by later ploughing, building and the activities of burrowing animals. So only the exceptional site can be expected to survive. It then needs to be discovered, which often happens by accident. However, some sites are found by deliberate survey, when archaeologists look for clues on the ground or in changes in the growth of crops where they are planted over richer, disturbed soil, or for slight humps and bumps which are often best seen from overhead, in a low-flying aeroplane. The time and cost of modern excavation, together with all the scientific analysis necessary to gain a full understanding of the site, means that only a small proportion of known sites can be excavated. Excavation itself is a skilled business, in which archaeologists must notice and record every slight change in the colour and texture of the soil, which may be the only trace of building foundations or the activities that once took place in it, and they must carefully record and lift the remains of artefacts used there. Post-excavation work usually takes far longer than the excavation itself. This includes the study of the various data recorded on the site: samples of soils are analysed for traces of seeds and other minute remains, and the artefacts are researched by specialists. Though burials and other deliberate deposits will normally have been placed carefully in the ground, they too are not immune from the processes of decay and disturbance. So archaeology will only ever provide a minute fraction of the information we could want to obtain about a past society. How much will depend on the quality and quantity of excavation, but more significantly on the way the raw data from excavations is interpreted.[3]

Archaeological evidence in itself tells us little. It needs to be interpreted. All archaeologists would agree with that, but how far that interpretation can go and on what basis it should be made, is the subject of considerable controversy. Some argue that archaeology should limit itself to the most fundamental matters like the date of a site or artefact, its basic function and how it was made, and perhaps expand from there to consider its implications for the economy of the society responsible for its creation. Since the 1960s more and more archaeologists have been taking the opposite view, maintaining that the challenge of the subject lies in using the available data to give the most likely answer to any question that may be asked about a past society. Most, perhaps, would take a middle course, attempting to put forward theories about some aspects of the social, political and possibly the religious life of the society, while remaining sceptical about the possibility of using archaeology to draw inferences about certain other aspects.[4] The life of women in societies now represented only by archaeological evidence is an excellent example of a subject which would have seemed unknowable to a past generation of archaeologists, but should present a valid challenge within the context of today's 'theoretical' archaeology.[5] The difficulty of interpretation may partially explain why the study of this subject has been attempted only rarely, and then only in respect of one particular society or problem. It is also extremely important to be constantly aware that nearly every idea put forward by archaeologists is theory or hypothesis, rather than firm fact. Good archaeology is selecting the theory which best fits all the available evidence and is not contradicted by any relevant data which may, or may perhaps not, be known to the archaeologist in question. Of course, new data may subsequently come to light and either refute a previously perfectly sound theory or strengthen one which was based on comparatively little evidence. So the ideas which I will put forward here, about how women lived in prehistoric Europe, should and will be judged on how well they fit the often sparse archaeological evidence.

And how are these theories formed? That too is a controversial point amongst archaeologists. Traditionally, theories were supposed to emerge empirically from the evidence, and be apparent to anyone sufficiently familiar with the facts. But inevitably the range of possibilities will be limited, or at least coloured, by the experience of the archaeologist. Many theories about prehistoric societies began to develop in the nineteenth or early twentieth century, and if we examine many well-established archaeological assumptions, we can discern the biases of scholars educated in the classics and history, from a middle- or upper-class élite and certainly a male-dominated background. No one would have questioned whether men, rather than women, were the hunters, or whether some men would have had more wealth or power than others. In seeking to know how a prehistoric society operated, we first need a broad understanding of how societies operate in general, and what range of variation might be conceivable. Many modern archaeological theorists base their hypotheses on one or other of the many current sociological doctrines, such as Marxism, structuralism or materialism, and consider how a particular behaviour pattern might show up in the archaeological record. Others, aware of the limited number of such patterns manifested in modern Western society – which is almost invariably that best known to the archaeologist and also most frequently considered by sociologists – look for inspiration to the rest of the world, and in particular to the cultures studied by social anthropologists.

But even anthropology is limited in the range of models it can provide. For instance, anthropologists studying women in other cultures around the world today show us a wide range of patterns of interaction between women and men, and in the tasks and roles usually allocated to each sex. But it cannot be assumed that the lives of women in prehistory were identical to those of other cultures today or in the more recent past. No two societies are identical in all aspects of their social, economic, political or religious behaviour; their material culture (such as the houses they build, tools they use and art and design they create) will be different from anyone else's. Broad patterns certainly exist, both within regions of the world and within similar subsistence economies, and this recurrence will be used as a basis for much of the discussion throughout this book. Where archaeological evidence indicates similarities with present-day societies, these may be acknowledged, but equally, where it does not, we must be prepared to consider that behaviour patterns may have existed in the past which are quite unlike those found today. Rather than using ethnographic data to give definitive guidelines for understanding how women lived in the past, we may be prompted by the variety of patterns and behaviour that they show to grow more curious about our own ancestors in the distant past.

The use of anthropological evidence by archaeologists is discussed in the following section, before a consideration of the various types of direct archaeological data which are available to the prehistorian.

Anthropological evidence

One of the ways in which archaeologists can construct hypotheses about life in prehistoric societies is by looking at present-day societies with traditional lifestyles based on economies and technologies much simpler than those of the Western world. Such lifestyles may resemble those of the past more closely than most of our own do. These societies are studied principally by ethnographers, who look at all aspects of a single society in depth, and by social anthropologists, who are interested in how a particular aspect of social behaviour varies between different societies and types of society. The use of ethnographic and anthropological data by archaeologists is controversial.[6] Initially it involved simple comparisons of artefacts discovered in prehistoric contexts with objects used by one or more groups elsewhere in the world today. An archaeological artefact which resembled one used by a present-day society was assumed to have had a similar function, and other implications about the archaeological society were then construed on the basis of what was known about the present-day one. Such an approach holds many pitfalls and must be used with great caution. It is easy to note a few similarities between an archaeological culture, such as the Ice Age inhabitants of Europe, and a single ethnographic example, such as the Inuit (Eskimos), and assume that the two societies had other things in common as well. It is far better to look for more generalised and recurring patterns amongst anthropological cases, as more recent studies have done, and to include as many criteria as possible in the comparisons. If all, or nearly all, known societies with a similar economic and technological base and living in a similar type of environment as a past society share a certain form of social organisation, it seems reasonable to take this as a working model for the archaeological case. However, it is important also to remember that the societies and people studied by anthropologists have had just as long to evolve as people in the Western world, and even if the technology or subsistence base of these societies seems to us to be rather simple, their social and religious behaviour may be very complex.

The chief problem with using ethnographic parallels in this way, even with the greatest caution, is the very real possibility that no societies either today or in the recent past share social, political or religious patterns with some of those in the distant past, even if they do share superficial technological and economic features. Supporters of this view argue that to assume they do, or even might, is to deprive archaeological research of its own goals and to make it a sub-field of, and dependent on, anthropology. In the USA, archaeology is treated as just that, and in my view this is not unreasonable. Both disciplines are seeking to learn about the behaviour and lifestyles of people in other societies: those studied by archaeologists just happen to be in the past. The key difference lies in the methodologies involved. A model derived from anthropology still has to be rigorously tested against archaeological data, and the possibility that a past society

was totally different from anything in existence today must certainly be considered if the data warrants it. However, in other cases some behaviour patterns recur so regularly that to ignore them without good reason seems just as perverse. I have therefore attempted to use all the available direct archaeological evidence as a basis for a hypothesis, but have not hesitated to draw heavily on anthropological data in considering patterns of behaviour with regard to gender roles and the status of women when this helps to complete the picture of women's lives at particular periods and places in the prehistoric past.

Anthropological evidence is of course much fuller than archaeological evidence. An anthropologist will ideally live with a particular group of people for a full year or more, learn the language, and get to know the people and gain their confidence. Behaviour patterns can be observed, and

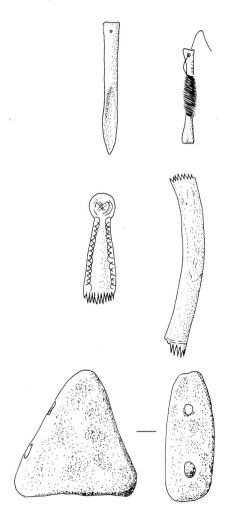

1 (*left*) A traditional craft: a Navaho Indian woman weaving a rug.

2 Typical archaeological evidence for the same activity: bone needles or shuttles, bone weaving combs for pushing down the weft threads, and loomweights of baked clay.

17

members of the group can be asked to explain why they do things in a particular way. A large and varied body of material can thus be collected, although nowadays most anthropologists concentrate on a single aspect of behaviour. However, even here bias may creep in: on the one hand, the people being studied may unwittingly or deliberately withhold information; on the other, and probably more frequently, the anthropologist may only observe and record those aspects of behaviour which concern him or her, even though these are not necessarily central to the life of the group. Unfortunately, the sphere in which this seems most commonly to occur is precisely that which concerns us here, namely the lives of women.

Although women, including some very well-known names, have been anthropologists, most anthropologists, especially before the 1960s, have been male. Whether deliberately or as the unconscious result of coming from a male-dominated society and academic background, they have generally been concerned principally with male activities, and have failed to observe female tasks and behaviour. Furthermore, all the societies that can be studied today have had some contact, however minimal, with the 'modern' world, and this may have caused some changes in their behaviour. For example, during the eighteenth or nineteenth century, a Western, and almost certainly male, explorer, missionary or anthropologist finding himself in an African village would have expected to meet and talk to the male inhabitants. After a few encounters, whatever the pre-existing situation, the men would have acted as spokespersons. They would have acquired Western trinkets, which, as novelties, would almost certainly have been highly regarded, thereby enhancing their own status. After perhaps a century or so of infrequent contacts of this kind, modern anthropologists, however objective their own observations, will find native men and women behaving in patterns remarkably reflective of Western culture. If a society has been influenced by the attitudes of missionaries, or by early nation-state government 'aid', Western gender roles are even more likely to be in evidence. Moreover, the earliest Western accounts of traditional societies were usually written by men, who only described topics of interest to themselves, or those activities which they were allowed to witness. Women of the society in question may not have wished to explain their behaviour to men of their own group, let alone outsiders, and may have performed tasks and rituals away from their sight. Thus, important women-only or women-dominated activities may never have been recorded, and in some cases may have ceased to be practised as a result of direct or indirect Western pressure. Any comparisons between women's roles and status in modern or very recent societies and their possible position in prehistory must therefore be treated with very great caution.[7]

Since the early 1970s an increasing number of women have been involved in anthropological fieldwork, and American anthropologists especially have studied aspects of the lives of women and gender relationships in traditional societies. The anthropology of women is now a well-accepted subject-area within the discipline, and early records of traditional societies have been reanalysed to pick out fleeting references to the lives of women.[8]

An additional problem faced by an archaeologist wishing to make use of anthropological conclusions is that most recent anthropological fieldwork has not concerned itself with the physical traces left by aspects of social behaviour. It is thus not possible for archaeologists to discover what material evidence a particular set of behavioural patterns might leave behind by studying anthropological accounts alone. The field of 'ethno-archaeology' has therefore been developed by archaeologists who themselves carry out fieldwork in ethnographic contexts to study just such problems.[9] An ethnoarchaeological study might, for example, look at the debris left by a modern forager band after a few nights' stay at one camp or homebase. The nature of the debris and its distribution can be analysed to see what archaeological pattern would be left after most of the organic waste had decomposed.

One of the very few studies dealing with the problem of how past gender roles can be inferred from archaeological evidence adopts this ethnoarchaeological approach. Using a method she calls Male/Female Task Differentiation, Janet Spector[10] argues that studying gender differentiation in archaeological contexts necessitates prior background work in ethnographic contexts, detailing the tasks performed by women and men, the areas within the settlement used for each activity, the equipment and the value given to the task. If this information is viewed against a full picture of a society, to ensure that it provides an appropriate model for comparison with a particular archaeological context, it should be possible to suggest far more detail about gender roles in prehistory than has hitherto been possible.

As an example, Spector has reanalysed accounts of the Hidatsa Indians of the Great Plains of North America. Although the group is no longer extant, it was studied in detail in the early twentieth century; informants described its way of life in the mid-nineteenth century, when the people were sedentary hoe agriculturalists living in 'earth lodge' villages. The accounts are sufficiently detailed to allow the identification of at least some of the tasks performed by women and men respectively, the time of year these tasks were carried out, where in the village they took place and the materials and equipment associated with them. For example, Hidatsa women procured and processed all food resources, with the exception of killing and butchering animals and growing and processing tobacco, which were male tasks. There were also important differences in the locations in which male and female activities took place. Other tasks which must obviously have been performed, such as child-rearing, are not mentioned in the early accounts; this highlights the need for archaeologists interested in this type of approach to carry out their own fieldwork among present-day peoples. However, as Spector herself admits, it is clearly not feasible for any one person to study more than a few groups, and the findings then have to be compared with the evidence of different archaeological cases, so it will be a long time before this promising method produces substantial results.

The behaviour of other animals and primates

Another area of research which can be of use to anthropologists and archaeologists investigating human behaviour is the comparative study of other animals, especially the primates, whose physiology most closely resembles our own. Important research of this kind includes observing the animals, such as chimpanzees and gorillas, in their native habitat over a long period of time, and without any human interference, and has been carried out by a number of scholars, such as Jane Goodall in Kombe, Tanzania, and the late Dian Fossey in Rwanda.[11] Differences in the behaviour of males and females, unencumbered by millennia of human cultural conditioning, have important implications for natural or genetic behavioural differences between the sexes in humans, and provide a particularly useful basis on which to build hypotheses concerning aspects of the earliest human behaviour such as the significance of motherhood or the origins of tool-using (Fig. 8). Recent detailed studies of the behaviour of other animals have also proved useful in research aimed at distinguishing natural sexual differences in behaviour from learnt gender behaviour in humans. Many traits previously thought to be unique to humans are now known to be common throughout much of the animal world. Group hunting and co-operation are found, for example, amongst wolves and lions; tool-using is seen in thrushes, which break open the shell of a snail by hitting it on a stone; and male birds of several species help the female to feed the young while they are still in the nest. Primate behaviour studies are particularly relevant to the earliest stages of human evolution and are discussed in more detail in Chapter 2.

Later documentary sources

By definition, the study of prehistory is concerned with the period in the human past before history, or in other words before the advent of any written records. The term is usually applied separately to each area of the world, referring to the period before the use of writing in that particular area. Even within Europe writing developed in different areas at different times, and in many parts of the continent written records are scarce until the medieval period. Some of the earliest inscriptions or evidence of writing remain undeciphered or illegible to modern scholars. Moreover, most of the earliest written records which can be interpreted list rulers or kings, commemorate battles or the erection of buildings, or name the owner or maker of the object on which the inscription is found, rather than describing lifestyles or behaviour. In many areas a number of intermediate stages may be recognised, which fall between the totally prehistoric, where there are no records at all, and the fully historic, where a fairly detailed picture can be built up from written records alone. Let us take Britain as an example. Although it is just conceivable that there was writing on perishable material which has not survived, as far as we know nothing was written in Britain in any form before inscriptions on coins in the first century BC, and even these are restricted to a few characters, usually the initial letters of names of people and tribes. But in Egypt and Mesopotamia writing had been practised since about 3000 BC, and in Greece the alphabet was first used about 700 BC. Greek and Roman writers and travellers such as Posidonius and Strabo had described some aspects of Britain from the second century BC; the most notable classical writer on Britain was probably Julius Caesar in the first century BC. So although the people of Iron Age Britain did not themselves write, a few descriptions do exist written by foreigners.

Under the Roman empire the way of life of the inhabitants of Europe would have continued very much as before, but they would have been in closer contact with people who could write. Some Romans living in the provinces have left descriptions of the lifestyles of people who lived there before the Roman conquest. Tacitus' accounts of Germanic tribes in *Agricola* and *Germania* are good examples. If it can be assumed that the key aspects of life had not altered significantly, descriptions like these may shed light on prehistoric, as well as slightly later, times. However, when evaluating them, the circumstances in which they were written must be borne in mind. In many cases it is unlikely that the author had ever visited the area himself or witnessed the events or behaviour he was describing. For example, Caesar's main concern was to report on his battles with the inhabitants of Gaul (modern France) and his attempted invasion of Britain to influential people in Rome. It was in his interest to make his enemies seem as fierce as possible, yet he would hardly have witnessed their behaviour off the battlefield, but would have relied on rumour and the reports of informers. On the other hand, even rumour usually has a grain of truth in it, however garbled it has become in the telling. So an archaeologist or social historian must study most early sources critically, and balance the value of the information they provide with the possibility that it may be confused or sometimes even positively incorrect.

Later sources sometimes refer back to earlier periods, and traditions may have been passed on orally before being written down. Again it is necessary to evaluate the reliability of such sources. From the early medieval period, around the eighth century AD onwards, documentary accounts become more frequent. For example, there is a large body of documents including laws, myths and legends from the Celtic western seaboard of Europe, particularly Ireland, which originated as part of a larger oral tradition which was not written down until the early Middle Ages; by that time they had become augmented and distorted by the adoption of Christianity and by the many other changes which divided the medieval from the prehistoric world. Ireland itself was never incorporated within the Roman empire, and social changes there may have been less marked than in Britain during that period. There are many clear indications that the Irish sagas refer to a prehistoric time of pagan tribal warfare, though it is usually uncertain precisely when the remembered events took place, and details which are crucial if they are to be used as historical sources may have become adapted to suit the cultural expectations of the later listener or reader. This may be particularly true of incidental detail, which is easily modified without altering the essential aspects of the story but which tells us most about social patterns and behaviour. If they are to be used to throw light on prehistoric life, therefore, these post-Roman Celtic sources must be used with considerable discretion. It would, however, be foolish to discount their evidence altogether, since they are unique in giving us at least a hint of the Celts' own view of the world, rather than a picture of pagan Celtic society from a classical standpoint.[12]

In all these sources references to women are comparatively rare, though probably not as uncommon as many scholars would at first admit. Careful analysis, with a view to discovering what they can tell us about the lives of women, can certainly be very rewarding, and an attempt to use some of the sources is made in Chapter 5 on Iron Age Europe.

The relevance and potential use of mythology as a source of information about an earlier period is particularly problematic. Many feminist writers, especially, have sought to use myths of a mother goddess to suggest that at some time in the past women played a much more important role in society, or even as supposed evidence for the existence of matriarchies.

Goddesses form part of the mythology of many societies, including those of the Mediterranean civilisations and of the Northern European traditions. Many, such as the Greek goddess Demeter, have special responsibility for obviously female aspects of life such as fertility, first of humans and animals and then of plants and especially crops, but others, such as the Celtic goddess Mórrígan[13] and the Roman goddess Minerva, are goddesses of war and other areas which are usually male-identified within the society itself. A key question is how a belief in these female deities came about. Does it relate to a distant memory of women, or a particular woman, whose roles included overseeing war, for example? If an earth or mother goddess was worshipped, possibly as the most important deity in that society, did women once have high status? It may be useful to consider the distinction between myths and legends made by anthropologists, even if it then begs the question of whether a particular story or saga is a myth or a legend. While a legend may embody a past event, albeit in very altered form, a myth, among other functions, serves to explain some aspect of the natural or human world. For example, every society asks how the world came about, and has a myth which explains this in terms understandable to that society. So just as everyone knows that women alone give birth to children, it is not surprising that many societies will also explain that the earth and crops are born from a supernatural female being of some kind. This need not, however, have any implications for the roles of real women, other than the obvious one of childbearing, and still less for their status. It cannot even be taken as evidence that the society thought that giving birth to large numbers of children was particularly advantageous, but merely shows that the factual relationship has been observed! A deity may be worshipped or venerated for the qualities she or he is held to embody, but even this is not always so. Even if a goddess is held responsible for creating some aspect of the world, and myths about her are retold, perhaps illustrated by pictures or models, she may not be thought to play any active role in the day-to-day life of the actual society. Nor can myths be seen in any sense as history; as an explanation, they may go back many generations, though the details of a myth which is orally transmitted will change almost each time it is told. There is, therefore, no obvious correlation between the existence of goddesses and the roles and status of real women, and it is extremely dangerous to use mythology as a source of evidence for history.

Archaeological evidence

Archaeological evidence for the lives of women in the past falls into various categories. Probably the most obvious is that from burials, but settlement sites and prehistoric art may also provide much valuable information.

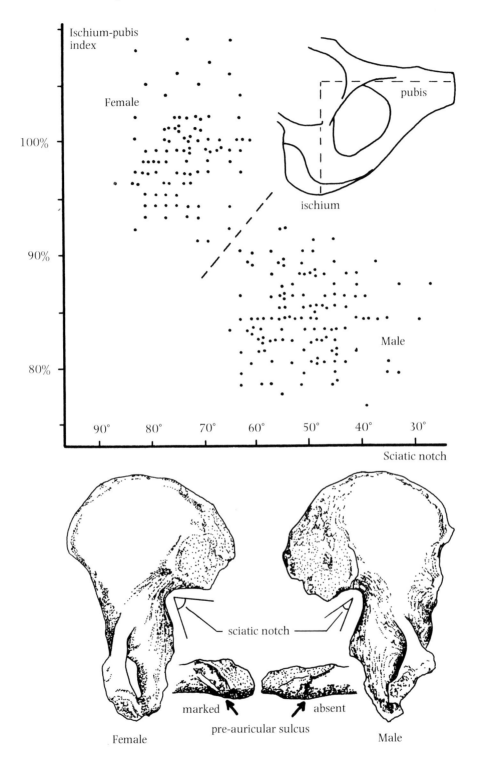

Ischium-pubis index

Female

100%

90%

80%

pubis

ischium

Male

90°   80°   70°   60°   50°   40°   30°

Sciatic notch

sciatic notch

marked   absent
pre-auricular sulcus

Female   Male

Burials, bones and grave goods

In burials where the skeletons or cremated remains of prehistoric women survive, adult women can usually be distinguished from adult men by looking at certain diagnostic bones, such as the skull and the pelvis. However, there is considerable overlap in the limits of shape and measurement of these features for each sex, which can make reliable sexing of skeletons difficult.[14] Studies of the bones themselves can also indicate the approximate age of death of the individual and sometimes the cause of death, as well as certain diseases she or he may have suffered from in life. The age of an individual at death may be estimated by studying various

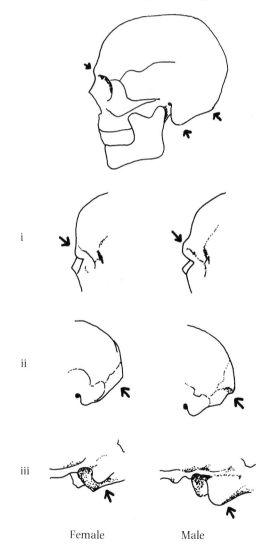

3 The diagnostic differences between female and male skeletons.
(*Left*) The range of variation found in two measurements of the pelvis, the proportion of the ischium-pubis index and the angle of the sciatic notch.
(*Right*) Three differences in skull shape:
i. the supra-orbital ridges,
ii. the nuchal crest, and
iii. the mastoid process.
After Brothwell, 1981.

Female   Male

anatomical features, including the degree of fusion of certain bones, especially in the skull, pelvis and long bones, and from the amount of wear or attrition on the teeth. Comparing the mortality patterns of women with those of men may suggest differences in the care given to each when ill, differences in health resulting from nutritional defects and benefits, and, in the case of children, possible differences in the treatment of girls and boys.

Damage to bones, such as breaks, or arrow or dagger wounds, might be seen to affect women and men with different frequency if, for example, one sex but not the other hunted or fought. Diseases such as osteo-arthritis, which are easily detectable in bones, may have affected women and men differently if they regularly carried out different tasks. A recent study[15] of the well-preserved skeletal remains of Canadian Inuit hunter-gatherers from the turn of the last century concentrated on identifying which parts of the body showed signs of bone and joint disease, especially osteo-arthritis, and whether they were more prevalent in women or men. There was enough ethnohistorical information about the people to know which activities were carried out by which sex. For example, women spent considerable time preparing leather and sewing skins for clothing: this seems frequently to have resulted in osteo-arthritis in the bones of the right hand, while softening skins with the teeth often led to tooth loss and osteo-arthritis in women's jaws. Men hunted with harpoons, which sometimes caused disease of the right shoulder and elbow; kayak paddling also resulted in distinctive wear of the bones. In a study of Neolithic skeletons from the Sahara,[16] it has been suggested that it is possible to distinguish the effects of frequent javelin throwing, wood cutting and archery by studying bone lesions or rough patches of growing bone which form where frequently used muscles or ligaments are attached to it. The incidence of different activities amongst different societies or between women and men may be distinguished, as well as the incidence of individual craft specialists within a population. This method clearly has great potential for looking at differences in gender roles: while it might be possible to relate some types of osteo-arthritis to specific activities, many activities may result in similar stress patterns – for instance, grinding corn, scrubbing floors or polishing stone tools may all cause 'tennis elbow' – particularly when the range of possible activities is not already defined by other information about the society, as it is in the first example above.

Although it may often happen that, for one reason or another, not all members of a community were buried together, in cases where it is likely that they were, a study of the whole cemetery may provide a wide range of population statistics. From these it is possible to calculate whether women generally outlived men, or vice versa, and to estimate the proportion of women who died in childbirth, as well as the infant mortality rate, e.g. Fig.

34. If the sample is sufficiently large, the number of children each woman would have borne can also be estimated.

Attitudes to the care of young children and babies are often reflected in infant mortality. In societies in which one sex or the other is considered to be more important or more valuable, deliberate or subconscious behaviour by the parents may affect the incidence of infant death in females or males. If, for instance, girls are more highly valued, the birth of a new female infant may lead to the neglect of an older brother, and so occasionally to his death. If this behaviour were regular within a society, we would expect to find more boys than girls in the cemetery (but a similar pattern might occur if dead female infants had such low status that they were not buried in the cemetery at all!). In extreme cases a preference for one sex over the other may give rise to preferential infanticide: in a cemetery this might be observed either in the number of infant burials of a single sex, or in an unnatural outnumbering of adults of one sex over the other. Again, however, caution needs to be exercised and other possibilities considered: for instance, death away from home may have been more common in one sex than the other, or women and men may have been given different burial rites.

In many societies, one way in which the status of individuals and the different value placed on women and men is reflected is in the quantity and quality of food they consumed. For example, where men are more highly valued than women they may be given a very high proportion of the meat or other protein available. Recent studies[17] have shown that analyses of skeletal remains can reveal some aspects of diet, particularly nutrient deficiencies. Infant and child mortality, in particular, may be caused directly or indirectly by malnutrition. Of course, in many cases, the community may not understand the cause of the disease or death, and may even resort to treatments or changes in diet which further aggravate the problem. If there is a shortage of milk or other foods, babies and children who are most valued will be given the most. Thus, if either girls or boys are particularly favoured, this may be revealed in different child death rates. Studies of tooth wear and pathological deformities of the bones caused by malnutrition, and chemical analyses of bones have also been used to find out, for example, whether women and men were fed or treated differently. Of the chemical analysis methods which are used, the measurement of the ratio of strontium to calcium in the bones seems to be the most promising.[18] Plants absorb strontium along with calcium, and when animals or humans eat plants these minerals are ingested too. However, the animal's body discriminates against the strontium, so that a smaller proportion of it becomes incorporated into the bones and body. If these animals are in turn eaten by other animals, for example humans eating meat, the strontium is again discriminated against. The proportion of strontium in the bones of people who have eaten a largely meat diet will therefore be considerably lower than in the bones of people who have eaten a mainly plant diet. This technique has been used to study changes in diet through time on a particular site, and comparing the findings with the quality and quantity of grave goods may indicate whether people thought to be 'rich' or of 'high status' on the basis of the grave goods ate more meat than other members of the community. A number of studies have also compared the amount of meat eaten by women and men within the same society. A difference in diet might either be related to the different types of agricultural work with which each sex was involved, or (on the assumption that meat-eating implies higher status) might indicate a difference in status between the sexes. Most of these studies have been carried out on prehistoric native American skeletons, and have routinely shown that women do have higher strontium/calcium ratios than men in the same communities, suggesting that they do indeed eat a smaller share of the meat available. However, this suggestion needs to be treated with caution, as it has also been shown that pregnancy and lactation alter strontium levels, and, especially in societies where most women would either be pregnant or breast-feeding throughout most of their adult lives, this fact must be taken into account. Although little analysis of this sort has yet been reported for European prehistoric data, and clearly the results need to be critically studied, the technique seems to be one of the most promising ways of studying differences in female and male work patterns and status.

Other techniques which might prove useful include carbon isotope analysis, which might be able to show if some members of a community were eating certain plants, including the leaves of plants which contain the C_3 form of carbon, while others ate grasses which contain the C_4 form.[19] Differential care and nutrition of female and male children might show up in radiographic analysis of bones, which can reveal transverse lines of increased bone density, known as Harris lines, reflecting periods of malnutrition during growth. A study of a prehistoric Californian population using this method showed that these lines were more common in modern Americans, and that women and men had identical line patterns. As males normally develop Harris lines more readily than females, it was suggested that in this community women were less well looked after than men.[20]

Wear on teeth can also be a very good indication of the type of diet to which an individual or community was accustomed, and may also sometimes give evidence of working at certain crafts. The greater the amount of abrasive material incorporated in the foodstuffs, the more wear will show on the teeth, and chewing different materials will result in recognisably different patterns of wear. So women's and men's tooth-wear patterns may be different, either because of differences in status or because they were primarily involved in different agricultural or food foraging tasks and then mainly ate those products for which they were responsible. A study of prehistoric Californian hunter-gatherers of around 2000–1000 BC showed different wear patterns in the teeth of women and men, though in slightly later horticultural communities the pattern of wear was the same for both sexes. A small number of women, but not men, from one of the horticultural communities had a rather unusual wear pattern which was thought to be the result of holding or pulling fibrous materials with the teeth, such as in basket-making. This, then, is very persuasive evidence for women being responsible for a particular craft within that society.[21]

Many prehistoric communities were accustomed to burying grave goods with all or some of their dead. From these archaeologists may be able to obtain a fairly clear picture of the artefacts associated with each sex and the relative quantity of goods appropriate to the burials of male and females, and thus to make hypotheses about the wealth and status of different individuals and of women compared with men. There are, however, certain pitfalls which such a study must avoid. Assumptions that the grave goods were owned and used by the dead individual during her or his life must be justified. The objects may have belonged to, and be gifts from, mourners or relations, or reflect the status of the head of the household or family rather than that of the deceased. Custom, ritual or fashion may dictate the types of grave goods appropriate for different groups of people. While these may relate to roles and status in life, they are perhaps more likely to reflect quite different aspirations for life in an afterworld, or may even be an attempt by the mourners to convey a deliberately false picture of the deceased and her status to the onlookers at the funeral or to the spirits or deities of the afterlife. But on the whole, most archaeologists are happy to base their interpretations on the majority of ethnographic cases where there is some, albeit tenuous, link between grave goods and the life of the deceased.[22]

Perhaps the most obvious clue to differences between female and male behaviour in a society is the presence in burials of any tools or other equipment. For example, for much of the later part of prehistory, from the Neolithic onwards, arrowheads, daggers and other weapons, used either for hunting wild animals or in warfare, are regularly found in male rather than in female burials. This seems to confirm the common assumption that these activities were male-dominated even in the prehistoric period. It will therefore be of particular interest if, even occasionally, an arrowhead or spearhead is found in a female burial. However, even where such apparently clear evidence has been found, the interpretation of the finds seems to have caused problems. An example from the New World which has led to debate is the discovery of atatls, or spearthrowers, in some female burials of the

Indian Knoll culture who lived in the North American Midwest in the second half of the third millennium BC. A variety of arguments were put forward in the early literature to avoid the obvious conclusion that women, as well as men, hunted: that they had a purely ceremonial function, that they belonged to a platoon of Amazons, or that they were part of the inheritance of some families or groups.[23] Another related problem is that, until quite recently, once a pattern had been established for a particular society, archaeologists often used the grave goods to identify the sex of the burial, rather than achieving this by analysis of the human remains and the grave goods independently, so exceptions to a rule might have gone unnoticed. Individuals who performed other tasks or crafts such as agriculture, spinning and weaving or metalworking might also be buried with

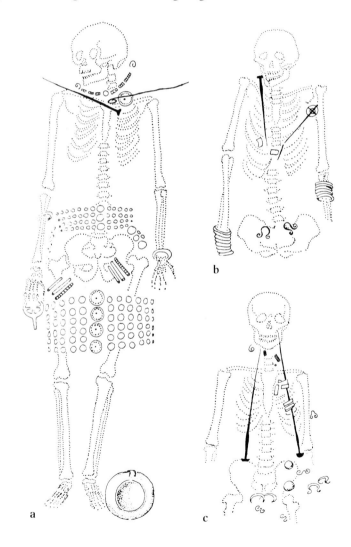

4 Burials of women from south Germany, mid-second millennium BC, showing the position of dress-pins and other ornaments:
a. Mühltal,
b. Wixhausen,
c. Asenkofen,
From Piggott,
1965.

the 'tools of their trade'. Where this seems to be the case it may be possible to identify which sex usually or invariably carried out a particular craft.

Dress is another area in which grave goods may provide particularly valuable information. Where bodies were buried fully clothed with ornaments, it is often possible to obtain a very clear picture of gender differences. In rare cases, such as some of the Danish burials from the Bronze Age and Iron Age which have remained preserved in oak coffins or waterlogged, the clothes themselves have survived (Fig. 32), though more usually only metal or bone ornaments and fastenings are preserved (Fig. 4). The location of brooches or belt buckles may give clues to what the clothes looked like and such ornaments will themselves reflect differences in gender behaviour within the society.

A major assumption which recurs in virtually all archaeological literature needs to be questioned in the present context. The grave goods found with men are assumed to have been 'earned', or 'won' by the individual and to reflect his own status, achievements or inheritance. On the other hand, when a woman is found with elaborate grave goods, or ones reflecting some activity usually carried out by men in our own society, these are almost invariably attributed to the prowess of her husband or father. Even where in a particular society women consistently have richer grave goods, it is usual to read that the men chose to display their wealth as jewellery on their wives or daughters. While by ethnographic analogy this may frequently be the case, the possibility that the women achieved their own wealth is hardly ever considered. The few serious attempts to rectify this situation and provide some basis for establishing how a woman may have acquired her grave goods depend on assessing the relative wealth of different burials within a cemetery – a procedure in itself fraught with problems – and then comparing the degree of wealth with the age of the individual.[24] If young girls and female infants are as likely to have rich grave goods as adults, then it may be assumed that this wealth was inherited from one or both parents, or some other relative (not necessarily the father); if women become progressively wealthier as they grow older it may be argued that the woman herself achieved that wealth, particularly if the pattern is not exactly mirrored by increases in male wealth. If women over a certain age usually have certain grave goods, while younger ones do not, it may be argued that goods were transferred at marriage (although I have not seen this argument used for male grave goods!) or reflect some age-related change of status normal in that society. All possible interpretations of such grave goods must be considered before any can be ruled out.

The location of burials within a cemetery, or the actual manner of burial, such as the side on which the body is laid or the direction in which the head is facing, might be determined by a wide range of factors, such as belief, status, cause of or age at death, or the sex of the individual. At some periods and places, mounds (or tumuli) were constructed over burials, and it may be possible to see that one particular individual was the first to be buried within such a mound and other bodies subsequently buried around it. Or it may be possible to tell from the layout of a cemetery that one individual was the focus either of the cemetery as a whole, or of a cluster of burials. Very occasionally the possibility that a cluster of burials represents a family group may be confirmed by the regular occurrence of a minor physical deformity common to, and therefore inherited within, the group. Studies which attempt to analyse the blood group of an individual from bones are still in their infancy, but they may also be used to distinguish family units within a cemetery. The relevance here of such techniques is that if it is possible to recognize the focal individual of a group it will be of considerable interest to know whether that individual is always male, always female, or if no regular pattern is apparent. In such a case, too, in theory at least, it should be possible to tell whether the individuals without the genetic trait or different blood group are older females or males, and thus whether it was women or men who moved into the family upon marriage. As we shall see, matrilocality or patrilocality (moving to the woman's or man's parental home respectively on marriage) is likely to make a considerable difference to the roles and status of women in any society.

Crafts and activities

A key question in the study of women in another society is whether there is any division of labour within it, and if so whether different tasks carry differences in status. One of the most obvious ways of studying this from archaeological evidence is to look at craft tools found with burials of a particular sex, as discussed above. Anthropological parallels may also provide suggestions as to which sex was responsible for which activities in a particular type of society, though without direct archaeological evidence this will of course remain hypothetical for any individual past group.

We can also consider clues such as fingerprints on pottery. If fingerprints remain on pottery they must have been impressed into the clay before it was fired, almost certainly by the manufacturer or by her or his assistants. Hypotheses about descent patterns and post-marital residence arrangements within past societies have been built upon assumptions that women made all the pots.[25] Small fingerprints have been interpreted as belonging to women potters (although they could equally well belong to young assistants of either sex, the complete lack of big 'men's' fingerprints within a large assemblage of pots might argue against the involvement of adult

5 A Njemps woman from the Baringo district of Kenya, smoothing the sides of a pot before firing. From Hodder, 1982.

men in potting). It is argued that women would have learnt the skills from the older women in the community, and copied the shapes and decoration from them. If they did not move away on marriage, and each family made all its own pots, then all the pots found on a site are likely to be very similar. If, on the other hand, women who had been taught to pot were dispersed after marriage, each moving to her husband's home, far more variety of style would be expected within each settlement site. This theory depends on knowing the sex of the potters, and assuming they are all of the same sex. If, however, there is any doubt about this, the ensuing arguments clearly carry no weight.

In cases where the sex of the manufacturer of a particular commodity is known from archaeological, or perhaps documentary, evidence, anthropological studies should warn us against having preconceived views about the status conferred by this work. Spinning and weaving, for example, are undertaken by women in some cultures around the world, and by men in others. But the status derived from the craft also varies tremendously; in some societies – usually, it seems, those in which the task is performed by men – it is well regarded, whereas in others, often those in which women are the spinners and weavers and where women have low status, the craft confers no particular status on the craftswoman.

Settlement sites

For many societies early settlements provide the best source of archaeological evidence, and information about the shape, size and number of houses is often comparatively easy to obtain. The types of artefact found in a particular building or room may often enable its function to be reliably determined. If it is known which tasks were allotted to which sex it may be possible to work out which rooms or buildings were used, and thus how much domestic space each was assigned. In a few societies, for example in the Neolithic of the Near East, burials are placed under the floor or under raised platforms, thought to be beds, in the corners of rooms. If it can be assumed that the exact position represents a place within the house formerly used specifically by the dead person, this may be another means of identifying the amount of space allocated to each sex, though it is also possible that the relationship and implications of the burial position may be considerably more complex.

A number of hypotheses, generated by anthropological data and relating to social organisation, have been based on the size and shape of houses. It has been argued that where houses are round, polygamous marriage patterns are more likely, and monogamous ones where houses are rectangular.[26] Arguments for patrilocal or matrilocal post-marital residence have been based on house size, suggesting that patrilocal patterns are more likely to result in small houses, whereas matrilocal family units are more likely to prefer large houses.[27] These hypotheses and their implications for Neolithic and Iron Age society are discussed in more detail in Chapter 4.

Apart from burials, direct evidence for the presence of people of a particular sex on archaeological sites is rare. This is undoubtedly partly because archaeologists have not usually tried to find it, but also because there are few occasions when women and men will leave unambiguously different remains. However, one very striking example showing where women had been and where they probably had not been within a large settlement comes from a waterlogged medieval site at Bergen, then an important trading post on the Norwegian coast.[28] Extensive excavations in several locations in the medieval town uncovered a number of latrine pits. The contents of such pits are always of interest to archaeologists, because the microscopic study of the remains of faeces often yields important evidence of diet. Latrines were also useful places into which to throw unwanted items, and precious objects such as rings or coins were sometimes accidentally but irretrievably lost there. In Bergen it was common to find moss, which had clearly been used as toilet 'paper', intermixed with remains of faeces. In some parts of the town, especially in domestic areas, small pieces of textile were also sometimes found in the latrines, whereas in other areas, most notably in the warehouse area beside the harbour, no such textile pieces were found. The suspicion arises that the textile had been used as sanitary protection, although it does not seem to have been possible to detect the presence of blood. That these textile fragments may therefore indicate the presence or probable absence of women in certain areas of the town is strengthened by documentary sources for the Hanseatic League, of which Bergen was part, which show that all the merchants were men.

This very clear example of the value of careful excavation, combined with detailed, if fairly straightforward, scientific analyses of the excavated materials and samples, has not, to the best of my knowledge, been paralleled on other sites, and depends on the right conditions of preservation for the evidence to be available. However, if such evidence were found on other sites it could be used to study questions such as whether women or men were restricted to certain parts of a settlement, or lived in separate houses. Alternatively, we might find evidence for the practice, known from a number of anthropological examples, of women spending the duration of their menstrual periods away from men, or in complete isolation. Whether this women's rite or ritual is seen as a chance for a rest from the daily toil of life, and a time to be venerated by women, or from the male perspective of the need for 'unclean' women to keep well away from men, is another question!

Art

Some, but by no means all, societies depict humans in their art. Often these depictions are so stylised that it is impossible to distinguish females from males; alternatively the artist may make it unclear, at least to an outsider or later observer, which sex is represented. But many other societies distinguish clearly between women and men in their art, either by the representation of the physical form, or by different dress or behaviour, or by some other convention such as painting the skin of women and men in different colours. Sometimes these conventions are obvious to archae-

6 The Venus of Willendorf, Austria, one of the best-known female figurines from the Upper Palaeolithic. Vienna, Naturhistorisches Museum.

ologists, but in other cases they may be suspected but not certain. Pre-historic art which does show gender differences is of course highly relevant to the study of women in prehistory. Minoan art, for example (see Chapter 4), in which women and men are shown involved in different activities and wearing different dress, provides the basis for much speculation about gender roles in that culture. Modelled or carved figurines of humans, whose sex is clearly apparent, are common in many early prehistoric societies in Europe, especially of the Stone Age. In Palaeolithic Europe female figurines predominate over male ones, and they are often obese and possibly pregnant. The function of these figurines has been much debated, and is discussed fully in Chapter 2.

A few general considerations need to be mentioned here. Although the functions of art within society are frequently considered by art historians, they are all too often ignored by archaeologists. It is very dangerous to assume that depictions of women in particular contexts necessarily reflect their true position within a society. A moment's thought about rep-resentations of women in our own society will make this obvious. Far from having the aesthetic value of the statues and paintings of the classical world or the Renaissance, pictures of naked women may be used for pornographic purposes. The naked female figurines of the Palaeolithic are usually inter-preted as goddesses or as having something to do with fertility magic, and the assumption is then made that this is a reflection of the high status of women in the society. But today, while images of women within the Christian and especially the Catholic Church may represent one particularly revered woman, the Virgin Mary, they certainly do not reflect the status of ordinary women in contemporary society. Therefore, although prehistoric works of art which depict women are a very important source of information about women in prehistory, they too, like any other source, must be studied and interpreted with caution.

2 The Earliest Communities

The earliest periods of prehistory form a very significant contrast with the later ones, and indeed with the whole of the rest of human history. The Palaeolithic and Mesolithic, or Old and Middle Stone Ages, are characterised not so much by the use of stone tools which give these periods their names, as by the means of subsistence which was universal at the time. Agriculture had not yet been adopted, and all food was acquired by foraging, gathering naturally growing plants and hunting wild animals. Today this distinctive subsistence pattern is practised by only a very small number of human groups; but several characteristic features which regularly accompany it can be discerned from them, including a nomadic lifestyle, setting up a new camp or homebase at frequent intervals, and much greater social equality, both between women and men and between different families or people of the same sex, than is typical of agriculturalists. There is good reason to suggest that many aspects of the lives of modern foraging societies resemble those of Palaeolithic people, so although there is little direct evidence for how women lived at this period, we can argue by analogy with these modern foragers about the role which Palaeolithic women may have played.

The Palaeolithic and Mesolithic[1] spanned roughly 2–2.5 million years, that is, about 250 times as long as all the rest of the prehistoric period: even in Europe the period was about 35 times as long as all the rest of the human past. During this time major changes in the climate and vegetation of Europe occurred; the human as well as the animal population had to adapt to them, and important developments in the human body and in technological and social abilities resulted. The climatic variations ranged from hot, dry, desert conditions in what is now Africa, where the earliest stages of human evolution took place, to freezing glacial temperatures in which very little vegetation grew and where the most common animals were mammoths, woolly rhinoceroses and hyenas, to the wet, temperate climate of north-west Europe in the Mesolithic, which encouraged the growth of dense deciduous forest. Archaeologically, just as much variation in the cultures and lifestyles of the first human populations can be expected. The earliest stages of human evolution seem to have taken place in East Africa, in the Great Rift valley, where the first recognisably human-like beings split from other primates around 8 million years ago, and are first seen in skeletal evidence between 4 and 3 million years ago. Although the precise dating of the various chronological landmarks is the subject of fierce debate amongst specialists in the field, some other points in human development include the first preserved tools around 2.5–2 million years ago, the first definite appearance of humans in Europe around 350,000 years ago, and the first humans who would have looked similar in all ways to ourselves, that is the development of *Homo sapiens sapiens*, about 40,000 years ago.

Most of the evidence for the period takes the form of stone tools, used for almost all daily activities and especially the acquisition of food. Hand axes were probably used as a sort of all-purpose pocket knife in the earlier (or Lower) part of the Palaeolithic, though in the later (or Upper) Palaeolithic and Mesolithic more specialist stone tools were used for tasks such as scraping clean animal skins, preparing plant foods, cutting wood, bone or meat, drilling holes and hunting.

Animal bones are very frequently found on sites of the period, and this has led archaeologists to make two major assumptions, firstly that all the animals would have been wild, and therefore hunted, and that no animals had yet been domesticated or were kept confined, and secondly, that meat was the most important part of the Palaeolithic diet. The first is based on the species of animals such as reindeer, red deer and bison, and on the context in which they are found. Although scavenging the meat of dead animals may have been common in the earliest stages, during most of the Palaeolithic most animals were in fact probably hunted. The second assumption arises from the profusion of bones on such sites; indeed, it is often suggested that meat was eaten almost to the exclusion of plant foods. However, the occurrence of bones and absence of significant evidence for plant foods is common everywhere in the archaeological record, and is a reflection of the differential preservation of the evidence, rather than a true indication of diet. In the Palaeolithic and Mesolithic the question of balance between meat and plant foods is particularly important, since it is often argued that it reflects the relative importance of women and men as food providers.

Palaeolithic and Mesolithic sites are frequently little more than collections of stone tools and bones, but excavation in recent years has suggested how the sites were occupied. Simple houses were built at some sites at this period, though elsewhere only rough shelters or windbreaks were put up. Natural caves were often occupied in the Palaeolithic period, but the small quantities of human debris in these and on the open-air sites strongly suggests that occupation at any one site was usually by only a small group of people and was of quite short duration, perhaps from a few days to no more than a few months. This picture equates very well with the ethnographic evidence of people living similar lifestyles today and in the recent past. Present-day foragers, or hunter-gatherers, as people leading this kind of life are commonly termed, almost always live in small nomadic groups, moving as and when the various food resources determine. The similarity of the archaeological evidence for the Palaeolithic and Mesolithic will be examined in more detail with the relevant ethnographic evidence, and used as the basis for arguing that the life of a Palaeolithic woman may not have been very different from that of her modern counterpart.

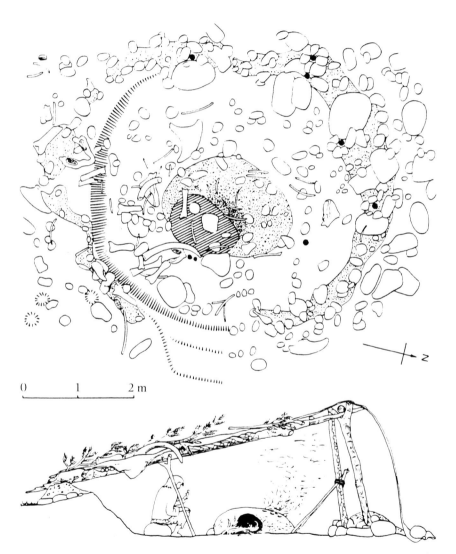

0   1   2 m

7 Plan and reconstruction of the Upper Palaeolithic hut at Dolni Vestonice, Czecho-slovakia, *c.* 23000 BC, constructed by digging out a slight terrace in the hill slope and building a low wall in front. A few shallow holes indicate the position of upright posts which presumably supported a light roof. Inside the hut were a hearth and a clay structure interpreted as a kiln in which clay figurines were fired. From Wymer, 1982.

The role of women in human evolution

Human evolution has traditionally been discussed in terms of the role which 'Man the Hunter' played in devising weapons and tools for catching and slaughtering animals for food, how he needed to walk upright on two feet to see his prey above the tall savanna grass, and how he was more successful than other species in his hunting exploits because he teamed up with other men and learnt the value of co-operation. And what of 'woman', meanwhile? Was she sitting at home, twiddling her thumbs, waiting for 'man' to feed her and increase his brain capacity and abilities until he became '*Homo sapiens sapiens*'? The argument went that as human evolution progressed, more and more time was needed to look after infants, so females no longer had time to hunt, and male co-operative hunting became essential in order that the men could bring enough food home to feed the family. As a result, male-female bonding in monogamous unions was an essential and a very early development. While most accounts of human evolution have assumed that all the advances in human physical and cultural development were led by men, a number of recent studies suggest alternative possibilities and have pointed out the vital role which must have been played by women.

Research into the earliest stages of human evolution is based on three strands of evidence. Physical anthropologists study the remains of early human skeletons, to assess the way in which they developed. For example, it is possible to tell from the structure of the legs and back whether an individual would have walked upright on two legs, or used the forearms for balance. Changes in the size of the skull through time give an indication of brain capacity. Secondly, the study of the behaviour of other animals, and especially primates, particularly those species closest to humans such as apes and chimpanzees, reveals some patterns which may have been shared by the earliest humans before cultural norms began to play an overriding part. For example, chimpanzees may be studied to see if males and females eat or collect different foods, or to find out whether they share any of the differences in child-care practices seen in human women and men. Thirdly, archaeological evidence for tools, settlements, environment and diet sheds light on the social and cultural development of the earliest humans.

Some scholars within all these three areas have turned away from the traditional male-dominated view of evolution and have begun to formulate an alternative model, allowing that female primates and hominids have played an important part, if not the key role, in the development of human behaviour. Different authors have stressed different factors in this development. Adrienne Zihlman[2] argues that changes in the environment were

41

crucial in necessitating social and economic changes in human populations in order to exploit this environment efficiently. Sally Slocum[3] points out that the only division of labour by sex amongst other primates is that females take primary care of their young, while males tend to dominate in protecting the group. She argues that a division of labour in food collecting is therefore unlikely to have been a key feature of early human behaviour. Other feminist writers[4] suggest that the female's choice of a co-operative and gentle mate was a critical factor in human evolution, as the chances of survival were improved by caring more closely for near relatives; in all mammals, and especially in primates, this is much more a female task or trait.

Among the physical changes which took place in the early stages of human evolution were increases in the size of the brain and the teeth; a decrease in sexual dimorphism (difference in size between males and females); increased hairlessness over the body; and bipedalism, or walking on two feet, rather than using the forelimbs for support, as chimpanzees and apes do. While an infant chimpanzee can cling to its mother's cover of body hair, leaving her hands free for walking or carrying food, a young human or early hairless hominid would need to be carried by the mother: this seems a much more likely stimulus both to bipedalism and to the invention of tools for carrying the infant as well as food than is the need to see prey animals over tall savanna grass and to throw simple weapons at them, which has been the traditional explanation for these changes.

A key aspect of the debate about the evolution of sex-role behaviour centres on food collection, and the way in which females and males may have foraged for different foods. Many discussions, including those written by some feminist anthropologists, assume that from a very early stage in evolution females primarily gathered plant foods, while males mainly hunted animals, the pattern usual in modern hunter-gatherer societies. Many recent arguments about other aspects of the role played by females in human social and technological evolution depend on this belief, even though it is rarely argued out fully. At one end of the scale other primates show little evidence for differences in food collecting behaviour between females and males, while at the other all modern foragers apparently divide subsistence tasks on the basis of sex. The question, therefore, is when and why this difference came about, and whether looking after young offspring would have a limiting effect on hunting by females. One view[5] suggests that although males unburdened by young might have caught meat more often than females, a regular division of labour would probably have come quite late in human evolution, as the physical differences between females and males are insufficient to make one sex or the other more suitable for either task. Recent work has also questioned whether meat actually filled a significant part of the early human diet, suggesting that this would have been far more like that of other primates, based almost entirely on a wide range of plant foods. What meat was eaten in the earliest phases of the Palaeolithic was probably scavenged, rather than hunted. Both these factors are problematic for the traditional view, as they suggest that hunting was neither an important factor in physical evolution, nor in the social and economic balance between female and male activities. Both sexes would have obtained vegetable foods and occasional meat, and brought some of their day's collection back to the homebase for sharing.

If there was little division of labour in the earliest phase of human development, when and why did it become usual? Two chronological points may have provided possible contexts. Initially, hominids would have been content to catch small game or to scavenge meat caught by other animals, or to collect those that had died naturally, but perhaps around 100,000 years ago they developed suitable tools and techniques for hunting large animals. While hunting small game would not have been hazardous, big-game hunting might often have resulted in death or injury to the hunter rather than the hunted. In small societies, such as these early human groups and present-day forager societies, every unexpected death is a serious blow to the viability of the community, particularly the death of women of child-bearing age. Mobility would also have been more important in hunting large game; the hunter would have to move rapidly and quietly, with hands free to throw a spear or shoot an arrow. It would not be possible to do this while carrying a bag or basket of gathered food, nor a young child, who might cause an additional hazard by making a noise at a crucial moment. Thus gathering and hunting become incompatible as simultaneous occupations; pregnant women and those carrying very small infants would have found hunting difficult, though gathering is quite easily combined with looking after young children. It is therefore possible that at this stage women began to hunt less, until a regular pattern of dividing subsistence tasks was established.[6]

Another possible context for the origin of the division of labour[7] is the change in environment which hominids found when they first entered Europe. It is argued that this spread could not have occurred until the perceptual problems of coping with a new environment had been resolved, by splitting food foraging into separate tasks. During the Lower Palaeolithic in East Africa, plants and animals would have been abundant, so vegetable foods and small game would have provided plenty of easily obtainable food with only the occasional large game caught to supplement the diet. As the hominid population increased and went in search of new territory, some hominids moved north into Europe. There they encountered colder conditions in which plant foods were harder to come by, so meat would have

8 Mother chimpanzee fishing for termites while her three-year-old daughter watches and learns from her. C. E. G. Tutin.

formed a more significant part of their diet. If this problem was not serious enough to necessitate a solution when hominids first moved into Europe, it would have become so with the onset of the last glaciation when conditions became very much colder and vegetation more sparse (this period equates archaeologically with the Upper Palaeolithic). The time and danger involved in hunting large animals became more worthwhile, but would not have provided a regular, guaranteed source of food, and would have been more dangerous. A solution might have been for only part of the community to concentrate on hunting, while the rest continued gathering plants and small animals. It is likely that this division would usually have been on a female-male basis for the reasons already suggested.

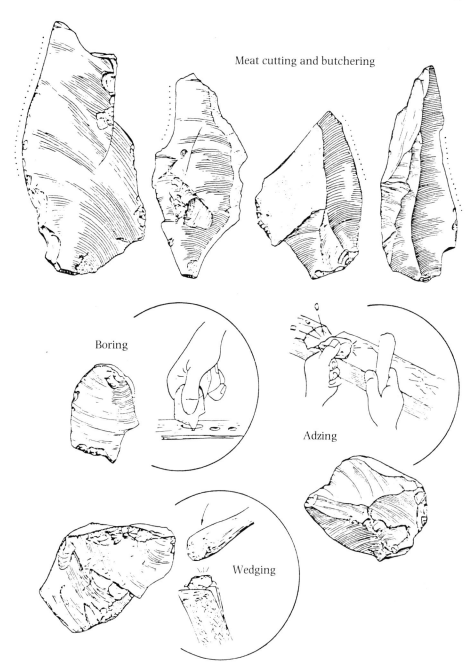

Meat cutting and butchering

Boring

Adzing

Wedging

9 Some Lower Palaeolithic flint tools from Hoxne, Suffolk, showing the way in which they would have been used. This has been demonstrated by the method of microwear analysis: microscopic examination of the edges of the tools can detect different traces of wear depending on the use made of the object. The dotted lines around the flint indicate the part of the flake that was actually used. From Wymer, 1982.

On the other hand, more detailed studies of chimpanzee behaviour suggest that there may be slight differences in the food collecting behaviour of females and males of non-human primates, which could argue for an early gathering/hunting division.[8] Although chimpanzees eat very little animal flesh, males make nearly all the kills and eat more of the meat; however, termite fishing, involving the use of sticks as fishing rods to poke into the termite mounds, a skilled task requiring patience and simple tool use, is far more commonly carried out by females. Whether the 'changing environment' theory or the latter argument is preferred, both hypotheses suggest that a division of labour on the basis of sex would have been an early development in human history.

Tool-using was once thought to be a distinctly human attribute, but in simple form it is now known to be shared with several of the higher primates, and even other animals and birds. Most early theories suggested that tool-using by humans was intimately linked with hunting, which in turn was assumed to be a male task, and that the earliest tools would have been spears for hunting animals and stone knives or choppers for butchery. This idea was partly encouraged by the archaeological evidence of the early stone tools, most of which are thought to have had such functions. However, this is partly a circular argument, as on the one hand the function of these tools is far from certain, and many would have been just as useful for cracking nuts or digging roots, and on the other, the very earliest tools would almost certainly have been made of wood, skins or other perishable material. Artefacts such as digging sticks, skin bags, nets, clubs and spears can be made entirely of organic materials, and would not have survived, so the extant stone tools are probably quite late in the sequence of hominid tool use. The evidence of tool use by other primates and by modern foragers, combined with a more balanced theoretical view, suggests that other factors and possibilities need to be considered.

One of the most significant human tools must be the container. Whether it be a skin bag, a basket, a wooden bowl or pottery jar, it allows us to carry items around or store them safely in one place. The container may have been one of the earliest tools to be invented, though unfortunately there is little archaeological evidence to demonstrate this. Chimpanzees can carry things in the skinfold in their groin, but when hominids became bipedal this skin was stretched and the fold was lost. The use of a large leaf or an animal skin, carried over one arm or the developing shoulder, or tied to the waist, might have replicated this lost natural carrier.[9] One of the most important things that a female hominid would need to carry would be her young offspring. The complex interaction of bipedalism, food gathering, the loss of hair for the infant to cling to, and changes in the structure of the toes which made them useless for clinging to its mother would have

10 !Kung forager women gathering plant food and carrying it in their *karosses*, or slings.
Richard Lee.

made it necessary for the mother to carry the child. The development of a sling for supporting the infant, found in almost all modern societies, including foraging groups, is likely to have been among the earliest applications of the container.

The first tools to aid in foraging and preparing foodstuffs are perhaps more likely to have been used in connection with plant foods and small animals than in the hunting of large mammals. The tools and actions required for termite fishing, for example, are not unlike those required for digging up roots more easily. Modern foraging groups often choose a particularly suitable stone to use as an anvil for cracking nuts, which they leave under a particular tree and then return to it on subsequent occasions. Higher primates also use stones for cracking nuts, so it is very likely that early hominids would have done this even before tools were used for hunting. The role of women as tool inventors, perhaps contributing many of the major categories of tools which are most essential even today, cannot be dismissed.

The introduction of food gathering, as opposed to each individual eating what food was available where it was found, was another significant advance which would both have necessitated and been made possible by the invention of the container. More food might be gathered than was needed immediately by one individual, either for giving to someone else or for later consumption. With the exception of parents feeding very young offspring, this behaviour is unusual among other animals and presumably would not have been common amongst the very earliest hominids, but gradually developed to become a hallmark of human behaviour. Another change would have involved carrying this food to a base, which would imply both conceptual and physical changes, made possible by the use of containers, and may also have made it necessary to walk on two legs, leaving the hands free to carry the food, either directly or in containers. The development of consistent sharing, not only with offspring but with others in the group, and exchanging food brought from different environments of savanna and forest would have been a stage towards living in regular social groups.

Environmental changes would also have led to social changes within early hominid groups. In savanna grassland, as opposed to forest, it would have been more difficult to find safe places to sleep overnight, and water would have been harder to obtain. Once a suitable location was discovered, there would have been a greater tendency to remain there as long as possible rather than sleeping in a different place each night, thus introducing the idea of a homebase.

Women also played a key role in social development. A major difference between human development and that of other animals is the greater length of time during which infants need to be cared for and fed: this has probably contributed to a number of human characteristics, including food sharing and long-term male-female bonding. The sharing of food between mother and offspring would necessarily have continued for longer in early hominids than in other primates, and it is argued that when a mammal too large to be consumed by the hunters alone was killed, the males would have shared it with those who had shared with them in their youth, that is their mothers and sisters, rather than with their sexual partners. This argument is supported by a primate study[10] which shows that banana sharing almost always takes place within matrifocal groups rather than between sexual partners. This has important implications for the primacy or otherwise of monogamy and marriage. Several scholars have also pointed out that in this situation the female would choose to mate with a male who was particularly sociable and willing to share food with his partner while she was looking after a very young infant. As well as preferring those most willing to share, females would choose those males who appeared to be most friendly. Not surprisingly, female chimpanzees will not mate with males who are aggressive towards them. The more friendly-looking males would probably have been smaller, or nearer in size to the female, and would have had less pronounced teeth, and therefore have been less aggressive-looking. Over thousands of years this female sexual preference would have led to gradual evolutionary changes in favour of smaller, less aggressive, males.

The stronger tie between mother and offspring caused by the longer period of time during which human infants need to be cared for would have resulted in closer social bonds than are found in other species. The primary bond between mother and offspring would be supplemented by sibling ties between sisters and brothers growing up together. Older off-spring would be encouraged or socialised to contribute towards the care of younger siblings, including grooming, sharing food, playing and helping to protect them. The natural focus of such a group would clearly be the mother rather than, as is so often supposed, any male figure. Moreover, this group behaviour would lead to increased sociability in the male as well as in the species in general. The role of the female, both in fostering this increased sociability in the species and as the primary teacher of technological innovations during this long period of caring, must be recognised.

An increase in human sociability, and particularly female sociability, would have had a number of other positive side-effects. As a result of a mutual willingness to share food and food resources, each individual would have had more access to overlapping gathering areas when a particular resource was abundant. This in turn might greatly increase the chances of the offspring being well fed and therefore surviving, and thus of the survival of the species in general. As the ability to communicate precisely increased with the development of language, it would have become possible for humans to have ordered social relationships with more individuals and other groups. This would have evolved into a pattern very similar to that found in modern foraging groups, many of which include distant relations who regularly meet up with other groups in the course of their annual movements. Males who had moved out of the matrifocal group in order to mate would have learnt a pattern of friendly contact with their ancestral females when they met them in the course of their foraging.

It can therefore be argued that the crucial steps in human development were predominantly inspired by females. These include economic and technological innovations, and the role of females as the social centre of groups. This contrasts sharply with the traditional picture of the male as protector and hunter, bringing food back to a pair-bonded female. That model treats masculine aggression as normal, assumes that long-term, one-to-one, male-female bonding was a primary development, with the male as the major food provider, and that male dominance was inherently linked to hunting skills. None of these patterns, however, accords with the behaviour of any but the traditional Western male. Other male primates do not follow this pattern, nor do non-Western human groups, in particular those foraging societies whose lifestyle in many ways accords most closely with putative early human and Palaeolithic cultural patterns. We will look at these modern foragers in more detail in the next section.

Women in modern and Palaeolithic foraging societies

It has been estimated that over 90 per cent of people who have ever lived have been foragers. However, foragers now make up less than 0.003 per cent of the world's population. In the past, particularly in the Palaeolithic and Mesolithic, foraging peoples were able to use large tracts of land, choosing the most favourable environments available at the time. Today's foragers are forced to live in the extreme environments which no other groups are able or want to use, and are frequently restricted to much smaller areas than they need in order to allow the environment to regenerate fully while they utilise another area. Today very few groups of foragers are completely uninfluenced by technologically more sophisticated groups, or by the politics of the nation states. And apart from these more overt differences it must always be remembered that, unlike the Palaeolithic and Mesolithic peoples, modern foragers have developed their culture over the same length of time as the people of the Western world, and in many respects are just as sophisticated as any other groups. These factors make any analogy between them and Palaeolithic and Mesolithic foragers uncertain; indeed, some archaeologists reject any attempt to make such analogies, particularly where details of social or religious life are concerned. Nevertheless, the obvious similarities between the two groups lead me to believe that it is justifiable to use modern foragers as a basis for a picture of Palaeolithic and Mesolithic life, albeit with due caution, where direct evidence is unavailable. It is, however, to be hoped that it will be possible to test the model in the future against data from new archaeological research.

Today's foragers are widely, if sparsely, scattered around the world, and the extreme environments in which many live closely match those of various Palaeolithic and Mesolithic societies. The Inuit, or Eskimo Indians of northern Canada, live in the extremely cold tundra, which is not dissimilar to the cold phases of the Upper Palaeolithic in much of Europe, although the difference in latitude and therefore in the amount of daylight would always mean that vegetation in the Arctic would differ from that of Europe. The !Kung of the Kalahari desert of southern Africa and the Australian aborigines, by contrast, live in an environment very similar to that in which the earliest stages of human evolution took place, while the Mbuti pygmies of central Africa live in tropical rain forests which are probably not unlike some of the hot phases, or interglacials, between the cold phases of the Ice Age. Despite these huge variations in environment, numerous similarities exist in the social organisation of all modern foragers, and we can therefore have confidence in the hypothesis that early foragers also shared similar patterns of organisation.

Foragers are often referred to as 'hunter-gatherers'; this term arises from the two major facets of their diet – meat which is hunted, and plant foods which are gathered. Although we shall consider some important exceptions, these two tasks are almost always divided between women and men: women gather and men hunt, and in the previous section we considered why this division might have come about in the earliest stages of human evolution. The term 'Man the Hunter' is also commonly used, and the implication is that man's principal food is meat, and his principal occupation hunting; this has been assumed to be invariably a male task which gives the men high status. It has been shown, however, that this view is not entirely correct, and may be largely a reflection of the interests and preconceptions of nineteenth-century Western male anthropologists and of the status of hunting as an upper-class pastime in nineteenth-century Europe. The diet of modern foragers has been studied intensively in recent years and the results of this work have had important implications for understanding the position of women in these societies, and by analogy in the Palaeolithic and Mesolithic. In all but the extremely cold ice and snow conditions in which the Inuit or Eskimos live, forager diets comprise a high proportion of plant foods, supplemented with a small proportion of meat as and when it can be obtained. The range of plant foods available in most environments is greater than the modern Western imagination allows for. As well as the more obvious fruit, nuts, leaves and roots, the stems, bark, rhizomes and bulbs of many species are edible, not to mention fungi, seaweed and other water-plants, which are tasty and nutritious. Furthermore, the gathering of plant foods in most environments is much more time-effective and reliable than the hunting of animals. In most communities the traditional picture of men hunting large wild animals seems to be correct, but large quantities of plants are gathered by women, who will also pick up small animals such as lizards and turtles, as well as insects and eggs. Women in forager societies, therefore, are the major food providers, and this is recognised in the status given to them. Perhaps the most significant contrast between forager societies and almost all others in the modern world is the equality between individuals found there, which contrasts with the very marked variations in status found in most other societies, particularly between women and men.

The most intensive studies on the diet of foragers have concentrated on the !Kung of the Kalahari.[11] The exceptionally wide range of plant foods available even in a desert region causes some surprise. Roots, leaves, berries and shoots of many different plants are eaten, though preference is given to a few species, including the highly nutritious and readily available mongongo nut. It is estimated that plant foods make up 60–80 per cent of the diet by weight of the !Kung and virtually all of this is supplied by the women, who gather enough food to feed themselves, their young children and aged relatives, and also their husbands, if the men return to the camp after an unsuccessful day. Like the women, the men will pick and immediately eat much of their daily food but they will not bring any plant foods back, whereas the women will return to the camp laden with bags or baskets. It must not be thought, however, that this gathering is an easy task, because although shortages are rare and it does not usually take long to gather sufficient food, great knowledge and skill are required to distinguish those plants which are edible from poisonous species, and to notice sometimes very slight above-ground traces of roots growing below the surface. It takes the !Kung women comparatively little time to gather the day's food, and as surpluses cannot be stored there is little point in gathering more than will be consumed within a day or two. On average, 240 calories of plant food can be gathered in one hour, whereas, taking into account the high failure rate of hunting, it has been estimated that one hour of hunting produces only 100 calories of food. Plant foods are eaten every day and the women will ensure that some food is always available. The successful killing of a large mammal, however, is an

11 A !Kung woman packing mongongo nuts. Richard Lee.

occasional occurrence, but it causes excitement and since it is usual for portions of the meat to be given to other members of the group – in contrast to the plant foods gathered by the women which are eaten by her immediate family – it gives prestige to the hunter. Nevertheless, the importance of the constant supply of food by the women is also well recognised.

In the proportion of plant foods eaten and the role of women in their collection, the !Kung seem to be very typical of modern foragers. It has been estimated[12] that two-thirds of forager societies depend on gathered food for 60–70 per cent of their diet. Some of the Australian aborigines practise a slightly different division of labour.[13] Women gather plant foods, but also hunt small game and kangaroos with the help of hunting dogs which they train. Usually men hunt large animals, but sometimes women and men will hunt or fish together. Amongst other Australian aborigine groups, such as the Tiwi,[14] men concentrate on acquiring food from the sea and air. The Agta of the Philippines are another important exception, in that women sometimes join in hunting,[15] but gathered food plays only a small part in their diet as they exchange meat for plant foods grown by neighbouring horticulturalists. Of all the recent foragers, only the Inuit eat a very low proportion of plant foods. The extreme environment in which they live poses special problems. Whereas a characteristic of all other forager societies is that food is not hoarded or saved, the Inuit store food over winter, preserving it either by smoking or freezing in the ice. Skins need to be prepared for making into clothes, whereas in warmer climates foragers typically wear very few clothes, or none. These special tasks have become the role of women, while, as in other forager societies, the men hunt.

Can we assert that Palaeolithic and Mesolithic women gathered large quantities of plant food, and as a result enjoyed greater equality than most women today? Three questions arise. Firstly, was the diet in the Palaeolithic and Mesolithic balanced in the same way as that of today; secondly, if it was, were tasks alloted in the same way, and thirdly, did this confer similar status on women?

To judge the balance of diet from archaeological evidence is, as we have already discussed, extremely difficult. One of the main features of most Palaeolithic and Mesolithic sites is a profusion of animal bones, many of which show clear signs of butchery. So meat was clearly a part of the diet, but the fact that it is the only food for which we have definite evidence does not prove that it was the most important one. While work on Neolithic and later sites now often includes sieving or flotation studies of soils in which small quantities of plant remains may be found, this is less common on forager sites as there is less expectation that seeds or other plant products will be recovered. This attitude will obviously reinforce the existing picture, rather than throw new light on the question.

The animals represented at any site depend mainly on the climate, but usually include a high proportion of deer, either reindeer or red deer. In the colder phases of the Palaeolithic, mammoth, woolly rhinoceros and horse prevailed, while at warmer times and further south, roe deer, ibex and chamois were important. In the dense woodland of the Mesolithic of temperate Europe, red deer, pig, elk and aurochs were more common. All these are big mammals, with large bones which under most conditions of preservation will remain intact and will be easy to find on archaeological sites. The smaller animals such as lizards and turtles, as well as birds and fish, whose bones are relatively small and fragile, and also eggs, are much rarer finds on most excavations, yet they form a significant part of the diet of most modern foragers. However, bones of these creatures are found on sufficient sites to show that they were also eaten by Palaeolithic and Mesolithic communities. Fish bones, for example, often include deep-sea and river species such as cod, haddock, pike, salmon and carp, to name but a few from a wide and varied list. At Shanidar cave, a site in Iraq first occupied in the Mesolithic, snails, river clams and tortoise are among the species which seem to have been eaten, and the shells of shellfish are commonly found, discarded in huge mounds or middens, at coastal sites in northern Europe.

It is very rare to find evidence which shows whether it was women or men who foraged or hunted for these animal foods, although anthropological accounts suggest that in most modern forager communities hunting is primarily carried out by men. In traditional societies it is also usual for a person using a particular tool to have made it themselves. Conventional archaeological wisdom seems to assume that Palaeolithic men would have made and used stone axes. One may, however, cite a few instances which contradict this pattern and remind us that the rule is not invariable. The lives of women of the Tiwi group of Australian aborigines, who still lead traditional lives on Melville Island, share tasks in an unusual way. While men are concerned with fishing and procuring food from the sea and the air, women forage and hunt for all forms of 'land food', including land mammals. Until the introduction of steel tools, their principal tool was the stone axe, not unlike those used in prehistoric Europe, which they used for a variety of tasks including stripping bark to make baskets and striking death blows to prey animals. Significantly, the women themselves made these stone tools.[16] In the archaeological record there is also at least one instance which strongly suggests that women took part in subsistence activities other than gathering. In contrast to the example of the Tiwi, prehistoric women appear to have fished, at least at the time and in the area of the relevant find. In coastal areas of Scandinavia, in the Mesolithic and continuing into the Neolithic, there is considerable evidence of fishing in coastal waters, both from fishbones which suggest that small cod, of up to 30–40 cm in length, was the main species caught, and from bone or boar's tusk fishhooks. The cemetery of the Neolithic site of around 3000 BC at Västerbjers in Sweden contained the skeleton of an adult woman buried with a fishhook. However, another male Scandinavian burial also with a fishhook shows that fishing was not exclusively a female preserve.[17]

Another product highly prized by modern foragers is honey, since it is normally the only sweetener available. This, too, would leave no archaeological trace, so the depiction of a person gathering wild honey from a tree in a wall-painting in a rock shelter at Cuevas de la Araña, Bicorp, in eastern Spain is particularly interesting.[18] Although the person has sometimes been described as a man, other commentators interpret the figure as a woman, identified by large buttocks and perhaps also by the flowing hair, which seems to be much longer and thicker than that of the stick-like, sometimes phallic male hunters in other paintings there. The exact date of the group of Spanish wall-paintings to which this belongs is uncertain, but it almost certainly falls somewhere between 7000 and

4000 BC. This, then, is very satisfactory evidence, not only for the collection of honey in the early prehistoric period, but also for its being a woman's task.

If it is to be postulated that Palaeolithic and Mesolithic women enjoyed similar status to modern forager women, and that at least by the time Europe was colonised this status was related, to a certain extent, to the high proportion of food they provided, it would be helpful to be able to produce evidence that a lot of plant foods were eaten. Of the plant foods which are most frequently preserved, nuts, or at least their shells, come top of most lists, and would have been an important source of protein. The amount of evidence for other plant foods depends almost entirely on how

12 A Mesolithic rock painting from Cuevas de la Araña, Bicorp, Spain, depicting a woman with a basket gathering wild honey from a hive in the top of a tree. After Obermaier, 1925.

much attention was paid to the question when the site was excavated: if wet sieving or froth flotation techniques have been used to sift out minute traces of carbonised plant remains, some evidence that vegetable products were eaten is almost always found to be present. Although the evidence for the earliest phases in Africa is slight, the important site at Kalambo Falls has provided remains of palm nuts and syzyium fruits. In the colder periods of the Middle and Upper Palaeolithic, when more extreme environments prevailed, the choice of plant foods may not have been very great, though the vegetation in the higher latitudes of Europe would always have been greater than that available to today's foragers within the Arctic Circle. Towards the end of the period, however, especially in the Mesolithic, a wide range of plant foods is attested. Temperate Europe, during the Mesolithic, was dominated by mixed oak forests, and the marked seasonal changes and variety of environments provided by sea, river and lakesides and different altitudes would have allowed a wide choice of foodstuffs. On archaeological sites hazel-nut shells are often common, and water chestnuts have been found in some places. Other species are less frequently preserved, though this does not necessarily mean that they were less frequently eaten. Species represented include yellow water lily at Holmegaard (an important Mesolithic site in Denmark), bog-bean, fat hen and nettle at the British site of Star Carr, and raspberry at Newferry in Ireland.[19] In the Mediterranean region, which as today enjoyed a hotter, drier environment, a greater variety of nuts, such as pine-nuts, pistachio, almonds, chestnuts and walnuts, would have been available, and pollen either from wild cereals or from other large grasses has been found in human faeces from Icoana in the Danube Gorge in Romania; at Franchthi cave in Greece wild barley and oats were eaten, along with three varieties of legumes and two of nuts. Other evidence which suggests that plant foods were particularly important comes from the Mesolithic site of Téviec, in Brittany, where the tooth-wear patterns of skeletons was thought to be caused by a plant rather than a meat diet.[20]

Neither the collection of plant foods nor their preparation leaves much trace in the archaeological record. This problem is compounded by the probable multi-purpose nature of many Palaeolithic tools and the uncertain use of most flint and stone tools prevalent throughout the Palaeolithic and Mesolithic. Although it used to be asserted that the function of most tools was related to meat and skin preparation, the possibility that some were used in the preparation of plant foods has recently been discussed. A study of the microwear (minute traces of tool use which are only apparent under a very high-powered microscope, see Fig. 9) on the stone tools from a 1.5-million-year-old site at Koobi Fora in Kenya indicated that they had been used for working plant materials,[21] though other studies of similar material

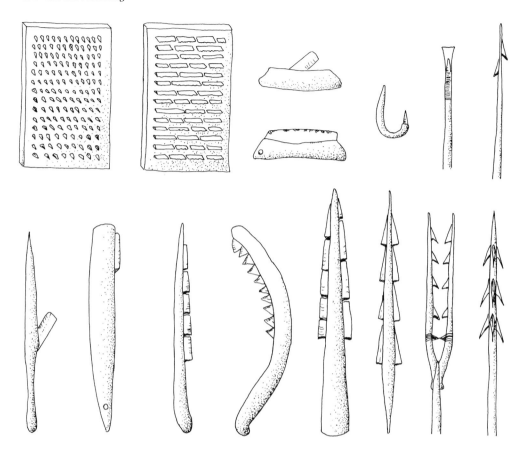

13 Various ways in which microlith flints can be hafted, resulting in very different tools, including graters, scrapers, a fish-hook, harpoons and arrows, and (bottom left) knives and sickles. After Clarke, 1976.

have so far proved inconclusive. The almost universal flint of the Mesolithic period is a tiny worked flake, known as a microlith. These are often only fingernail-sized, but are found in a variety of shapes. They formed part of composite tools or weapons set into wooden handles or hafts, as is shown by rare instances where the wood has been preserved, such as from the Shanidar cave in Iraq, or where careful excavation reveals the original positioning of microliths in relation to each other. Although reconstructions usually depict them as multi-barbed arrows, these archaeological examples – as well as very similar tools found in ethnographic contexts – show the very wide range of uses to which these tools could have been put. In the Mediterranean, microliths are often found associated with seed-grinding stones, suggesting they may have been used for related functions, such as cutting the stems of wild grasses or shoots. Roots could have been cut with heavier, straight-edged composite knives, or grated with microliths set in rows in a flat board. David Clarke,[22] who first pointed out the wide range of possible uses for microliths, therefore suggests that the large quantity of these flints found in Mesolithic contexts might imply an increase in the importance of plant foods in the diet, rather than a change in hunting techniques. If it is taken that women rather than men were the principal plant-gatherers, this might also imply an increase in the status of women in the Mesolithic.

Perhaps one of the most characteristic features of most modern forager societies is their nomadic lifestyle. The small social group, or band, which may vary in size from as few as six to over fifty people, moves its homebase as often as is desirable to maximise the ease with which food can be obtained. When the supply in the immediate locality of a homebase becomes exhausted, there comes a point at which it is more efficient to move than to have to travel out from the base in order to obtain food. This point may come after only a few days in one location, or after several months. There is often considerable seasonal variation in the length of time foragers will remain in one place. For example, during the spring and autumn the !Kung will only remain in one spot for about two or three weeks, whereas during the dry season a homebase near a source of water will be used for up to six months.[23] One result of these short stays at any one place is that it is hardly worthwhile to invest much effort in building houses or shelters. Typically, and especially when a very short stay is anticipated, rudimentary shelters are built, or even none at all. The Australian aborigines, living in a hot, dry environment, seldom build any kind of shelter, while the houses of the !Kung differ according to whether the season is hot or cooler. Other foragers, including the Palaeolithic people of Europe, would sometimes choose natural shelters, such as caves, where they were convenient, and these may not have required any modification. All these houses would be very difficult to recognise archaeologically: few posts or other structural features are dug into the ground, and the shelter itself is made entirely from organic materials such as branches, reeds or skins and would therefore leave no trace. Moreover, the short time of occupation means that little refuse accumulates. This has two effects: from an archaeological point of view, it is a further problem in recognising foragers' homebases, as refuse often provides the main focus of archaeological information on any site; but from the point of view of the inhabitants of the site, forager homebases are likely to be much more hygienic than the permanent homes of many farming communities. As a result, contagious or epidemic diseases are far less of a problem for foragers than for agriculturalists, since they move away before water sources become polluted and refuse tips become the breeding grounds for all sorts of pests and insects. Coupled with the very varied diet of most foragers compared with the limited diets of many agriculturalists, where one or two crops provide a high proportion of daily subsistence, most foragers lead relatively healthy lives.

Archaeological evidence suggests that this nomadic lifestyle was also, on the whole, typical of the Palaeolithic and Mesolithic. It is possible, however, that in the temperate environment of the Mesolithic of Europe, which would have been much more favourable than that enjoyed by most foragers today, some sites may have been occupied for much longer, or even more or less permanently. This could have led to several social adaptations more typical of the succeeding Neolithic phase taking place earlier than has been thought. However, most archaeological sites of the Palaeolithic and Mesolithic are typical of short-lived occupation; in some phases caves were occupied, while elsewhere 'open-air' sites are found. Sites are often recognised by one or more hearths, which would have been used for cooking, to sit around in the evening and to ward off predatory animals, surrounded by a usually quite small quantity of refuse, including food debris and waste flakes from tool-making. Occasionally evidence of, for example, stake-built huts or shelters is found. The extent and spread of the debris gives an indication not only of the length of occupation, but also of the size of the group which occupied the site. Further indication of the length of stay may be provided by a study of the ages of animals killed and the types of vegetation represented, which may indicate in which season or seasons the site was occupied. As an example, we can take the site of Terra Amata on the Mediterranean coast of France,[24] which dates from the Lower Palaeolithic, around 400,000 years ago. The remains of a shelter were found, with an oval setting of stones thought to have held the bases of branches bent over to form a central ridge. Inside the shelter were hearths and areas where tools were made. Pollen from fossilised human faeces indicates that the site was occupied in late spring.

An aspect of modern forager life which is of particular relevance to women is the careful spacing of childbirths invariably practised by these societies. Typically, a mother will not have another child until the youngest is three or four years old. Many explanations have been put forward for this. Some argue that this is the natural result of the child's total dependence on breast milk until it is able to eat normal adult food at the age of about four, as the cereal products onto which children in agricultural societies are normally first weaned are not readily available in most forager societies. Continuous breast-feeding on demand tends to suppress ovulation in the mother and thus prevents or reduces the likelihood of her becoming pregnant during this time. Others believe the spacing of births may be a deliberate policy, as the mother would not be able constantly to carry around more than one child unable to walk the long distances which the forager lifestyle entails. This could be achieved by the use of herbal abortion-inducing or contraceptive drugs – of which many traditional societies have a clear knowledge – or by infanticide. Whether this birth spacing was practised in the Palaeolithic and Mesolithic is difficult to determine. It is sometimes possible to estimate the number of children a woman has borne from the pelvic bones of a skeleton; however, to the best of my knowledge this has not been estimated for any Palaeolithic or Mesolithic skeletons.

Social equality between women and men is a key feature of modern forager societies, and is usually attributed, in part at least, to the fact that each sex provides an equal share of the food. Archaeological evidence for social structure can be obtained from burials and the grave goods associated with them (see Chapter 1). The very few burials known from the Palaeolithic or Mesolithic show interesting patterns, though it is not always easy to know how to interpret them.[25] Although we know of only thirty-six burials from the whole of the European Middle Palaeolithic, and not all of these are sufficiently well preserved to be identified by sex, a clear pattern does emerge in the presence or absence of grave goods. Nearly all men are buried with stone or bone implements or animal bones, or are covered in ochre,

14 A reconstruction of the Lower Palaeolithic hut from Terra Amata, Nice, France, *c.* 38000 BC. The size (approximately 8 × 4 metres) and shape of the hut were indicated by the distribution of stones and debris. From Wymer, 1982.

while none of the female burials has any surviving grave goods. In the Upper Palaeolithic, when considerably more burials are known, approximately equal numbers of women and men are buried with grave goods, though in the Mesolithic period men, and especially older men, are once again more likely to receive special treatment, being buried with ochre, antlers or stone artefacts. One interpretation of these differences in female and male burials might be that the social equality found in modern foraging societies did not exist in the Palaeolithic and Mesolithic, and that men received grave goods while women did not because men had higher social standing. On the other hand, if women had grave goods of organic materials, perhaps offerings of selected plant foods rather than joints of meat, and tools or ornaments of wood, these would not have survived. Alternatively it may be argued that women and men in modern foraging societies often wear different ornaments or items of clothing, and use different tools because of their different tasks, and yet their social status is equal, so perhaps it is not wise to use the few and modest Palaeolithic and Mesolithic grave goods to jump to any too hasty conclusions.

The life of a Palaeolithic or Mesolithic woman may have been quite pleasant. An often-quoted phrase describes modern foragers as the 'original affluent society', where everyone has sufficient food and there is little stress and jealousy as everyone has equal access to the very few commodities available.[26] By analogy with modern foragers, except at periods when the environment was particularly harsh, food would probably have been readily available. If women were, on the whole, responsible for gathering plant foods and perhaps small animals, this may not have taken many hours a day. Unlike hunting, which depends on quietness, plant gathering could be quite a social activity, carried out by all the able-bodied women of a band working together. Young children could play round about, receiving attention whenever necessary, or remain at the homebase with elderly relatives. The preparation of the gathered plant foods is another task which is usually performed by women among present-day foraging groups: nuts need to be shelled, and roots and tubers may be baked or roasted in the ashes of a fire. Although the building of whatever shelters are used is often a women's task in modern forager societies, there are few other domestic tasks; again by analogy with modern foragers, with the exception of very cold climates, the total lack of or very little clothing, the short duration of settlement in any one place and the small number of possessions of necessity typical of foragers would have minimised the need for virtually all the household tasks which twentieth-century Western living demands – even if not necessarily carried out by women!

Matriarchy, patriarchy or equality

One of the biggest debates in anthropology in the nineteenth century, which has been revived by modern feminists, was about whether there was ever a time when women were dominant over men as men dominate women in patriarchal societies. A matriarchy would be defined as a society in which women not only have equality with men, but also control, power and dominance. Modern feminists and nineteenth-century and modern anthropologists have sought an answer to the problem by looking for present-day societies which approach such a state. Most serious scholars have seen that there are no societies today where women are regularly in the prime positions of leadership, and consequently question whether matriarchy could ever have existed. But the answer lies in the realm of prehistoric time, and must therefore be seriously addressed here, although it is difficult to see what direct archaeological evidence might be forthcoming. Within Europe and the Western world, as will become clear in subsequent chapters, patriarchy was well established by the time that written records first appear in the fourth millennium BC in Egypt and the Near East. Although it will be argued that changes in social organisation took place during the early prehistoric period, if a matriarchal society ever existed in the distant past it must have been during the Palaeolithic, and the subject must therefore be seriously considered by any archaeologist interested in feminism or social organisation in general. This was appreciated by the renowned archaeologist V. Gordon Childe, writing in 1951,[27] though he rejected the possibility of recognising either matriliny or matriarchy in the archaeological record and pointed out that although small female figurines have been taken as such evidence, it is unlikely that they are any better an indicator of matriarchy than are images of the Virgin Mary in our undeniably patriarchal society. Many archaeologists today, however, would hesitate to reject with such certainty any possibility that evidence for matriarchy might yet be found, even if it is not clear quite what form such evidence might take.

The suggestion that matriarchal societies existed before a take-over by men was first put forward in the mid-nineteenth century by two scholars working from very different evidence. Johann Bachofen, a German classical scholar, based his arguments (in *Das Mutterrecht*, 1861) on the archaeological remains of female figurines which he took to be goddesses and especially on classical mythology, where some women are depicted as having considerable power and where descent is sometimes seen to be matrilineal.[28] For example, Bachofen points to examples in the Homeric and other Greek myths where matriliny is suggested. Oedipus, a penniless exile, becomes king by marrying the widowed queen Jocasta, and Menelaus becomes King of Sparta when he marries Helen. Both these instances imply that the women have inherited their respective kingdoms.

Lewis Henry Morgan, a leading American anthropologist and author of *Ancient Society*, 1877, was one of the first scholars to make careful studies of many native North-American peoples. He saw that in some of these, for example among the Iroquois (see Chapter 3), women had far higher status than in his own society and were dominant in aspects of the economic sphere; they played a crucial role in ritual and political activity, and descent was often reckoned through the female line (matriliny). Morgan argued that an original pattern of descent through women was overthrown by men when people first lived a settled existence and the accumulation of property became common. Morgan's arguments were taken up by Friedrich Engels in *The Origins of the Family, Private Property and the State* (1884). His theory was that women at first controlled the communal property of the family, but that when agriculture was introduced, men used, and therefore owned, the farming tools, especially ploughs and domesticated animals. Men thus became the first sex actually to own private property. In order to pass this on to their children, they had to introduce monogamy so that they could control the descent system. The role of the male in reproduction, which might not have been fully understood in a foraging society, would have been clearer once animals were kept in captivity, and it was perhaps observed that females would not breed unless they had contact with male members of their species. In a matrilineal system any-thing a man owns is inherited by his matrilineage, and so would go to his sister's children rather than his own; moreover, his children would belong to his wife's matrilineage. Under a system of patriliny, however, a man could have sexual monopoly over his wife, and economic or legal monopoly over her children. As a result women were subordinated economically, and restricted sexually.[29]

Like many scholars since, these early writers failed to make fully the crucial distinction between matriarchy, matriliny and matrilocality. Many societies today practise matriliny (descent reckoned through the female line) or matrilocality (where a married couple moves to the home of the woman's family, rather than the man's). But in all these societies men act in positions of leadership, which is usually considered the essential aspect of social organisation distinguishing patriarchy from matriarchy or equality. Bachofen also made the assumption that female deities described in classical mythology referred to an historical epoch of matriarchy, or at least that there was a direct relationship between the two. Both these points are controversial.[30]

In the last decade or two, feminist scholars have revived an interest in the question of matriarchy. Anthropologists have re-analysed the evidence for the position of women in societies existing today and those for which we have records written over the last few centuries. Most agree that no societies currently in existence can really be described as matriarchal, especially if this is defined as the exact opposite of patriarchy. However, at the same time as anthropologists point out that no such societies exist, most feminists doubt whether this would result in the Utopian past or future which they are seeking. Some anthropologists argue that although no truly matriarchal society exists now, such societies may only have died out or changed to patriarchy in the last few centuries, under pressure from outside. Early observers may have missed the true nature of other societies by assuming that men were the leaders and therefore the people with whom they should have initial contact, or by only observing or recording aspects of life of interest to themselves, such as warfare or hunting, rather than accurately reflecting the real character of the society itself.

Other anthropologists have taken an alternative viewpoint; they have looked at a range of traditional societies and found that the status of women is regularly higher in forager groups than in any other type, but that these societies are far from being a mirror image of patriarchy.[31] Their social organisation is based on equality between individuals and between the sexes. Everyone has equal opportunity to put forward suggestions and have them listened to, and every individual has the right to make her or his own decision about what to do in any particular instance. Obviously it will usually be preferable to go along with the majority, but if the band is split, for example over which area to move to next, each group may go off in a different direction with no hard feelings. There may, too, be one or more people in the band with outstanding skill in a particular task, perhaps gained through age and experience, whose opinion may be respected over those of others. However, this will not extend to other matters, nor will that individual be deferred to further if she or he is seen to have lost her or his skill or judgement. One key to this equality is the lack of private property or possessions within the society, and the impossibility for a nomadic forager band of storing food. One person cannot therefore own more than another, nor can dependence or debt to another build up in a way which makes oppression and submission a likely outcome.

Although in forager societies the differences between female and male tasks are not fixed or binding in the same way as they have been in the Western world until very recently, and there is quite a high degree of overlap, there does seem, on the whole, to be a fairly fixed division between the sexes in subsistence tasks and especially the provision of food. This, as we have seen, is probably related to the demands of childbirth and childrearing.[32] The key factor seems to be that women provide as much if not more food than men, and as a result of searching for it, they have equal knowledge of their territory and contact with other people; the importance of women's role as producers of the next generation in societies whose populations are small and could fall below a critical point is also appreciated. Women are therefore seen to be as important members of the community as men, and their tasks, though different, are rated as highly as the male skills of hunting.

Mother goddesses or Venus figurines?

Prehistoric human figurines dating from various periods are found in several parts of Europe and have attracted considerable attention over the last century. They have often been discussed as a single phenomenon, despite the fact that they cover an immense time-span, from the Upper Palaeolithic (*c*.25000 BC) to the Bronze Age (*c*.2000 BC), include many variations on the basic theme and should not necessarily be interpreted in the same way. I will do the same here, discussing the Neolithic figurines as well as the Palaeolithic ones, before considering other aspects of the former period in the next chapter. The female figurines have been considered almost to the exclusion of the male ones. This has led to the notion of a Mother Goddess worshipped and represented by idols throughout pre-historic Europe. Two aspects of this concept need to be examined here. Firstly, the figurines themselves must be reviewed. Where and when were they made? In what context are they found? Do they represent women exclusively, and is there sufficient similarity in their design and context to suggest that a single explanation is plausible for all the figurines from all over Europe? Secondly, the evidence for the belief in such a Mother Goddess needs to be considered, along with other possible interpretations.

Most of the figurines belong to one or two phases. Those from the Upper Palaeolithic are often referred to as 'Venus figurines' (from the Roman goddess of fertility), and come from a wide area of Europe stretching from Western France to Russia. A second, larger and more diverse group belonging to the Neolithic period is found in the Mediterranean islands and in Eastern Europe. We will examine these two groups separately before considering a range of possible explanations for them.

The art of the Upper Palaeolithic in Europe falls into three categories, the best known of which is perhaps the cave paintings from France and Spain depicting the animals that were hunted. Secondly, there are bone and stone objects with carved or engraved designs, often of animals; and thirdly, the 'Venus' or 'Mother Goddess' figurines.[33]

Over sixty Palaeolithic female figurines have been found in widespread locations in Europe. A few are made of moulded baked clay or carved in bas-relief, but most are carved from softish stone or in mammoth ivory and

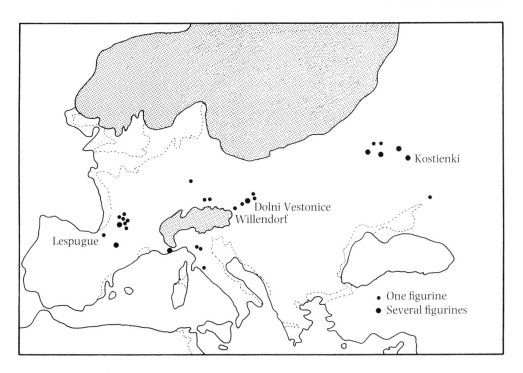

15 Map of the distribution of Venus figurines, showing contemporary (*solid*) and modern (*dashed*) coastlines, and areas covered by ice sheets (*shaded*). After Champion *et al.*, 1984.

are between 4 cm and 22 cm in height, mostly at the smaller end of this range. They show remarkable uniformity in style, and all are characterised by very large breasts, large buttocks and thick thighs. Other parts of the body, such as arms, feet and facial features, are sketchily represented or absent, and the women are naked, though some seem to be wearing ornamental girdles or chest bands. The care and skill with which these figurines have been executed varies considerably: some have clearly had a great deal of effort expended on them, while others appear to be very roughly made. They have been found from the Pyrenees in the west as far east as the river Don in Russia, an area of over 2,000 km from south-west to north-east, and seem to belong to a narrow timeband in the Early Upper Palaeolithic between around 25000 and 23000 BC.[34] Most are associated with houses or homebases, and they are usually found singly amongst assemblages of flint tools and debris, though sometimes, as at Kostienki-Borchevo on the river Don, several have been found together.

Among the best known are the baked clay figurines from Dolni Vestonice in Czechoslovakia (Fig. 7), which were found amongst domestic debris in a hut, along with bone and flint remains. In another hut on the same site

16 Venus figurines:
a. Dolni Vestonice,
Czechoslovakia (baked
clay);
b. Lespugue, Haute
Garonne, France
(mammoth ivory);
c. Willendorf, Austria
(limestone);
d. Sireuil, Dordogne,
France (calcite);
e. Balzi Rossi, Italy;
f–g. Kostienki, USSR
(mammoth ivory).
Approximately half
actual size. From Wymer,
1982.

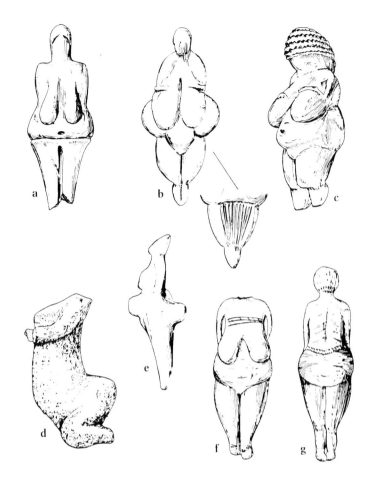

was a kiln thought to have been used for baking or firing such figurines, as well as clay models of animals. This is particularly noteworthy, as it is the earliest evidence of clay firing. Another well-known figurine is the 'Venus of Willendorf' in Austria, carved from limestone and 11 cm high; she has carefully arranged hair or a head-dress, but no facial features. Her arms are laid across her breasts, but her legs end just below the knees. The southern French examples from Abri Laussel and Abri Pataud are carved in bas-relief, and are considerably larger than the portable figurines. The Laussel example is 44 cm high and holds a horn in one hand, while the other rests on her stomach. Also from the same rock shelter, however, is a male figure, the presence of which must be taken into account when the function of these figures is considered.

Although the female 'Venus figurines' must be seen to form a group, they should also be considered as part of a much larger, and usually neglected, series of carved figures of Palaeolithic date. Some, but by no means all, of these are female, though most have naturalistic rather than exaggerated proportions, while others are clearly male, and most appear to be sexless.[35]

The second group of clay or carved prehistoric figurines dates from the Neolithic period. The introduction at this time of clay for pottery-making provided a new medium for the sculptor, which allowed far more detail and flexibility in the figurines than was possible in the Palaeolithic, when they were normally carved. The distribution and eventual decline in importance of these figurines may shed interesting light on the changing status of women during the early prehistoric period. They are found throughout much of Europe and in south-west Asia, including especially south-east Europe and the Mediterranean islands from the Cyclades in the east, through Crete to Malta and Majorca in the west, but interestingly not in central or north-west Europe. Although many of these figurines are of female form, it cannot be ignored that animal models are also sometimes found. Moreover, many figurines show no obvious sexual characteristics, and although male figures also sometimes occur, like the animals they are often left out of the discussion. Many of the figurines from each area and island in the Mediterranean have specific characteristics which mark them out from those of other areas; also the contexts in which they are found vary from one area to another.

One of the groups of European Neolithic figurines which has been studied in detail is that found on the island of Crete. These figurines belong mainly to the Middle and Late Neolithic, from around 5500 to 3000 BC. Many authors have linked the Cretan Neolithic figurines with those of later, Minoan, Crete, which will be considered in a later chapter, but a number of important contrasts have been noted by Peter Ucko in a wide-ranging discussion of the interpretation of prehistoric figurines.[36] Although thirty-three figurines are definitely female, six are clearly male and another forty-

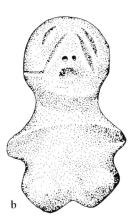

17 Neolithic figurines from Crete:
a. Petra tou Limniti (height 18 cm);
b. Ayia Mavri (height 16 cm).
After Ucko, 1968.

a   b

two are without sexual features. The existence of even a few male figures makes the interpretation of the females as an all-important 'Mother Goddess' difficult, without allowing the possibility of the equal existence of a male deity. Do the sexless examples represent children, or 'humanity'? Unlike figurines from other places, the Neolithic Cretan female images do not have particularly marked sexual characteristics. They were nearly all found in rubbish pits or piles of debris outside houses. None come from any context which might be regarded as a shrine, and none from burials, though no tombs are actually known from this period in Crete.

Another remarkable series of early Neolithic female figurines comes from Anatolia (modern Turkey). This area is particularly important as it is one of the few areas in which fertility cults and a 'Mother Goddess' are historically attested at a later period. The site of Çatal Hüyük is of especial interest in this context, and the implications of the symbolism of the figures have been discussed by the excavator and other authors.[37] The site lies in the Konya plain of Anatolia, and is the largest Neolithic site in the Near East. The village or town, with an estimated 1,000 houses and perhaps a population of around 5,000–6,000, was occupied over a long period, from around 6250 to 5400 BC. The figurines fall into two groups. The first have crudely shaped female forms, with pointed legs, stalk-like bodies and a beaked or pointed head. They are found tucked into crevices in the brickwork or shrines, but never actually inside them. The second group are carved in stone or clay, and do come from shrines. They include a variety of representations of both men and women. The men have penises; the women have breasts and some seem to be pregnant. While most are naked, some are clothed. A series of plaster reliefs on the walls of the shrines depict women giving birth to bulls' heads. The only humans represented in this way are women, and the excavator thought that men might be represented by bulls and rams.

Another site of similar date and in the same area, Hacilar,[38] has also produced a number of clay statuettes. None of these represent animals, and the human figures fall into two categories. Twenty-five figurines are clearly of women, while another twenty have no breasts or other sexual features. The excavator of the site, James Mellaart, considered these to be representations of younger women, though other scholars have been less certain about whether one particular sex was intended. Many of the figurines are described as steatopygous, meaning that they have over-large buttocks, but Ucko[39] has pointed out that these are not out of proportion with the other, ample dimensions and stomachs of the figurines. Unlike at Çatal Hüyük, the figurines were found inside houses, and were therefore presumably kept there, rather than in communal shrines.

The figurines from the Cycladic islands include representations of both

18 Two Cycladic figurines:
(*left*) from Amorgos, *c.* 3200–2800 BC (height
11.1 cm);
(*right*) Spedos type, *c.* 2800–2300 BC (height
20.9 cm).
British Museum.

women and men.[40] They cover a wide chronological span from the early Neolithic to the Late Bronze Age, and it is possible to see typological changes from simple clay models to the highly schematised figurines, characteristically with folded arms, carved from local marble in the Bronze Age. In contrast to the Cretan figurines, they have usually been found in graves, rather than on settlement sites. Although male figures do occur, most of the representations are of women, some of whom may be pregnant. Most have very stylised faces, their arms folded below the breasts, and an incised triangle representing the genital area. We do not know whether these female figurines were buried with women or men, or whether the possibly pregnant figurines were perhaps buried with women who died in childbirth, though these are questions which future excavation should be able to answer. Some are carved in semi-relief, giving a flat appearance, while others are more naturalistic. Others again, particularly of the later phases, show people, who always seem to be male, involved in activities such as playing the flute or the harp and hunting. Interpretations of the Cycladic figurines have been varied. It has been suggested that they may have been designed to satisfy the sexual appetite of the deceased; that they were substitutes for human sacrifice, images of venerated ancestors, or toys to amuse the dead. Often they are seen as images of deities, perhaps a great Mother Goddess or one who would care for the dead on their journey to the underworld. Although none of these theories outweighs the rest, some questions may help to strengthen one or other of them. If the figurines are intended to give satisfaction to the dead, why are examples – however simple – not found in all graves? Often they seem to have been put into the grave in a manner not particularly suggestive of reverence, such as one might expect towards a deity. Sometimes broken images are found in the graves, which may suggest that they were used in funerary or other rituals before being placed with the dead.

The function of both the Upper Palaeolithic and the Neolithic figurines and the significance they had for the societies which made them have been the subject of much speculation and debate. As the majority of them are representations of women, their interpretation is clearly central to our theme. Most of the Palaeolithic figurines show marked similarities, which strongly suggest a common meaning and linked social or religious tradition throughout Europe. By contrast, in the Neolithic the figurines of each separate area have different distinctive features, and so although at a very basic level they may all have a link – which may be merely a common ancestry in the Palaeolithic figurines – each group needs to be considered separately, taking into account the detail and the context in which they are found in each culture. It certainly cannot be assumed that every human figure modelled in prehistory had the same function.[41]

As we have seen, there are significant differences between the Palaeolithic 'Venus' figurines and those of the Neolithic and Early Bronze Age. Also, because in most ways the contrasts between the Neolithic figurines of different areas of the Mediterranean are more notable than the similarities, it has been argued that it is unlikely that the whole area shared one belief system or common set of meanings. On the other hand, in recent times large areas of Africa were populated by completely autonomous, and sometimes hostile, tribes which nevertheless shared many characteristics of ritual and religion, even if each tribe manifested the belief in a slightly different way. As the same arguments, ethnographic analogies and considerations are relevant for discussing the numerous possible interpretations for the figurines of both phases of the Stone Age, these will be considered before turning back to think about specific groups of figurines.

The majority of writers discussing the Palaeolithic 'Venus' figurines emphasise their sexual characteristics, especially the large breasts and pubic triangle, and the fact that many of them may be pregnant. These figurines may, however, simply depict women who to our eyes would be obese; yet this obesity may have been a highly desirable state to generally thinner, less well-nourished women. These characteristics, it is often argued, demonstrate that the figures are concerned with fertility. Fertility is much more important to small societies who are dependent on maintaining a constant birth-rate simply for their survival than to larger societies in the modern Western world. Two lines of argument have been taken. Some people believe that a goddess of fertility or a Mother Goddess is represented, while others have suggested that the figurines are part of sympathetic magic rituals aimed at making individual women pregnant.

The likelihood of a significant continent-wide cult of a Mother Goddess has been greatly exaggerated.[42] However, the worship of a fertility goddess is attested in historical records in Anatolia, some several thousand years after the Neolithic figurines were produced in the area, and this strengthens the possibility that the earlier Anatolian figurines are representations of the same goddess, particularly when their form and context are examined.[43] If this interpretation is correct, is a single goddess represented in different postures and forms, or is a series of different goddesses intended? It does not, however, automatically follow from this that every figurine in prehistoric Europe must be interpreted in the same way. A universal religion based on a specific female goddess is unlikely in a society such as that of Palaeolithic Europe, both because it assumes closer and more detailed contact between different groups over a wide area of Europe than is implied by links in other aspects of material culture, and particularly because religion based on deities would be very unusual in similar societies today. The belief systems of forager and other small-scale societies, who are closely in touch with the natural world and whose own social systems are based on greater equality than that of later socially stratified societies, typically centre on general spirits and forces, rather than on personified gods and goddesses. Such beliefs in deities are characteristic of, for example, the classical Greek and Roman world and have inspired archaeologists to refer to the Palaeolithic figurines as 'Venus' figurines by analogy with the Roman goddess of fertility. They are typical of complex societies where social stratification and craft specialisation is closely mirrored in the 'pecking order' and special tasks assigned to the deities. While the origin of the classical belief systems is worthy of consideration in its own right, it seems unlikely that such a system would have prevailed in the Palaeolithic and early Neolithic periods. By analogy with other social and economic changes in the later Neolithic and early Bronze Age (see Chapter 3), these periods are probably more likely to have provided a context in which such cults could have originated.

Another interpretation of the Palaeolithic figurines[44] stresses the domestic context in which many of the Venus figurines are regularly found, often near hearths in some of the earliest huts and houses. A link is made between women's role within the family and home and as 'fire-makers' in many traditional societies. The figurines are thus interpreted as spirits, if not images of 'goddesses', connected with protecting the newly 'invented' home and hearth.

A related interpretation which has sometimes been put forward for the later figurines is that they represent votaries, or priestesses, sometimes in a particular attitude of prayer, sometimes taking part in actions appropriate to the worship of the relevant deity. As argued above, religions involving deities, let alone priestesses with specialised functions, imply a political and social organisation far more complex than that likely to have existed at the periods in question.

The figurines might also represent pseudo-historical characters who formed part of the mythology or explanatory framework of the society. In parts of Africa, for example, figurines are used as teaching aids in initiation ceremonies, to illustrate characters in myths or to demonstrate appropriate behaviour within society. After use these models are thrown away, and might thus be expected to be found in contexts similar to those of the Neolithic Cretan figurines. The predominance, even if it is sometimes over-emphasised, of female representations would then be particularly interesting. Could they perhaps have been used in women's ceremonies, or to explain pregnancy to girls at puberty? Or, if they represent specific historical or mythical women, do they argue for the importance of women within the history and mythology of the society? It may be objected that even if women are revered within a religious context such as in the modern Catholic world, this may give little indication of their true status within society. But this objection has also been counteracted by the suggestion[45] that there is a much closer link between ideology and behaviour in egalitarian than in hierarchical societies, where inequality and exploitation are deliberately veiled by ambiguous and contradictory ritual and rhetoric.

The use of figurines in sympathetic magic[46] to aid fertility is attested in many ethnographic examples, and may have been perceived as even more important in societies where the link between male impregnation and childbirth was not fully understood. A woman wishing for a child would make, or have made, a model either of herself pregnant, or – more commonly in known ethnographic examples – of the hoped-for child, perhaps shown as the adult they would eventually become. She might then carry the image around, perhaps sleep alongside it, or use it to perform other rituals. Amongst several North-American Indian tribes, such as the Zuni, a woman wanting a baby carries a model around, keeps it in a cradle or places it on an altar until she becomes pregnant. After the successful birth of a child the model is in some cases thrown away and in others carefully kept by the mother to ensure the child's future prosperity. In some West African groups it is common for a pregnant woman to carry a model on her back, while among other peoples in the area, such as the Senufo, fertility figures are given to children at puberty; they are looked after and eventually buried with the individual upon their death. The sex of the desired child might be specified by the model, or left undefined. The small size of some of the prehistoric models would make them easily portable. The fact that both the Palaeolithic and many Neolithic figurines are commonly found within houses or homebases, and often among debris, would strengthen this possibility if the image could be cast aside once it had fulfilled its function, while the idea of discarding the image of a specific deity seems less likely. If some of the early prehistoric figurines are intended to depict a desired child, the implication of the dominance of female figurines, followed by sexless representations over male figures, would have to be that girls were more highly desired than boys, while some parents were indifferent to the sex of their child.

In some modern societies figurines are commonly employed in other forms of sorcery and magic. To do harm to an individual it might be necessary to carry out an equivalent action on the model, such as breaking it to imitate death, or sticking pins into it to represent wounds. Alternatively, a model might be used for good, such as healing, perhaps by anointing it with a particular substance.

On the other hand, more mundane explanations of the figurines are possible. For example, in many areas of the world figurines are played with by children as dolls, and such an interpretation of some of the prehistoric models cannot be dismissed. The use of cheap materials such as clay, the occurrence of animals as well as humans in some areas, and the apparent carelessness with which they are sometimes disposed of makes this a possible hypothesis for some of the groups of figurines.

Clive Gamble[47] has looked at a rather different aspect of the Palaeolithic figures, which is not necessarily incompatible with any of the interpretations which we have discussed. He emphasises their role as a means of communication, linking far-flung communities through a common symbolism. The date of the figurines coincides with the period of maximum glaciation, when communities would have needed extra social safety nets to cushion imbalances in resources. The figurines come from open-air sites and rock shelters rather than from the deep recesses of caves, suggesting that they could be viewed, and therefore their 'message' read, by anyone at any time. This interpretation might be considered additional and complementary to whichever hypotheses are preferred for explaining why the 'Venus figurine' was chosen as the medium for communication, even if the implication of a far-flung and important link is accepted.

We have now considered a range of possible interpretations for the figurines of all periods, and it is clear that 'mother' or fertility goddesses are by no means the only possibilities. We have also seen that some interpretations are more or less likely for some groups of figurines, due to the context in which they were found, whether in graves or in domestic or rubbish deposits, because of the cheap or, on the other hand, the rarer or harder-to-work materials out of which they are made, or the regularity of distinctive features of the body form or posture. The social, environmental and economic contexts of the societies which produced the Palaeolithic and the Neolithic figurines are very different: the contrasting roles of women as food-providers in each society must be considered, and the huge chronological gap between the two groups must be appreciated. The Palaeolithic figurines are the products of hunter-gatherer communities living in extremely cold climates, on the edges of the glacial ice-sheets, where meat probably acquired largely by men would have been a mainstay of the diet, whereas the Neolithic figurines were made thousands of years later within simple agricultural societies, where, as we shall see in the following chapter, women played the key role in food production. It is therefore not necessary to use any one explanation to account for all the figurines. And, as with any works of art, their role in creating and reinforcing a particular ideology, which might not relate directly to the actual role of the object portrayed, in this case women, needs to be borne in mind. The reader must in the end make up her or his own mind, and only be aware of the problems involved in the interpretation of any archaeological material. Whichever interpretation is preferred, the dominance of female representations over male, even where the forms are not uniquely female, must be significant.

3 The First Farmers

From the point of view of the lives of women, the Neolithic period is perhaps the most important phase of prehistory. As we saw in the last chapter, it is likely that at the end of the Palaeolithic and Mesolithic, women enjoyed equality with men. They probably collected as much, if not more, of the food eaten by the community and derived equal status from their contribution. But by about four thousand years ago, in the Bronze Age, many of the gender roles and behaviour typical of the Western world today had probably been established. The implication is that the crucial changes must have taken place during the Neolithic period.

The chief characteristic of the Neolithic was the establishment of agriculture in south-west Asia and south-east Europe, perhaps around the seventh millennium BC or earlier. The innovation progressively spread across Europe, until it became established in Britain by the fourth millennium BC (Fig. 23). Numerous other inventions and adaptations in lifestyle seem to have occurred more or less at the same time. These include the change from a nomadic to a sedentary settlement pattern, the invention of pottery and the use of polished stone tools. It is likely that important social changes followed from these developments.

The discovery of agriculture

One of the most momentous changes in the history of the human species was surely the domestication of plants and animals – the invention of agriculture. The social consequences of the switch from foraging to agriculture would have been as far-reaching as the economic consequences, but not all the implications of this change would have been realised for many generations or even centuries. The transition from foraging to farming would have made profound differences to nearly all aspects of the lifestyle of prehistoric women and men. Rather than moving around in search of food, the discovery of agriculture allowed, or perhaps necessitated, a sedentary lifestyle. It would also have given rise to, or perhaps was precipitated by, an increase in the size of the population. There is a lot of discussion in the archaeological literature about which of these changes were causes and which effects, and why the changes came about, or were adopted eventually over almost the whole of Europe. The discovery of farming techniques has usually been assumed to have been made by men, but it is in fact very much more likely to have been made by women. On the basis

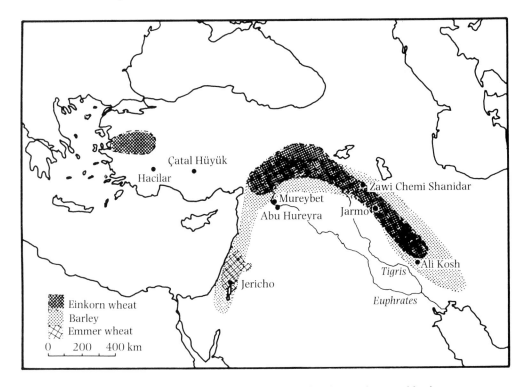

19 The natural distribution of the wild cereals emmer and einkorn wheat and barley, with the key sites in the early history of agriculture in south-west Asia. After Bender, 1975.

of anthropological evidence for societies still living traditional foraging life-styles and those living by simple, non-mechanised farming, taken in conjunction with direct archaeological evidence, it seems probable that it was women who made the first observations of plant behaviour, and worked out, presumably by long trial and error, how to grow and tend crops.

This transition from foraging to farming, which marks the change from the Palaeolithic and Mesolithic or Old and Middle Stone Ages to the period known to archaeologists as the Neolithic or New Stone Age, seems to have taken place initially in south-west Asia some time after 10,000 BC. By 6000 BC farming was well established throughout that part of the world. From there the ideas and skills of agriculture spread throughout Europe.

Over the last decade or so, tremendous steps forward have been made by archaeologists in discovering when and where agriculture first came about, and some of the stages by which the transition happened.[1] Scientific methods of dating, especially radiocarbon or C^{14} dating, have allowed us to ascertain the date by which fully agricultural, sedentary populations were living in various parts of Europe and south-west Asia, and palaeobotanical and zoological studies have shown which plants and animals were first domesticated. The earliest agricultural communities lived in the areas often known as the Fertile Crescent, around the rivers Tigris and Euphrates, now within the modern countries of Iran, Iraq, Turkey, Syria, Jordan and Israel, where the grasses which were to be domesticated grew wild.[2] Other archaeologists argue that human groups could have evolved through the stages of transition to agriculture quite independently over a very much wider area, possibly including parts of south-east Europe. In the early phases at sites such as Ali Kosh in Iran, Çayönü in Anatolia and Jericho in Israel, wild cereal seeds and animal bones have been found which differ in the detail of their form or morphology from their domesticated successors, whereas in the later phases at the same sites the same species

20 The difference between wild and domesticated wheat: ears and grains of **a.** wild einkorn (*Triticum boeoticum*) and **b.** domesticated einkorn (*T. monococcum*). After Bender, 1975, and Cole, 1960.

a

b

occur in their domesticated form. One of the key sites is Mureybet in the Euphrates valley, where about 200 round houses were built on low-lying land. The site is located at least 100 kilometres from highlands, which are thought to be the nearest location where wild cereals would grow naturally. The presence of wild wheat and barley seeds at Mureybet, therefore, is most easily interpreted as evidence that cereals were brought as seed corn from the higher land and planted near the site, at a date of around 8500–8000 BC.[3] A similar case, but even earlier in date (about 9500–8500 BC), occurs at the site of Abu Hureya, about 25 kilometres downstream from Mureybet, where wild einkorn wheat was found in immediately 'pre-Neolithic' levels, but would not have grown naturally in the area. A study of seeds of weeds found with the wheat, however, showed species typical of the vegetation of the area around Abu Hureya rather than of the higher land away from the site, and strengthens the hypothesis that the cereals were being grown locally.[4]

How and why did this change to agriculture take place, and, more particularly, what can we say about the role of women in this process?

In the last chapter we discussed foraging societies still living in the world today. They gather and hunt food in a way similar to Palaeolithic societies before the invention of agriculture; among these people there is a regularly recurring pattern of food procurement. As we have seen, women are mainly concerned with gathering plant food, which provides the bulk of the diet of nearly all foragers, while men spend much time hunting animals. Although animal products form an important source of proteins in the diet, meat actually makes up a relatively small proportion of the food intake of these societies. We can also study other groups of people in places such as New Guinea and parts of Africa who still grow crops and keep animals with the aid of only the very simplest technology, in much the same way as we may imagine Neolithic societies would have done. These societies do not use ploughs or artificial irrigation, and they keep few, if any, animals. To distinguish them from people using more mechanised agricultural technologies, anthropologists usually call this type of farming horticulture, and the people using it horticultural societies. By studying the way of life of these groups and considering the type of archaeological evidence that would remain from their various activities, and comparing this with the actual archaeological evidence for the earliest farmers in Europe and south-west Asia, some insight can be gained into lifestyles in Neolithic Europe.

The problems involved in using ethnographic examples as a model for past societies, and in particular for considering possible gender roles in the past, have already been discussed and must be borne in mind here. But in addition to the more general difficulties associated with making such comparisons, a number of significant differences between Neolithic and modern horticulturalists must be noted. Most present-day horticulturalists live in areas such as New Guinea, the Pacific Islands, South America and parts of central Africa. The climate and natural vegetation in these areas is quite different from those in which the earliest horticulturalists lived, and the crops grown by these people have different growth and harvesting requirements from the cereal crops grown in Europe and south-west Asia, and require different techniques to prepare them for consumption. These factors will have made some difference to the social and economic organisation of the communities, but just how much, and how they would have affected gender roles and the status of women is difficult to establish. However, although present-day horticulturalists live in a wide variety of places around the world, many remarkably regular patterns of behaviour can be observed, and this gives us some degree of confidence in using their lifestyles as a model for the Neolithic, particularly if some of the behaviour patterns can be seen to be reflected in evidence from archaeological sites.

Studies of the roles of women in different types of agricultural communities show a remarkably consistent pattern.[5] In societies where plough agriculture is practised and animals are kept on a significant scale, most of the agricultural work is done by men, with women playing no direct part, or only a very subsidiary role. On the other hand, in horticultural societies, in which hoes or digging sticks are used for making holes or drills in which to plant roots or seeds, women are usually almost wholly responsible for agricultural production. A study of 104 horticultural societies existing today showed that in 50 per cent of them women were exclusively responsible for agriculture, in 33 per cent women and men shared various tasks, and in only 17 per cent were men wholly responsible for farming, and this is after decades or even centuries of contact with societies whose ideology would encourage men to take on greater roles in production.[6] Horticultural societies are still widespread, mainly within the Tropics, in many parts of Africa, central America and Asia. The typical pattern in these areas is one of shifting cultivation, where patches of land are worked for a few years, and then when soil fertility declines another plot is cleared and cultivated. Although men often help to clear the plots of trees and undergrowth, women usually hoe, sow, tend and harvest the crops. Studies carried out early this century suggest that this pattern of cultivation was more common then than it is today. It also seems very likely that it was even more typical before most parts of the world had contact with European traders and missionaries, with their preconceived ideas about what it was right and proper for women and men to do.

Today's horticulturalists, living mainly in tropical rain forest areas, have to clear dense forest and undergrowth before they can begin cultivation, and, as we have seen, this is usually the men's task. In south-west Asia, in the areas where agriculture was first practised, the natural vegetation was very different. Analysis of pollen preserved on Neolithic sites shows that natural grassland would have predominated, with oak and pistachio forests on the higher land. Clearing this grassland would have been a relatively easy task, and it is possible that initially the chosen cereal grass seeds may have been scattered on bare sandy patches with little natural vegetation, or that wild grasses could have been pulled up or burnt off before seeds were scattered. The clearing task allotted to men in present-day horticultural societies would therefore hardly have existed; in any case, men would presumably still have been involved in hunting, as they had been when the society was wholly dependent on foraging and indeed as they were in many recent horticultural societies before pressure on the land and modern government interference reduced the importance of hunting in many areas.

Most traditional horticultural societies keep no or very few animals. Wild animals may be hunted, or one or two domesticated species may be kept in limited numbers, usually living around the farmyard, rather than being herded on a large scale. In New Guinea and the Pacific Islands, for example, pigs are bred; they are highly valued and considerable effort goes into their care, but because animals are not used for ploughing and animal manure is not spread on the fields, the symbiotic relationship between plant crops and domestic animals which is found in more sophisticated agricultural regimes does not exist. In south-west Asia, however, the first evidence for domesticated sheep, goats and pigs dates from almost the same time as the earliest crops, and often occurs on the same sites, though at Abu Hureya, one of the very earliest agricultural sites, for example, it seems that in the first phase when crop husbandry was practised, meat was supplied only by hunting wild animals.[7] It may be that the parallel invention of plant cultivation and animal domestication is a real and important difference between the present-day and the Neolithic horticulturalists. On the other hand, it is impossible to work out the relative proportions of plants grown and animals kept at a site from archaeological remains, because animal bones usually survive well, whereas seeds and plant remains are rare, and are not found unless special techniques for their recovery are used during excavations. It is likely that a high proportion of the animals kept on the site will be represented, while most seeds, and remains of other food plants, will either have been eaten or resown and thus leave no archaeological trace. On most early Neolithic sites, bones of wild animals are commonly found with those of domesticated species, and hunting must have continued alongside agriculture. How were gender roles balanced in these early Neolithic communities? Did some men transfer their knowledge of animals learnt through hunting to the tending of domesticated animals? Or did the men continue to hunt, as in today's horticultural societies, while women or children looked after a small number of domesticated animals, perhaps the young of a mother who had been killed by hunters, which had been 'rescued' and tended by a group of children?

As women are responsible for plant food gathering in virtually all foraging societies about which we have information, and are responsible for growing plants in horticultural societies today, it can be argued that it is very likely that they would also have been responsible for these tasks in the past.[8] It also follows that women would have been in a position to hit upon the various stages towards the cultivation of plants, as well as all the vital concomitant inventions associated with it, such as the hoe, and storage and preparation procedures. Two questions arise. How might we imagine these stages evolved? Would it have been a huge and sudden breakthrough, or a gradual process? And secondly, can we find any archaeological evidence from the excavated Neolithic sites in the areas where we know agriculture first occurred to suggest or prove that it was women who made this revolutionary change?

The archaeological evidence for the early stages of the transition to agriculture is hard to recognise. Morphological changes take place in plants by both unintentional and deliberate selection of certain characteristics, but only after years of cultivation. Species of animals kept separate from wild populations with restricted breeding partners also change in the details of their form after several generations. However, these mutations occur long after the socially far more significant step of people actually manipulating the lives of the wild species, by keeping them in captivity or providing food. If wild grass seeds are found on an archaeological site it will not, therefore, be easy to tell directly whether they were gathered by a pre-agricultural woman or grown in a place deliberately chosen by a 'Neolithic' woman.

A number of very important excavations which have taken place in south-west Asia in the last decade or so have produced vital new evidence for the stages in the transition to agriculture.[9] The settlements and house types of the first farmers and their material culture have become better known. However, most of these excavations have been on quite a small scale by the standards of excavations in north-west Europe. If larger areas of these sites were excavated it might be possible to show that some areas or houses within them were used for one task and others for different ones. For instance, concentrations of flint debris have shown where flint tools were made, but corresponding evidence for different food-producing task areas has not yet been reported on Near-Eastern Neolithic sites.[10] If this could be done, it might be possible to correlate this evidence with the sex of the skeletons which are quite frequently found buried under the floors of the house. Assuming that the dead person lived or worked in that particular house, as seems quite plausible, this correlation, calculated for a large enough sample, might provide real evidence that women were regularly associated with one set of tasks and men with another. Although, to the best of my knowledge, such a study has not yet been attempted, it would be well within the scope of archaeology and requires only a larger body of relevant material, which will undoubtedly be forthcoming from excavations in the near future.

How may we imagine the discovery of agriculture was made? By analogy with present-day foraging societies, as we have seen, it was almost certainly women who were responsible for gathering plant foods, which, it is important to remember, make up the bulk of the diet in nearly all traditional societies. They would therefore have been aware of the most likely place to find a certain plant growing: for example, one plant food may have grown beside a river, another under the shelter of trees. After a lifetime of watching plants growing, these women would have understood a great deal about the complicated business of plant biology; they would have recognised the young seedlings which had become fully grown crops when they returned to the same place later in the year. They would soon have realised that if there was less rain or less sunshine than usual the plants would not be so big and there would be less to eat, and they would have realised also that the seeds needed to fall to the ground if more of that food was to grow in the same place the next year. If the whole plant was pulled up or eaten, none would grow there the next season, but if some of the seeds were dropped or sprinkled somewhere else then that plant might grow there instead. Undoubtedly many thousands of foraging women would have realised this, but to most there would not have seemed to be any advantage in controlling the places where the food grew. As we saw in the last chapter, foraging lifestyles have many advantages, and agriculture does not necessarily make life any better. Many present-day foragers, for example the !Kung of the Kalahari desert, are well aware that their neighbours practise agriculture, and even of how it works, but they choose to retain their traditional, easy practices: 'why bother to grow crops when there are so many mongongo nuts in the world?'

The transition from foraging to horticulture would inevitably have led to many other changes in lifestyle, not all of which would have been foreseen by the earliest innovators. Around 10,000 BC women all over Europe and south-west Asia would have spent part of their days gathering the crops and plants which grew around them; the men would have spent their time hunting. When the women thought that a plant growing some way from home would be getting ripe, or the men noticed that there were fewer and fewer animals nearby, they would take their small collection of belongings and move perhaps a few miles, perhaps many, till they came to a better source of supply. How often such a move was necessary would have varied tremendously. In some parts of the world, or at certain times of the year, it would have been necessary to move every few days, while at others they could have stayed several months in one particularly rich spot. Indeed, in some of the most favourable parts of Europe it might only have been necessary to move two or three times a year, alternating between a few regular living places, or perhaps the only reason to move might have been to harvest one particularly favoured crop which grew some distance away. The foods that were actually eaten, of course, varied from area to area, and some would have been more obvious candidates for domestication than others. In the mountain valleys of south-west Asia there grew a number of grasses, the seeds of which, it was discovered, could be boiled or ground into flour, and were particularly tasty and nutritious. These grasses, which we know as the cereals wheat and barley, were only found in the mountain valleys, but other foods eaten in the area seem to have grown on lower land, near the river valleys. Cereals only ripen once a year, but the seeds could be kept and eaten in a later season. Foragers do not as a rule carry food around with them, but some of the women gathering these cereals may have found that they could easily gather enough food in a few days to last for some time; some people would probably have stayed where the seeds were harvested, while others may have preferred to carry them some distance to other places, where perhaps other foods were to be found.[11]

These discoveries would probably have had two important consequences: firstly, a change from a nomadic lifestyle to sedentism, and secondly a significant increase in population.[12] In the first place it would have been difficult to carry heavy bags full of cereals around; and if they were left somewhere, with the intention of returning to them later, someone or some animal would be very likely to find them, and eat them before the harvesters came back. For these reasons, therefore, it would soon have been discovered that it was best to leave at least some of the group guarding the grain stores. Perhaps the elderly members of the community stayed behind while the others went off looking for other foods. If sufficient grain was collected to last for a considerable part of the year, it may have become easier to stay in one place for many months, provided that some other sources of food were also available nearby. When the cereal grain was moved from its storage place to where it was to be eaten, some seeds would inevitably have dropped on the ground, and some may eventually have germinated. If the group was still living in, or had returned to, the same place the next spring, some of the women would no doubt have noticed the new plants of wheat and barley growing there. Some particularly observant women, or perhaps even a child, may have watched as the seed lying on the ground sprouted, and gradually grew bigger and bigger, until it was recognisable as a cereal plant. This would have happened year after year in many different settlements around the natural sources of wheat and barley. However, it would have been a major and significant step deliberately to drop or sprinkle some precious seeds near the homebase and to be confident that new plants would grow there. On the other hand, once this step had been taken, it would have saved the trek to the place where the cereal was normally harvested. It would then have been important to remain nearby while the young plants were growing in order to ward off scavenging animals and people. And once the ripe grain had been harvested, it would have had to be carefully stored and protected while it was gradually being eaten over the winter. So, without any original intent, the group would have had to remain in the same place all year round; at no season could the whole community have easily moved away. From a nomadic foraging society the group would thus have become sedentary horticulturalists.

Modern nomadic foragers typically build only rudimentary forms of shelter or none at all. They do not remain long enough in the same place to make building substantial structures necessary; moreover, they usually have very few material possessions, as these would only be an extra burden to carry around. But as soon as a group no longer moves frequently, but instead remains in one location, both these factors change. It becomes worthwhile spending some time building a house which will last, and horticulturalists nearly always construct substantial buildings for sleeping and, perhaps more importantly, for storing the food they have produced. The same pattern is clearly seen in the archaeological evidence for the transition from foraging in the Palaeolithic and Mesolithic to food producing in the Neolithic. In the immediately pre-agricultural phase in the southern Levant, known as the Natufian phase after a key site, and dated between around 10000 and 8000 BC, seasonally occupied base camps comprised round or oval huts with stone footings but probably flimsy superstructures, and were perhaps little more than windbreaks. But in the next archaeological phase in the area, when there is evidence of agricultural activity, the houses were more carefully constructed. At Mureybet, a site to which I have already referred, quite substantial rectangular huts were built, some of cut blocks of limestone, others with clay walls in a wooden framework, built on stone footings. Storage bins were built into the floor of the houses, and the fact that the walls had been replastered implies that the houses were occupied for a considerable time.[13]

As people became committed to living more or less permanently in one location because of the agricultural cycle, and began to build places to store things, they would have found it easier to accumulate possessions, such as ornaments, storage containers and tools. Tools used by foragers must be either light enough to carry around or simple enough to be made as and when they are required, and then discarded after use. If, on the other hand, they can be kept and looked after, more effort can be expended on their manufacture. Early agricultural tools would initially have included such things as pointed sticks for making holes in the ground for sowing seeds, and stone querns for grinding grain into flour. As women were discovering the need for this equipment, so they, rather than men, would have solved the problems and invented the necessary tools.[14] While prehistoric foraging women might have used skin bags to carry the plant foods they had gathered back to their base, just as their modern counterparts do, horti-culturalists would have needed more solid containers for keeping food in their houses, but which they would not have had to carry around. Carved wooden vessels may have been used, and pottery has been used by most horticultural societies, both past and present, but rarely by foragers. Indeed, because it is usually so well preserved on archaeological sites, pottery is often the first thing an archaeologist will mention when discussing a site or period. It was invented in south-west Asia, in the same areas in which farming was first practised, but probably several hundred years after the people had become accustomed to a sedentary lifestyle. As pottery was

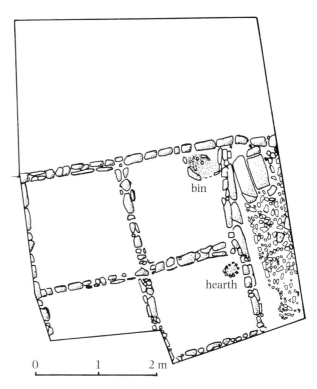

21 The plan of an early Neolithic house in the farming village of Mureybet, Syria, built of cut bricks of soft limestone set in clay mortar. One of the four rooms (lower right) contained a sunken stone-lined hearth, while another (top right) had a storage bin. Outside (right) was a paved courtyard. After Mellaart, 1975.

bin

hearth

0   1   2 m

87

probably used initially for storing cereals, or for cooking plant foods, both of which were within the women's sphere of activity, women are more likely than men to have discovered the processes of moulding clay and then firing it.

Another consequence of the ability to keep material possessions and to store food was that for the first time some people could accumulate more than others. If someone needed a tool or an emergency supply of food that someone else had in surplus, it could be borrowed or accepted as a gift, and the borrower would become indebted to the lender or giver. So wealth, debt and obligation, and hence social stratification based on differential ownership, could have begun to develop for the first time in the Neolithic period, and this is a key theme to which we will return later.

Young children, too, would no longer have needed to be continually carried around. As was discussed in the previous chapter, forager women, facing long treks every few days or weeks, rarely have more than one child under the age of three or four years at any one time. Carrying one child around constantly would be hard enough; carrying two almost impossible.

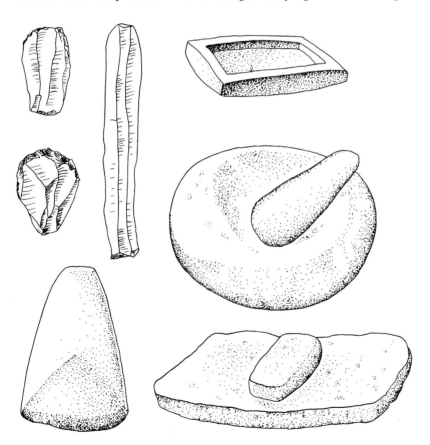

In forager societies the lack of suitable foodstuffs for very young children delays weaning; continual breast-feeding, which would have been necessary in the absence of other food, tends to suppress ovulation in the mother, so also determining the minimum spacing of births. But once long journeys became less common, and food – particularly cereals which are more easily digestible by young children – more certain, an increase in the number of children born, perhaps coupled with a slight decrease in infant mortality, would soon have led to a growth in population.[15] On many Neolithic sites in south-west Asia, a rapid increase in the size of the community is shown by the increasing number of houses on successive phases of the site. The well-known Neolithic site of Jericho is a particularly remarkable example, where the homebase of a small foraging group seems to have developed suddenly into a thriving small town.

Farming must have made this population growth possible, but it would also have led to the beginning of a vicious circle of social and economic change from which there was no escape. More food could be produced from each unit of land, but everyone would have had to work harder to produce

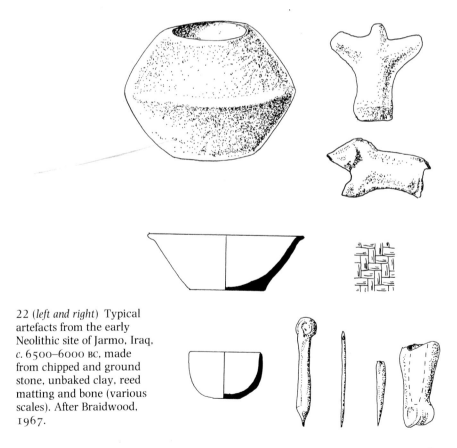

22 (*left and right*) Typical artefacts from the early Neolithic site of Jarmo, Iraq, *c.* 6500–6000 BC, made from chipped and ground stone, unbaked clay, reed matting and bone (various scales). After Braidwood, 1967.

89

that food. More people in the group would have meant more women to work in the fields, but also more mouths to feed. The invention of pottery and other new skills would have created a desire or perceived need for new material possessions. The manufacture of these items would have taken people's time away from agricultural tasks, though they too would still have needed to be fed. A major area of debate amongst archaeologists studying the period is whether an increase in population necessitated the adoption of agriculture, or whether it was the advent of agriculture which made population growth possible. But once the change had been made, everyone would have had to work harder to get more out of the land, and the option of returning to a foraging lifestyle would have become less and less feasible. The people of south-west Asia and then of Europe had become enmeshed in the ever-continuing spiral of increasing populations and more and more labour needed to feed the people, but perhaps also began to enjoy a more comfortable, and certainly a more materialistic, lifestyle. At any rate, agriculture is generally regarded as an advance, and a positive and important step in the progress towards civilisation; and it is very probable that this hugely significant discovery was made, not by men as has generally been assumed, but by women.

The expansion of agricultural communities

Over the three or four millennia after agriculture had been adopted in south-west Asia, the knowledge and skills involved gradually spread through most of Europe. With the success of the new method of food production the population was able to grow; as a result, every so often a community would become too big to be viable and part of it would probably move away in search of fresh land to cultivate. Sometimes, too, forager women probably learnt agricultural skills from a farming group which they encountered. Over the millennia and over the huge area which is Europe there is a great deal of variety in the archaeological evidence for these first farmers, which cannot be considered here in full, but as an example we shall look at perhaps the best-known complex of sites, known as the Linear Pottery Culture, in some detail.

The Linear Pottery Culture,[16] so called after the type of decoration on its pottery, flourished between roughly 5500 and 4800 BC. Settlements are found along the river valleys of the Danube, the Rhine and other major rivers and tributaries of Central Europe, where fine loess soils would have been particularly favourable to agriculture. The areas actually cleared and exploited were very restricted:[17] only limited clearance was made in primary forest, and the bones of wild animals found on the sites which have been excavated suggest that hunting would still have been important in the

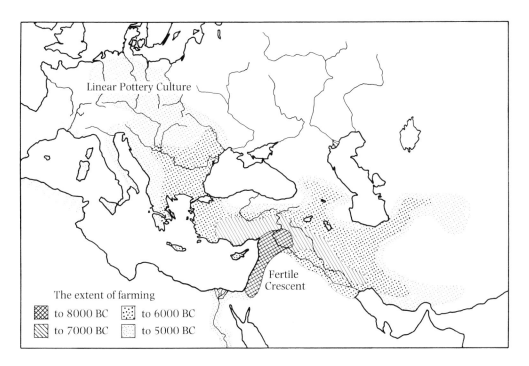

23 The spread of agriculture, based on the evidence of radiocarbon dates. After Sherratt, 1980.

surrounding forests.[18] If, as will be argued in more detail, women were the primary crop producers in these new settlements, it can probably be inferred that they, rather than the men, recognised the ideal soils and chose the land to be cleared, even if, by ethnographic analogy, we may allow that men took part in the actual clearance. The problems of agricultural exploit-ation of the primary forest of central and north-west Europe would have created different tasks and problems from those of the drier bush or scrub of the lower-lying areas of south-east Europe and the Near East. In the latter areas the preparation of fields for planting would have been a relatively easy task, whereas the clearance of heavy forest undergrowth would have been more akin to the forest clearance which present-day horticulturalists must undertake in areas such as New Guinea or South America. There, the usual pattern is that everyone – or sometimes just the men – clears the forest by ringing the bark of large trees so that they die. Smaller trees and under-growth are cut down. After the vegetation has been allowed to die and dry out for a few weeks or months, it is burnt, providing valuable nutrients in the ash at the same time as clearing the land. After this the men return to their hunting, while the women carry on with their agricultural tasks.

The crops grown by the people of the Linear Pottery Culture were much

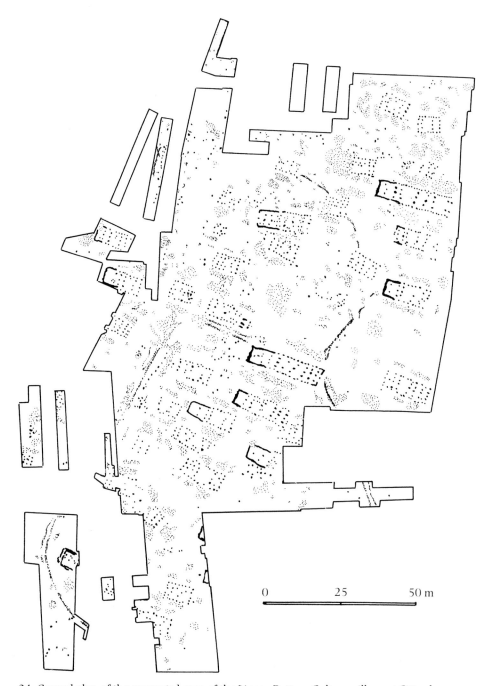

24 Ground plan of the excavated area of the Linear Pottery Culture village at Sittard, Netherlands, fifth millennium BC, showing the rectangular longhouses with post holes and bedding trenches. Beside the houses are shallow pits, and parts of the ditches surrounding the village are clearly visible. After Piggott, 1965.

25 A group of typical Linear Pottery Culture artefacts, including pottery vessels, flint knives and arrowheads, and 'shoe-last' adzes. Bonn, Rheinisches Landesmuseum.

the same as those cultivated by the first farmers in the Near East. Wheat was by far the most important cereal, and peas, beans and various other plants were also grown. Technologically, too, the agricultural processes would have been similar to those of the first farmers, before simple hoeing was superseded by the plough. Women would almost certainly still have been primarily responsible for most, if not all, agricultural work. Querns used to mill flour have sometimes been found in female burials of the Linear Pottery Culture, but never with men,[19] which strongly suggests that women were responsible for food processing, even if that does not necessarily imply involvement in the first stages of food production. Bones of domesticated animals are common on Linear Pottery Culture sites, with cattle pre-dominating over pigs. In addition, wild animal bones suggest that hunting was still important, probably accounting for at least one-third of the number of animals eaten,[20] and fishing and fowling would also have been practised. The question still remains as to how important animal products were, compared with plant foods, in the economy, and who was responsible for the animals. If, as has frequently been suggested, they were overwintered in one end of the longhouses typical of the Linear Pottery Culture (see below), this would imply that the number of cattle kept was limited. The location of settlements on soils ideal for growing crops rather than grazing animals and the predominance of forest around these settlements have been used to support the argument that crops would have been a far more significant part of the economy than domesticated animals.[21] The work of tending and feeding small numbers of cattle and pigs might have fallen to the women, while men continued to hunt and fish.

One of the most distinctive aspects of the Linear Pottery Culture is the large, rectangular longhouses (Fig. 26), about a dozen of which are usually grouped together to form villages occupied by several hundred people. The shape and size of houses of any society will be, at least in part, a reflection of its social organisation, and particularly of family structure, and in turn reflect the position of women in that society. Two studies,[22] which might be applicable to archaeological evidence, have used ethnographic data to substantiate this correlation. Melvin Ember has argued that residence patterns after marriage are reflected in the size of houses, while John Whiting and Barbara Ayres suggest that polygamy or monogamy may be inferred from their shape. According to Ember, in matrilocal societies, where women stay in the same settlements after marriage, larger houses used by extended family units are more common than in patrilocal societies, where smaller houses are occupied by nuclear units. Sisters and their unrelated husbands are more likely to share household tasks and live under one roof, than are brothers sharing houses with unrelated wives in patrilocal societies. Obviously the matrilocal extended families will need more space within each house, which will thus have a larger floor area than a house designed for a nuclear family. A survey of ethnographic cases where sufficient data was available both for house sizes and for residence patterns suggested, with clear statistical correlation, that houses in patrilocally organised societies average 30 square metres in floor area and nearly always less than 55 square metres, whereas the ethnographic data available for albeit a fairly small number of matrilocally organised societies shows houses averaging 80 square metres, with only one known exception under 55 square metres. While this latter study showed a statistically significant pattern, sufficient data was only available for thirty-seven societies. Whiting and Ayres' study suggests that rectangular houses, such as those found in the Linear Pottery Culture, are more likely to be associated with monogamy than with polygamy. Caution must clearly be exercised if we wish to apply this pattern to archaeological examples. The small sample size and the ever-present possibility, indeed sometimes the probability, that a past society behaved in a way unreplicated in the present world should warn us against feeling that the hypothesis can be turned into a law-like certainty. Nor is it always possible to distinguish domestic space from areas used for storage or other functions. However, difference in house size can often be easily detectable from excavation plans, and on the basis of Ember's study, such evidence might form part of a hypothesis as to whether the society was matrilocally or patrilocally organised, particularly if this is supported by other data.

The houses of the Linear Pottery Culture and its successor cultures in central Europe, the Lengyel, Rossen and Tripolye, stand out within the prehistoric period for their great size. They are rectangular in shape and have a width of between 5 and 6 metres. This is probably the maximum that can easily be spanned with gabled roof timbers and a roof slope sufficient for rain water to drain off efficiently. In length the houses vary from 7 to 45 metres, though 6 to 20 metres is most common, and 17 metres the average.[23] These figures give house areas of between 30 and 120 square metres, and an average of around 100 square metres, which certainly falls within the pattern suggestive of matrilocal residence, though it must be borne in mind that we do not always know the function of each part of the house. The structure of the houses shows remarkable regularity. One-third of the house has a more solidly built outer wall than the rest, and this is often interpreted as winter stalling for cattle. An alternative interpretation is that it is merely strengthening against the prevailing wind, as studies of phosphate levels, which might provide evidence of stalling of animals, and artefacts distributed within the house show more uniformity than might be expected if different areas were used for very different functions: this is important, as it will significantly affect the calculation of domestic space and hence the number of people likely to have lived in each house. The other end of the house invariably has very sturdy internal posts, which probably supported an upper floor. This would have been strong enough to have been used for storage, though the area below may still have had a domestic function. Therefore, probably one-third, and possibly two-thirds, of the floor area of each house was not actually used as domestic space. Other clues, such as internal partitions or hearths which might suggest space allocated to nuclear units within an extended family, have not been found on any Linear Pottery site, but this is as likely to reflect the poor state of preservation of the sites as the lack of such features. Several houses of the Tripolye culture of the Middle Neolithic, on the north side of the Black Sea, which are of similar shape and size, have between one and five ovens, and the number of hearths correlates closely with the length of the house. On the basis of this, another study[24] has suggested that a 5–6 metre section of a longhouse might have been occupied by one family. Thus, for example, a longhouse of 20 metres would have housed four families. Many, but not all, of the Linear Pottery houses are over the 55

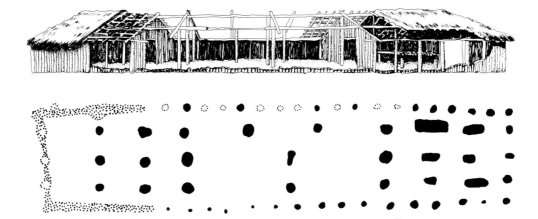

26 Reconstruction and ground plan of a typical longhouse of the Linear Pottery Culture, from Geleen in the Netherlands. After Clarke, 1977.

square metre dividing line between matrilocal and patrilocal residence proposed by Ember. The smaller houses may have been occupied by smaller, but still extended, families, whereas it would be harder to explain houses much larger than a basic unit if nuclear family residence was the norm. I would therefore suggest that the pattern here was one of matrilocal residence units based on the maternal grandmother and her daughters with their husbands and children. Families with only one or two daughters would require smaller houses than those with perhaps four or five daughters. As we have already seen, the evidence for the agricultural base of the Linear Pottery Culture is consistent with a high degree of economic, and hence political, involvement by women, which together with higher than average status for women is also characteristic of matrilocal societies.

The suggestion that matrilocal residence was the norm in the Linear Pottery Culture is supported by theories put forward in two important studies. Though they are quite independent, both relate, in general, to societies which are in the process of spreading or migrating: this is one of the clearest characteristics of the Linear Pottery Culture, as well as the other early Neolithic groups which occupied Europe between the sixth and the third millennium BC.

The first study[25] looked at societies which had recently migrated into new territory and found that these societies had a greater than average likelihood of being matrilocally based. The advantages for such a society in a new territory are easy to see. In a matrilocal society men move from their village of birth on marriage, so adult male relatives are dispersed among villages. They are therefore less likely to make war on other villages of the same culture, as in effect this would involve fighting and killing their own brothers. So the newly founded villages would be able to concentrate on the problems of clearing new land, building new houses and the like, rather than worrying about raids. On the other hand, when in danger from other peoples – perhaps the original inhabitants of the territory into which they had moved – it would be easier to call on the support of relatives in other villages.

Another theory[26] argues that the limiting factor on the success of a society moving into new, sparsely or unoccupied territory would be the size of the labour force to clear and farm land. As women are primarily responsible for increasing the size of a group through reproduction, somewhat higher value would then be placed on them than in societies which put less of a premium on enlarging the labour force. On the other hand, social tensions between descent groups over whether offspring belonged to the mother's or the father's family – that is, matrilineal or patrilineal descent – might become more significant as each group wanted new members. This contrasts with the situation found later when the critical resource became land rather than the size of the workforce, which would have given women less ability to negotiate their social position.

There is also another reason why peoples who had recently migrated are more likely to have been matrilocally based: in societies where women already had a greater say in subsistence issues, their arguments that more land was needed in order to feed the family, and therefore that the group needed to migrate, might take precedence over other, social, issues, such as remaining in the vicinity of close kin, which might incline patrilocal societies to remain in the same area.

As we have seen, burials and their accompanying grave goods can provide useful clues to the social structure of a society, and those of the Linear Pottery Culture seem to confirm the model of a society where women were not dominated by men. Cemeteries of inhumation, or more rarely cremation, burials are often associated with the Linear Pottery Culture villages. The burials have few grave goods, and perhaps most significantly there are no major differences in the quantity or apparent quality of the grave goods found with women and men. Arrowheads are only found in men's burials, while querns and awls are found with women. At some sites ornaments made of shell imported from considerable distances are only found with male burials, but at other sites both women and men are buried with these shells.

Before leaving the Linear Pottery Culture it will be of interest to draw some comparisons between it and the culture of the Iroquois Indians of the east coast of North America. Archaeologists have often been criticised for drawing one-to-one comparisons between their data and an anthropological example, as obviously no two peoples will be identical, and it is often tempting to see an archaeological site or culture as a carbon copy of the anthropological in order to fill in the missing details, or to try and use it as proof of an archaeological theory. There are a number of important differences between the Linear Pottery Culture sites and those of the Iroquois Indians, but there are some equally noteworthy similarities. These make a brief look at the Iroquois worthwhile, partly to help sketch one possible view of the Linear Pottery Culture, and on a more scientific level to provide a model or basis for further questions to ask of the direct archaeological evidence for the Linear Pottery Culture.

The Iroquois were living in what is now New York State at the time of the earliest European settlers in the area, and were described by a number of explorers and missionaries in the eighteenth and early nineteenth centuries.[27] They have been of particular interest to feminist anthropologists as one of the best-documented societies in which women had high status and quite a degree of power. The society was also matrilineally and matrilocally based. The Iroquois economy depended mainly on horticulture: maize, beans and squashes were grown, and supplemented by wild fruit, nuts, roots and mushrooms. The Linear Pottery culture used very similar hoe techniques to grow principally wheat and pulses. However, a most important contrast is that the Iroquois did not keep animals: while the women were almost wholly responsible for all agricultural activities, men hunted wild animals. The Linear Pottery people, on the other hand, kept cattle as well as some sheep and pigs. If the cattle were overwintered at one end of the longhouses, their numbers cannot have been very large, so it is possible that the task of tending the cows fell to the women in addition to their other agricultural tasks. Iroquois land was owned communally and cultivated by the women as a team. Like the Linear Pottery farmers, the Iroquois had to clear woodland in an environment not very dissimilar from that of Europe. Men, perhaps with the help of women, cleared the fields by girdling trees and then burning the undergrowth after they had been allowed to die off, just as is suggested for Europe.

One of the most striking similarities in the material culture of the two societies is in their houses. Like the Linear Pottery Culture, the Iroquois built massive longhouses which accommodated an entire extended family. In each Iroquois house an older woman, or matron, who was usually the grandmother of the children in the house, lived with her daughters and their husbands and children. Each smaller unit had an area and hearth of its own, but food supplies were communal and distributed by the matron, who had the power to exclude undesirable men from the house or to withhold food from them. This gave women the very powerful right of veto over virtually all male activities, including making war. Although discussion in inter-village or inter-tribal matters was in the hands of the men, it was impossible to implement a decision unpopular with the women.

Many aspects of the archaeology of the Linear Pottery Culture of early Neolithic Europe therefore suggest that its social organisation and economic base may have allowed women to be highly valued and play a leading role in many aspects of life, enjoying status at least equal to that of men, and this picture may perhaps be tentatively reinforced by the parallels which can be drawn with the life of Iroquois women.

The secondary products revolution,[28] or the great male takeover bid

In an earlier section it was argued that women almost certainly 'invented' or worked out the principles of farming as well as many of the concomitant skills and tools which go to make crop agriculture possible and profitable. As principal food providers they were probably respected and had equal status with men. But between then and now, in all but the most traditional hunter-gatherer and horticultural societies, the status of women has been drastically reduced, and in many areas farming has become a predominantly male preserve. Why the change, and when did it happen? Two facts are certain: firstly, by the time of the earliest written records, everywhere in Europe farming was primarily a male occupation, and men owned the farmland and the tools. Secondly, in those areas of the world where women are still the main agricultural producers, most of the farming is concerned with crop production, and if animals are kept at all, it is usually on a small farmyard scale, rather than as large herds or flocks.[29] The change to male dominance in agriculture, therefore, took place at some time between the first stages of the Neolithic period and the advent of written records, and may be related to the changing role of animals within the farming economies of prehistoric Europe. It also seems likely that such a drastic shift in lifestyle, whether it took place gradually over millennia or as a sudden 'revolution', would have been associated with other changes within society. Anthropologists have shown that in present-day societies a significant (though not 100 per cent) correlation exists between plough agriculture and patrilineal descent and land ownership in the same way as there is a correlation between non-plough agriculture and the heavy involvement, and consequent enhanced status, of women. We can look for evidence of this shift in the archaeological record: for example, changes in family structure, wealth or ownership patterns may show up in settlement sites or in burials, as we shall see in later chapters.

While I shall discuss the evidence for Neolithic Europe, the same transformations also took place in the Near East and have recently been discussed in similar terms by Autumn Stanley.[30]

The crucial changes in farming practice are thought to have taken place around 3000 BC, in the later Neolithic period. This would have been some five millennia after the introduction of farming in the Near East, and similar economic shifts can be detected in many areas of Europe at about the same time. Andrew Sherratt[31] has suggested that although domesticated animals were kept during the early Neolithic, they were used only as a source of meat; the consumption of milk or milk products was probably not significant, nor were the animals used for pulling ploughs or carts. All these innovations came later and not only revolutionised agricultural productivity, but also reduced the amount of labour involved in farming. Moreover, the greater importance of domesticated animals and their products would have reduced the necessity for hunting wild animals. As the balance of work changed from part hunting, part crop cultivation and tending a small number of animals to an economy dependent on mixed farming, so the roles and duties of women and men may have shifted. Let us examine the evidence and arguments in detail.

Both carts and ploughs first appear in depictions on clay tablets and cylinder seals in Mesopotamia, around the beginning of the fourth millennium BC, and both seem to have spread to Europe fairly rapidly over 500 years or so. One of the earliest depictions of ploughing (Fig. 27) shows an ox drawing a two-handled plough with a sowing funnel, a device used for sowing seed deeply in the soil and often associated with areas where irrigation is needed. Most significantly the two individuals involved, one guiding the animal from the front, the other guiding the plough, both appear to be men with beards. Early depictions of ploughs in Egypt, from Old Kingdom tombs, also show them being used by men. Elsewhere in Europe the earliest evidence for ploughs is found in the form of 'ploughmarks', where the subsoil has been scratched, leaving grooves sometimes preserved under later sites. These are found in the course of excavation, and examples from both Denmark and Britain are dated as early as the mid-fourth millennium;[32] however, unlike the depictions, these marks obviously give no direct evidence of whether the farmer was male or female. From about the same date we also find models of yoked oxen from Poland. Our earliest evidence of carts, which would also have greatly increased agricultural efficiency, consists of pottery models from Hungary, of mid-fourth millennium date, and actual wheels, found preserved by waterlogging in north-west Europe and dating from the late fourth millennium.

Another innovation which seems to have taken place at around the same time was the large-scale exploitation of milk and the herding of milk cows on a significant scale. Apart from milk's dietary advantages, if animals are to be bred for traction and herds maintained, it is much more 'cost-effective' to obtain milk from them regularly, rather than to eat them as meat only

once! Four or five times as much protein and energy can be obtained from a female animal by milking than by slaughtering it for meat. On the other hand, two problems arise. The first is that many human adult individuals and groups are physiologically intolerant of milk, so that it has to be processed into yoghurt or cheese before it can be consumed; and secondly, most female animals, other than the highly bred modern milk cows, are unwilling to give up their milk to anyone other than their own calves, and special techniques and devices need to be invented in order to milk them. Both these factors suggest that the milking of animals may not have been amongst the first inventions associated with agriculture. Milking was practised on a small scale from about the fifth millennium BC in the Near East. However, the herding of cattle as part of a mixed farming economy, and hence milk production on a significant scale, was delayed for several millennia in most areas of Europe, until the other developments towards mixed farming, including opening up large tracts of grassland, had taken place. Changes in the range of pottery vessel forms over much of Europe and south-west Asia may reflect the widespread adoption of a new range of activities such as would be connected with milking and milk processing.[33]
A number of illustrations of milking scenes from the Near East, Egypt and south-east Europe survive from the mid-third millennium onwards. In most of these the sex of the milker is unclear. However, in those illustrations where this is obvious, the milker is always male. An Egyptian scene from a tomb of the second half of the third millennium shows men handling and milking cattle, and a Minoan seal shows a cow being milked by a man. On

27 Men leading and guiding a two-handled plough, depicted on a cylinder seal from Mesopotamia, late third millennium BC. Oxford, Ashmolean Museum.

the evidence of the cattle bones, however, it is likely that milking was introduced slightly earlier than the date of these illustrations. The analysis of cattle bones from Swiss Neolithic sites of the early fourth millennium shows that many female cows were kept more than two or three years, a pattern which strongly implies dairy rather than beef production. Sherratt suggests that in north-west Europe small dairy herds may have been kept, though the heavy forest cover would have inhibited large herds. Although in pastoral societies (those which depend exclusively, or almost exclusively, on animal herding) the division of gender roles between tending, milking and the processing of animal products is more varied, when animal husbandry is part of a mixed farming regime, as it seems to have been in Neolithic Europe, the involvement of women often seems to depend on the scale of herding. When only a few animals are kept, women often tend and milk them, in addition to other farming tasks, while men continue to hunt. In full-time mixed farming communities, where herding is a large-scale activity, such as is postulated for post-'secondary products revolution' Europe, men tend to be more involved in herding and milking, often leaving women to process milk into cheese and yoghurt.

A third innovation, which can be more easily detected archaeologically, was the systematic spinning and weaving of wool. Wool itself sometimes survives where conditions of preservation are favourable, and spindle whorls and loomweights are common finds on archaeological sites. This innovation may be particularly significant in this context: in the Homeric legends, in Mycenaean Greek documents and later in classical Greece, as well as in the earliest documents of other areas, spinning and weaving are almost universally female tasks, often forming a significant part of the economy, and would probably have created an additional time-consuming role for the woman farmer. Perhaps they would not have been possible without a reallocation of other tasks to men. Although flax was grown and used as a textile early in the Neolithic, the breeding of sheep which produce wool which can be plucked, rather than hair, was probably the result of deliberate selection. This practice may have originated as early as the fifth millennium in Mesopotamia, but only became common in the third millennium when sheep herding seems to have become more widespread in several areas of Europe. At about this time, or perhaps slightly later, the skeletal features of the animals show a change which may reflect the increasing concentration on wool production. Most significantly, a high proportion of the sheep are seen to have been kept till an age well past that at which they are most efficiently bred for meat.

The innovations of ploughing and the extensive use of the secondary products of animals, involving milking and spinning and weaving, bring in their train many other important new tasks. Ploughs have to be made and maintained, and animals trained for the job from a young age. Milking needs to be done regularly, and milk products processed, often in specially made equipment. Sheep have to be plucked. Herds must be fed or tended in suitable pastures, and given access to water. Spinning and weaving wool into yarn and then textiles is especially time-consuming, though it can be carried out at the same time as other tasks, such as looking after children. So the range and amount of work produced by these innovations is not inconsiderable, particularly if added to the already substantial amount involved in arable agriculture, let alone child-rearing, even if each one of these tasks is carried out on only a small scale. By the third millennium, farming and food production would have changed from a comparatively small series of tasks which one woman, or group of women, could have performed with comparatively little equipment, to a series of complex operations which would have been a full-time occupation for the whole population.

Although there is considerable variation in the relative proportions of bones from wild and domesticated animals on Neolithic sites of different phases in different parts of Europe, on many sites of about this time the ratio of bones of hunted animals becomes comparatively small, whereas on earlier sites, such as those of the Linear Pottery Culture, a high proportion of meat (over 30 per cent in some cases) comes from hunted animals. This provides further indication that men were abandoning hunting in order to join in the farming process to a much greater extent, even, eventually, going so far as to take over agriculture entirely.

The 'secondary products' which develop in the later Neolithic all centre around the greater importance of animals, particularly cattle and sheep, within the farming context (pigs, which give no secondary products and are less time-consuming to manage, are not so significant in this argument). They mark a change from horticulture to intensive agriculture, in which the herding of animals directly for food, for the secondary products which derive from them and for their additional use as traction animals, is as important a part of the agricultural work of the community as arable farming. If the few artistic representations of the later Neolithic and sub-sequent prehistoric periods can be used to suggest that men now became more involved in agriculture, this can be backed up by a consideration of gender roles in societies with a similar economic base which have been described in the anthropological literature.[34]

In areas of the world where plough agriculture and the herding of animals are the predominant form of farming, men universally play the major role in agricultural tasks. Women either take no part in farming or only a small one. They may sometimes contribute to harvesting, or to the care of domestic animals, if these are kept only in small numbers. An important distinction exists today between Africa, where horticulture predominates, and Asia, where plough agriculture is far more common and where domesticated animals are kept. Even in those areas of Asia, for example, where women are involved to some extent in aspects of plough agriculture, they work fewer hours than men; whereas in Africa, where farming is predominantly carried out without the use of the plough, and primarily by women, they do far more work than men. The other main difference between these two farming regimes is that social and economic stratification is a far more significant factor, with greater extremes of poverty and wealth and of land ownership amongst the Asian plough agriculturalists than amongst the African hoe agriculturalists or horticulturalists. While bearing in mind the problem in using ethnographic comparisons, we may nevertheless consider whether the changes which took place in Europe during the 'secondary products revolution' had similarities with the differences between the African and the Asian form of agricultural organisation.

To return to Neolithic Europe, it is difficult to be precise about the exact date of these innovations and to know whether they occurred together over a short space of time or each individually as a gradual development. Looking for the earliest example of an artefact or innovation is notoriously difficult in archaeology, partly because we are never looking at more than one tiny sample of the sites or examples that once existed, and partly because it is rare to be able to date a particular instance exactly. There is also dispute about whether some of these innovations happened in different parts of Europe, or spread from a small number of centres. Whichever is the case, their adoption would seem to be a common response to a general problem, that of coping with an increased population and the necessity to expand out of areas of best possible soils and conditions into slightly less fertile ones. Moreover, the introduction of each individual aspect would not necessarily have immediately resulted in social changes. Sherratt[35] argues that the total impact of the large-scale adoption of all these innovations would not have been felt in north-west Europe till the late Neolithic or even the beginning of the Bronze Age. If the innovations were spread over many hundreds of years, or several generations of farmers, no single individual would have appreciated the change at the time; but from our retrospective viewpoint, they can certainly be considered revolutionary, not only from the point of view of farming itself, but in the social changes which must have followed.

These changes in agricultural production took place over much of north-west Europe, just as in the areas of south-east and central Europe, which we have so far considered; and throughout most of Europe they were secondary to an earlier phase of horticulture-type farming. As in south-west Asia and south-east Europe, the third millennium in north-west Europe is marked archaeologically by the expansion of the settled area onto poorer soils away from the river valleys. This expansion was accompanied by significant changes in settlement and house types, and new artefact forms.[36] Major changes in material culture are frequently the outward manifestation of deep-rooted social or political changes, and it will be argued that they imply significant consequences for the women of prehistoric and later Europe, right through to the present day.

Patterns of social organisation in horticultural societies today are quite different from those of intensive agriculturalists: these seem to be linked to the balance of agricultural tasks and to their allocation to each sex. One of the greatest differences is in the position of women. This reinforces the theory that it was in the later Neolithic, when men began to take over most agricultural work, that the social status of women declined.

As we have seen, it is likely that most of the tending of animals was done by men. Large-scale herding often takes place some way from the farm or settlement, as fresh grazing land is continually sought. Raiding by neighbouring tribes seems to be an endemic part of most cattle herding – almost a variation on hunting! This has been seen as the origin of warfare, when for the first time people owned a resource which it was both worthwhile and fairly easy to steal.

Secondly, the invention of plough agriculture, too, would probably have resulted in farming becoming predominantly a male activity, while on the basis of ethnographic analogy, at least, women would probably have spent more time in food preparation, child-rearing and textile and perhaps other craft production.

Thirdly, although less land is needed for the same amount of production, plough agriculture is far more labour-intensive than hoe agriculture: where land is poor, ploughing makes agriculture possible. In some areas of pre-historic Europe it had the effect of making large tracts of lighter, sandy soil available, but in other areas it may have allowed an increase in population where there was a real or perceived shortage of land. In the earliest phases of the Neolithic, land shortages would certainly not have been a problem, as witnessed by the rapid population spread discussed in an earlier section. However, in the later Neolithic there may have been a shortage of land perceived to be suitable for agriculture.[37] Women would therefore have been expected to produce more children and thus more labourers. This would have been seen as their major role. Moreover, male children might have been valued most highly, as future farm workers. Women, meanwhile, would have become less valued by men in their own right: as more time was spent in pregnancy and the care of very young infants, so less time could be spent on farming activities. As men took over many of their tasks, they no longer contributed so much to the daily production of food, which had been a crucial factor in maintaining the equal status they had previously enjoyed.

Fourthly, another social change which might have been an indirect result of the secondary products revolution was the switch from matrilocal residence and matrilineal descent to patrilocal residence and patrilineal descent. There is a very strong ethnographic correlation between male-dominated farming and patrilineal descent and patrilocal residence. A male farmer will teach his sons the necessary skills and expect them to tend his land and animals. In a matrilineal system his sister's sons, rather than his own sons, inherit these herds, land and equipment on his death. This is not in the male interest if men are the main agriculturalists. When women were involved in the land-based tasks, they would have learnt the basic skills from their mothers, so it would have been more obvious for them also to inherit their land and equipment. However, it also seems that individual land ownership is less common amongst hoe agriculturalists, and, by definition, less equipment is used. Therefore, at least in terms of material goods, far less is typically at stake in matrilineal than in patrilineal systems.

Finally, the development of agriculture brought with it a large increase, not only in the number of related tasks, including several which are very time-consuming, but also in the range of material possessions such as farming and food-preparation tools and storage vessels. Two consequences would have resulted. On the one hand, this may be seen as the spur to the development of craft specialisation, as some individuals concentrated on the production of one particular item, which they would exchange for other products or services. At first this could have been in addition to normal farming tasks, but increasingly some people might have found that they could acquire enough food and other necessities by producing only their specialised article. In this way exchange must have become more common, and more sophisticated. On the other hand these material possessions, as well as the domesticated animals themselves, would have constituted considerable wealth, which could be accumulated and handed on from one generation to the next. In the early stages of agriculture better luck or skill in farming may have meant more food, but without the means or the need to convert it into material goods, this would have had few social consequences. However, as one family accumulated more cattle, or acquired better ploughs, or were able to exchange more goods because of their specialist craft skills, the gap between their wealth and that of their neighbours would increase progressively. Many commentators[38] have seen this apparently slight shift to be at the root of the whole of the Western world's social system of hierarchies, class and stratification. A distinction between rich and poor, which is insignificant in forager societies, develops progressively as wealth is passed on from generation to generation within some families, while others are never able to achieve surpluses. The wealthy can become powerful by lending to poorer families in return for services, such as farm labour, or support in combat against other groups. By this means the rich are able to become more wealthy, while the poorer become indebted to other families, and have to produce more and more, or spend time on tasks other than directly for their own subsistence. So the vicious circle develops, and it is easy to see how from this point permanent hierarchies not only of wealth, but of power and status come about, in a way which is impossible in forager societies. This is also the context in which a society can begin to think of people, as well as material possessions and land, as objects of value and exchange. A child could be given as labour to a family to whom the child's parents were indebted, or a woman given to work or to produce extra children.

How such fundamental changes actually took place is not clear, even if we assume they were a gradual process in each community. The full consequences which have just been discussed would have developed very slowly, even over millennia, and are difficult to pinpoint chronologically. In any case, as women were increasingly relegated to secondary tasks, by the end of the Neolithic period they had fewer personal resources with which to assert their status. Presumably, as with so many innovations even in the modern world, the social and economic consequences of seemingly minor innovations would not have been apparent until it was too late to return to former *mores*. The discovery of agriculture, which at the beginning of the Neolithic had been such a positive step by women, was by the end of the period to have had unforeseen, and unfortunate, consequences for them.

4 The Bronze Age

The introduction of copper, and later its alloy bronze, used for making tools, weapons and ornaments, heralds the period known to archaeologists as the Bronze Age. The metal was known from the fourth millennium BC, though it did not become common in western Europe until the second millennium. It was eventually displaced for most of its uses by iron, around the seventh century BC. For archaeologists, bronze is particularly important as an easily recognisable chronological indicator before the advent of scientific or 'absolute' dating methods, such as radiocarbon dating. However, it is easy to overestimate the significance of the change for the people at the time; the new materials would not necessarily have been all important in everyday life. Archaeologists discuss at length matters such as the discovery of bronze and the nature of its impact. But social questions, such as what proportion of the population had access to the new material and what indirect effects it had on society, are equally important.

In every region of Europe a change from communal to single burials seems to have occurred at about the same time as the introduction of copper and bronze: this may suggest that individual wealth could be demonstrated for the first time. This individual wealth, in turn, led to the development of societies with a high degree of social stratification, intensifying a trend which, as we have seen in the last section, probably began to develop after the establishment of agriculture. Wealthy élites seem to have emerged, and there may have been a premium on portable and durable wealth, not only in the form of bronze, but also of gold, jet, amber and other materials, which were often exchanged or traded over large areas of Europe. This change within society must have had a significant effect on the lives of women. In some societies studied by anthropologists, women are used to display male wealth. Ornaments and jewellery may be worn by women, whether they are accumulated by them on their own account or by their male relations; in other societies, women themselves are used as exchange commodities in dealings between men. Could Bronze Age women possess and acquire their own wealth, or did some merely have rich husbands? Were they involved in trade, either as merchants or as commodities? And what was the overall impact of the new materials on their lives?

The evidence for women in the Bronze Age is rather different from that which we found in earlier periods. Over much of Europe the dead were now buried separately, each with their own grave goods and individual ritual. Women are therefore often clearly distinguishable from men, both by virtue of the evidence of their skeletons or cremated remains and of differences in the grave goods with which they are characteristically buried. The number and quality of objects found in graves varies considerably, and the significance of particular objects and of overall differences between burials has been the subject of a great deal of debate. In particular, much work has attempted to evaluate the relative wealth of different grave goods: for example, whether a small gold ring might be worth more or less than a large bronze axe. This is a very difficult task, yet very important, especially as women and men were regularly buried with different types of grave goods. It is also impossible to account for the possibility that there may have been highly valued grave goods made of materials which would usually have perished, such as fine textiles or rare and beautiful feathers. The results of these studies, which will be discussed in this chapter, have provided a number of indications of the relative wealth and status of women in different phases of the Bronze Age, and in different parts of Europe. Another potentially fruitful source of evidence is rock engravings found in parts of Scandinavia and the southern Alpine area, although their interpretation is in many cases open to question.[1]

But first we shall consider the subject of Minoan Crete. By the time of the Bronze Age the peoples of the eastern Mediterranean basin had developed urban life, architectural styles, technology and other features of their culture far in advance of the rest of Europe. This has led many people, including archaeologists, to describe them as 'civilisations', and to suggest that these people were far more sophisticated than the 'barbarians' else-where in Europe. Whether their architecture and the fact that their culture has been better preserved really reflects such a great difference in the lifestyle of the majority of the people of Minoan Crete compared with the rest of Europe, and in particular in the lives of, and attitude towards, women, is an open question. Nevertheless, the evidence for women's lives in Minoan society is certainly much fuller than for most other prehistoric women in Europe, so it will be discussed in some detail. Moreover, a particularly relevant aspect of Minoan culture is that it is often taken as a classic example of a matriarchal society.

Was Minoan Crete a matriarchy?

The Minoan civilisation of the Mediterranean island of Crete was at its height in the first half of the second millennium BC, and in technological terms it belongs to the Early Bronze Age. The remains of this society, including architecture in stone and works of art, are well preserved and far more elaborate than elsewhere in Early Bronze Age Europe. Yet Minoan

Crete is a prehistoric culture, as we have no written records of the people's lives or attitudes. Although clay plaques bearing inscriptions in Minoan hieroglyphics and 'Linear A' script have been found at a number of sites, unfortunately they have not yet been deciphered. Our understanding of the archaeological evidence is therefore just as dependent on the interpretation we put upon it as is the evidence of the Stone Age which we have already discussed.

Early Bronze Age Crete is well known for its huge palaces, the most famous of which must be Knossos, a huge site excavated by Sir Arthur Evans in the early years of this century.[2] Other palaces at Phaistos, Mallia and Ayia Triadha are almost as impressive. Each consists of a series of labyrinthine rooms built around three or four sides of a large open court-yard. Complexes of various-sized rooms have been interpreted as reception rooms, domestic suites and store-rooms. On the walls, or more commonly lying in fragments on the floor, of some of the corridors and domestic and reception rooms the excavators found fragmentary traces of elaborate wall-paintings or frescoes. Many of these have been reconstructed, sometimes from very small pieces, though the significance of the scenes depicted is not always unambiguous. Among the most celebrated of the artefacts found at Knossos is a series of figurines of bare-breasted women with full-length skirts, and with one or more snakes entwined around their arms.[3] These, and the subjects of some of the frescoes, have been the basis of one of the best-known controversies in the debate over the existence of matriarchal societies.

The frescoes should be a form of evidence which is easy to understand. Almost for the first time in human history, we find scenes showing women and men involved in a variety of activities, and, most significantly, it is usually possible to distinguish between the sexes. In most scenes they are easily told apart by major differences in dress and hairstyles, but in addition the Minoans seem to have adopted the convention of painting the skin of women white, while that of men is painted brown. The same convention occurs in Egyptian tomb paintings of about the same date, and enough other indications of sex combine with this to give us a reasonable degree of confidence in assuming that all white figures are women, and all brown ones are men.

In these frescoes women are depicted more frequently than men, and sometimes in more detail.[4] Some scholars have used this fact to argue that women were held in high regard in Minoan society. However, although it may be possible to gain some insight into women's roles from the activities in which they are portrayed, the mere fact of pictures of women certainly cannot be used as evidence of high status. As we have already discussed, in our own society, for instance, pictures of women – even naked large-

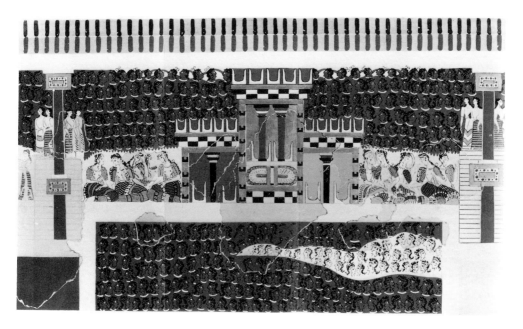

28 Part of the Grand Fresco from Knossos. From Evans, 1921–4.

breasted women, for which we find parallels in Minoan art – predominate in certain magazines and newspapers, in advertising and the like. But these images are created entirely for the pleasure of men, and far from reflecting female dominance, they are actually symptomatic of the low status of women in our society.

It should, therefore, be more profitable to look at the contexts in which women are portrayed, and at the things they are doing. If, however, we are to take the scenes at face value, we have to make the assumption that they are intended to show everyday activities rather than, say, scenes from mythology, legend or an imaginary world, or ritual, and this may not always be justifiable. Indeed many archaeologists specialising in the Minoan period believe that all the scenes portrayed on the frescoes do in fact depict ritual or religious activities. A number of the frescoes show scenes of crowds apparently watching some sort of entertainment or perhaps a religious event. In the best known of these, the Grand Fresco from Knossos, the front row is taken up by women, wearing elaborate jewellery and their hair in ringlets; behind, and on a smaller scale, women and men are sitting together, but sketched in less detail. Here men apparently outnumber women. What can be deduced from this scene? In the original excavation report,[5] Evans took the view that the presence of the women in the front row was more significant than the overall numbers of each sex. He assumed

29 Fresco from Knossos showing bull-leaping. The figures on the right and left are women, distinguished by their white skin. From Evans, 1921–4.

that the front-row seats would have been occupied by religious figures or granted to specially honoured individuals, as they later were in classical Greece. Many analogies were made with the classical period, as it was believed the Minoans were the direct ancestors of the Greeks. This has since been shown to be a mistaken view, and the Minoan evidence must now be reinterpreted in its own right. Some women, then, were present at the event. They were not prohibited from attending it, nor were they left at home.[6] Some occupied 'good seats', but this is hardly sufficient evidence to argue for their high or superior status in all aspects of Minoan civilisation.

The Camp Stool Fresco seems to show two rows of people, some male, some female, sitting in pairs on stools, with raised cups, perhaps drinking to the larger female figure in the centre of the group, who is sometimes interpreted as a goddess,[7] sometimes as a priestess. Another painting, known as the Priest King Fresco, shows a person, thought to be a man, leading a procession of women apparently carrying presents or offerings. It is often used as evidence that despite the supposed high status of women, the palace was ruled by a man, perhaps the legendary king Minos, who is shown leading the procession. However, there is some ambiguity: the figure, only the top part of whose body survives, is painted white, which elsewhere invariably indicates a woman, but the body shape, muscles and lack of breasts suggest that it is a man. So a number of illustrations show women in apparently important positions, suggesting some kind of leadership or dominance, but if these pictures had explanatory captions we might find that they had quite other meanings!

One of the best known of all the Minoan wall-paintings, and also one of the most interesting from the point of view of female activities, is the bull leaping scene. Three figures, dressed identically in kilts, are taking part. Two have dark skin and are therefore presumably male, and one has white skin and is presumably female. A similar scene is depicted on a cup from Vaphio, where a figure, thought to be a female on the basis of the hairstyle, seems to be being tossed between the bulls' horns. So women, as well as men, took part in bull-leaping, a sport, or perhaps a religious activity, which must have involved considerable agility and stamina, and hours of practice,[8] as well as surely entailing a very high risk of death or injury. What class of people took part, we do not know. Was it an honour to be chosen as a bull-leaper, or something to which slaves were condemned? It seems probable that the skill involved must have been either much admired or had religious importance for it to have been depicted on the fresco.

We also find depictions of women involved in certain agricultural tasks, tending fruit trees or gathering crocuses. These scenes are often assumed to show ritual activity, such as tending sacred trees, or goddesses performing crop fertility magic or ritual. Even if this interpretation is correct, it may also reflect some of the normal tasks carried out by women, which would not be at all surprising in the light of the evidence for the continued involvement of women in agriculture, discussed earlier.

Even more enlightening than the frescoes from Crete itself, perhaps, is a series of paintings from Akrotiri, on the island of Thera (Santorini),[9] northeast of Crete, where extensive remains of a town contemporary with the Minoan civilisation have been excavated. The site has been remarkably well preserved because it was covered by volcanic ash and lava after the island's volcano exploded and destroyed the town in the sixteenth century BC. One of the most impressive frescoes comes from the 'West House'. It extends around three walls of a room, and shows three towns, each on a separate land mass, separated by a sea on which ships are sailing. In each of the towns a variety of activities is taking place. If the rule that men are painted brown and women white also applies at Akrotiri, then the only women depicted seem to be watching from the roof-tops in one of the towns while others, wearing long full skirts with contrasting bodices, are shown carrying water jugs on their heads. There seem to be no women on the ships, nor in other active roles on the land. Where are these towns? On Crete, or Thera? And does this fresco show another ritual or mythological scene, or does it give a true perspective on the lives of Minoan women?

Turning to the architecture of the palaces themselves, the visitor to any of the excavated sites will not fail to be impressed by the complexity of their design. Numerous rooms of various sizes are arranged around an open courtyard: at Knossos one group of rooms has been labelled the 'Queen's Suite', containing the 'Queen's *megaron*' or hall and the 'Queen's bathroom'. This has led some writers to argue that as the queen had her own suite of rooms, she must have had privacy and independence: 'one can hardly avoid seeing in this arrangement a nice respect for the fair sex, as well as due appreciation of their company'.[10] Alternatively it has been argued that this shows that Minoan women were 'modest creatures', or that they were regarded as inferiors and relegated to an isolated part of the palace. Rather than argue with either of these almost equally unverifiable assertions, we need to look at the evidence which led to these rooms being identified as the queen's suite in the first place. Trying to work out the use to which a particular area was put, be it a room, a whole house or an outdoor space, is one of the greatest problems facing an archaeologist digging a prehistoric site. Occasionally the shape, size or location of the area will be helpful, or the presence of features such as a hearth, which suggests that cooking took place there or that the room was kept warm and thus used as domestic living space. More often, clues are provided by artefacts found in the room, and in modern excavations plotting the exact location of each artefact helps to provide an even more detailed picture. For example, large areas of the Minoan palaces consist of long narrow rooms, lined with huge ceramic jars or *pithoi*, in some of which have been found the residues of cereal crops, grapes and olives. These rooms, then, were clearly designed and used as store-rooms. In other rooms evidence for craft activities has been found. Tools connected with a particular trade or craft, raw materials ready for use or as waste pieces, and finished, partly finished or incorrectly made objects may identify a room as a craft workshop. For example, at Knossos there is the workshop of a stone-vase maker, with unfinished stone utensils and abandoned tools, and at Mallia a seal-engraver's workshop has been found.

But what might we expect to find in a bedroom, given that only in exceptional circumstances, which do not occur at Knossos, are wood, textiles or similar organic materials preserved? And how might a queen's bedroom look different from a king's (or anyone else's)? Perhaps the queen shared a bedroom with the king. Indeed, in Homer's *Odyssey*, written several centuries later but possibly referring in part to a period shortly after the heyday of Minoan Crete, Odysseus and his wife Penelope certainly share a bedroom. And anyway can we be sure that the people living at Knossos were in fact a king and queen?

In the south-east corner of the palace at Knossos a series of interconnected rooms opening off a huge staircase were found. Some of these rooms are large and lit by light wells open to the sky above. One, known as the Hall of the Double Axes, is a particularly large and airy double room with a veranda and finely carved ashlar masonry, with a double axe incised on each block. As the excavator, Arthur Evans, considered this room one of the pleasantest in the palace, he thought that it would probably have been the ruler's room, in which he dispensed justice and performed other duties. A few rooms away, and accessible by a number of different routes, is another large room, also well lit by light wells. In the light well outside this room fragments of frescoes, one with a sea scene and dolphins and the other depicting a dancing girl, were found. These scenes were restored on the walls of the room, and as they were imagined to show 'feminine subjects' it was thought that this room might have been used by the queen. Would modern analogy bear out the assumption that dancing girls are more likely to have been found on the walls of a woman's room than a man's? In more recent excavations at other Minoan palaces, similar suites of rooms have been discovered, almost identical in layout and in their location within the palace. While we can assume that they all had the same or similar functions, we need not accept Evans' interpretation of these functions. Perhaps he was right that the layout, lighting arrangements and decorations indicated domestic quarters, but numerous different interpretations could be made for the individual rooms. Why not a bedroom and a living room, or a morning room, a reception room or a dining room? To assume that the two best rooms were for the king and queen respectively is to make assumptions about the social organisation of the palace which are really not justified without much more detailed theoretical or practical evidence. Such assumptions probably tell us more about the attitudes and social behaviour of the late Victorian excavators than those of the Minoans.

Elsewhere in the palace of Knossos, Evans found the plaster remains of two seats, with a large hollowed centre, lower and wider than the throne in the 'Throne Room'. In the frescoes women are often depicted squatting rather than sitting, so he argued that this lower seat would have been more comfortable for a woman. He does not, however, discuss the other implication, that women with wider bottoms need wider seats![11] Both these lower seats are in rooms which seem to be workrooms, and probably kitchen areas, so it may be either that lower seats were more practical or comfortable for tasks which were carried out on the floor, or that women were employed in kitchen work.

Although Sir Arthur Evans himself was quite cautious about his interpretation of the 'Queen's Rooms', numerous writers since then have built on this clearly hypothetical identification in an attempt to prove their own hypotheses about the status of Minoan women: i.e., either that, having their own quarters they were 'modest creatures', or that it showed the high esteem in which they were held. Whatever conclusions about the position of Minoan women, even high-status women, can be drawn from the frescoes, it seems highly dubious that they can be backed up by the architectural evidence of the palaces themselves.

The final aspect of Minoan culture which has been used as a basis for hypotheses about the status of women is the so-called 'snake goddess' figurines.[12] Found frequently not only in the palaces, but also elsewhere on Crete, these figurines are made of terracotta or of faience, a glass-like substance. The figures are bare-breasted, with long hair tied at the back with a large bow. They wear full-length skirts. and one or more snakes are twisted around their uplifted hands. The figurines are usually found only in certain parts of the palaces, which, because they also regularly contain features such as structures thought to be raised altars, are interpreted as shrines or temples. The discovery of similar figures, along with other models of animals, birds, snakes and trees, in caves on top of some of the Cretan mountains, has led to these caves also being considered as shrines. Similar representations of women also occur in frescoes and on other objects, such as *sarcophagi*, or coffins, and smaller items such as rings and seals. In these depictions they are sometimes shown apparently being venerated by other people, mainly women. And women, too, are shown taking part in ritual activities, such as slaughtering animals on sacrificial tables and pouring libations. Notwithstanding the arguments put forward in Chapter 2 for the uncertainty of the function of earlier, Neolithic, figurines, which have some similarities with these Minoan figures, the consistent provenance and design of the latter and the way in which they appear on the frescoes all suggest that they represent some woman or women who held a special place in the society. Is this a goddess, as Evans and many other Minoan scholars have suggested, or a real woman, perhaps a priestess or votary, who made offerings to, or had a special place in the worship of, the deity or deities, or a queen or other woman who lived in the palace? The latter seems unlikely, unless she also fulfilled the role of priestess or goddess, as the dress and hairstyles depicted on the frescoes and on the snake women are quite unlike those of the apparently normally dressed women portrayed occasionally on seal-stones. The Neolithic figurines, by contrast, are much simpler and not found in special contexts.

So, what can we say positively about the position of women in Minoan society? Can any inferences about the kinship pattern, whether it was matrilineal or patrilineal, be drawn? Does the evidence described above

30 One of the snake goddesses from Knossos. From Evans 1921–4.

indicate that Minoan Crete might have been a matriarchal society, as has been suggested both by some of the earliest scholars and by recent feminists?

The frescoes certainly show women involed in a wide variety of activities, some physical. Other scenes imply their participation in aspects of the public sphere, for example watching some mass audience event and leading processions. There may well be some connection here with religious ritual, in which women, in the form either of goddesses or of cult leaders or priestesses, or both, certainly appear to predominate. But it is important to bear in mind that all the evidence comes from the palaces, which clearly were primarily occupied by the wealthy or higher strata of society, and that the frescoes presumably reflect the interests of these people. Taken at face value, it certainly seems that élite women may have had more status and participated in a wider range of activities than women in many other societies. But the question of how relevant the frescoes and other evidence are to the lives of most women living in Crete during the Minoan period remains unclear. We still have little or no basis for considering the lives of the majority of women living in the countryside, and it cannot be assumed that because high-class women enjoyed some status within their own society, other women did too.

Finally, as regards matriarchy, the meaning and implications of the idea have been discussed in detail in an earlier chapter, and I have also tried to show not only how little evidence there is in any living or documented society, but also how difficult it would be to prove from archaeological data. Even if we may hypothesise that women, or at least women of higher status, may have had a better deal in Minoan Crete than in many other later societies, it is impossible to argue that they actually held power. Equally, however, as in most other prehistoric societies, there is no evidence that men held power at the expense of women.

Burials, grave goods and wealth in north-west Europe

The archaeological evidence for the Bronze Age in north-west Europe differs greatly from that for Minoan Crete. Whereas most of what we know about the Minoans comes from the palaces, very little is known about the dwellings of the contemporaneous population north and west of the Alps. Instead, particularly in the early phases of the Bronze Age, we have the buried bodies of the people themselves. In most parts of north-west Europe at this period the burial rites usually involved inhumation with a variety of grave goods, most of which were probably the personal possessions of the deceased. From these we can get a very clear picture of the sort of things worn and used by women, and how they differed from those used by men. The quantity and quality of grave goods buried with different individuals can give an indication of the degree of equality or social differentiation within the society, and the bodies themselves can provide information about the relative ages at which women and men died, their stature, and some aspects of their health. The details which have emerged from studies of these burials vary considerably for different parts of Europe, and, as so often with archaeological evidence, there is much ambiguity and disagreement about how the burials are to be interpreted, and the implications of the grave goods.

Despite this, some features are common throughout the area. Most striking is the fact that the grave goods found with women are invariably different from those buried with men. For the first time in European prehistory it is clear that sex is a primary factor of social differentiation. It is possible, however, that an even greater contrast existed between those entitled to formal burial and those who were not, as it seems unlikely that the number of contemporaneous burials which have been found in any one area is sufficient to account for the entire population. However, among those who were buried, there is a greater contrast in the grave goods, and in some areas in the details of burial, such as the side on which the body is laid, between women and men than there is, for instance, between deceased individuals of different age groups.[13] The pattern follows modern Western expectations of sexual stereotypes. Woman are regularly buried with a variety of ornaments and jewellery, such as pins, necklaces and bracelets (and in some areas they frequently also have little knives, sometimes described as daggers, as well), while men are just as regularly buried with weapons. The detail of these weapons varies considerably, from daggers and spearheads to swords, but the distinction between them and the female ornaments is clear.

In Scandinavia a small number of exceptionally well-preserved burials provide evidence not only of contrasts in grave goods made of inorganic materials, but also in dress, as woollen clothes have survived. The bodies were placed in oak tree-trunk coffins which produced an effect like the tanning of leather, in addition to which the graves have remained waterlogged.[14] Men usually seem to have worn a kilt-like garment, a cloak and a cap, while women may have worn one of two different types of costume. One of the best-known burials is from Borum Eshøj in Denmark, where a woman, aged between 50 and 60 and about 1.57 m (5 ft 2 in) tall, was buried wearing a short tunic, perhaps over a full-length skirt, tied with two belts. She also wore a hair net and several pieces of jewellery. By contrast a younger woman, between 18 and 20 years old, found at Egtved, wore a knee-length loosely corded skirt and a short sleeved tunic, both made from brown sheep's wool. Like the Borum Eshøj woman, the Egtved girl wore a variety of bronze ornaments. Next to her body was a bundle containing the cremated remains of a younger girl, aged 8 or 9 years. The age difference is too small to suggest that she could have been the woman's daughter. Cremated bodies have been found in similar juxtaposition with inhumations elsewhere in the European Bronze Age, and have led to theories that servants or slaves were sacrificed on the death of a mistress or master.

These burials are good examples of the two types of female costume found in a number of graves in Bronze Age Denmark. A favourite ornament seems to have been a belt with a large bronze disc in the centre, and the women also almost invariably wore a hair-net or hair-band. The principal difference between the two styles lies in the length of the skirt, and has been interpreted as summer and winter dress or as marking a distinction between married and unmarried women.[15] The short length and 'revealing openness' of the skirt of the Egtved woman have led to numerous comments in the literature since the burial was discovered in the 1920s which are typical of Western stereotyping and prudishness. For example, 'it would have been more sensible and modest (even by the standards of primitive people) if the material [of the tunic] had been made into the skirt and the string work – a fish net – used to drape the upper part of the body . . .', and 'it is hardly fit to be called a skirt, being not so much as a covering for her

31 Reconstruction drawing of three different styles of women's dress and one man's, from Bronze Age Scandinavia. From Burgess, 1980; drawing by Angie Townshend.

32 The costume worn by the woman found at Egtved, Denmark. Copenhagen, National Museum.

nakedness'.[16] The long garment of the Borum Eshøj woman was deemed to be far more appropriate, and the short skirt has sometimes been reconstructed as an overskirt, which would have been worn over a longer one. However, one early but detailed study of the burial questioned whether full-length skirts were worn at all; the Borum Eshøj woman, it was suggested, was in fact covered by a burial shroud, and she too may have worn a much shorter skirt.[17] Bronze figurines, from the same area but of Later Bronze Age date, depict women wearing the same short skirts and confirm that they were worn alone, although one of these statuettes seems to be wearing a long skirt. There are also a number of other burials where the cloth of the skirt has not been preserved, but where small tubes of thin bronze sheet have been found, occasionally with enough textile to indicate that the tubes decorated the fringes of cord skirts similar to that of the Egtved woman and to the garments apparently worn by most of the figurines. It may therefore be that normal attire for women in Bronze Age Denmark included a short open skirt, or that it may have been a special garment for ceremonial, including burial, and that the figurines had some ritual function, or depict goddesses or votaries.

Before looking at the burial customs in more detail, two important methodological *caveats* need to be made. Patterns of burial practice were originally studied by comparing skeletal material with artefacts found with the body. More recent studies have also assessed the evidence of the bones quite independently of the grave goods, though the sex of many, and

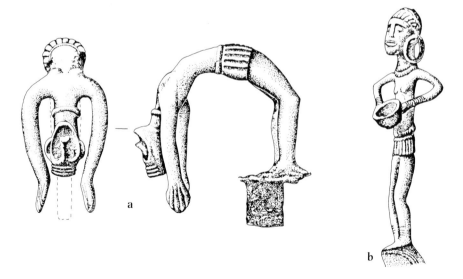

33 Small bronze figurines of women from Late Bronze Age Denmark: **a.** locality unknown; **b.** the handle of a knife from Itzehoe, Holstein. After Broholm and Hald, 1940.

probably most, burials has been assumed from the nature of the grave goods. Many problems are involved in reliably assessing the sex of excavated skeletons, but it is clearly essential, especially in the present context, to know of any exceptions to the usual rule of female and male grave goods. For example, were any of the 'weapons' used as badges of office, and, if so, did a woman occasionally, or even one or twice in very special circumstances, now unknown, hold that office or possess that 'weapon'? Or was there any way in which someone could opt out of the usual gender roles, a possibility well attested in the ethnographic record? These questions could only be answered if every skeleton were independently sexed.

Secondly, the majority of burials are found with no surviving grave goods at all, and the sex of these individuals has rarely been examined. It is therefore particularly difficult to make any assumptions about them. Other examples have one or more artefacts buried with the body, and the usual argument is that the more artefacts there are, the 'wealthier' or more important the individual. However, all burials may actually have been accompanied by other items which no longer survive, such as food offerings, simple or rich textiles and other artefacts made of organic materials, and which may have represented a completely different 'degree of wealth' from the more obvious grave goods.

Nevertheless, with these provisos, let us consider the grave goods found with Early Bronze Age burials in more detail. Bronze Age burial rites are similar throughout most of Europe, though in each area there are local differences in the details of the grave goods and the way in which the body is buried. We will examine three areas, south-west Czechoslovakia, southern England, and Denmark and southern Sweden, where interesting studies have been carried out which throw light on gender roles.

The Branč cemetery of south-west Slovakia

One of the very few archaeological studies which has specifically considered the status of women is the work by Susan Shennan,[18] who has analysed burials with grave goods excavated from a cemetery at Branč, in south-west Slovakia. Just over 300 burials were found here, and males and females were shown to have characteristically different grave goods and modes of burial. The sex of the bones was assessed by a palaeopathologist quite independently of the grave goods (though differences are only apparent in adults), and the age of each person at death was assessed. On the basis of the degree of wear on teeth and the fusion of certain bones and joints, the bones were ascribed to five- to ten-year age brackets. This information was then correlated with data about the way in which the body was buried and the type of grave goods placed with it. Hypotheses about what certain objects may have represented in terms of symbols of age, sex or status and how the goods may have been acquired by the individual were put forward on the basis of these data. While most men (69 per cent) in the Brančč cemetery were buried lying on their right side, most women (81 per cent) were laid on their left. Although it might be interesting to speculate about why the custom of burying men and women on different sides was not strictly adhered to, it seems most likely that the reason for the discrepancy is incorrect sexing of the skeletons, as 100 per cent certainty is not always possible.

Artefacts found with the bodies included ornaments, weapons and tools made of copper, stone and bone. The number and quality of grave goods varied considerably from individual to individual. Shennan devised a system of wealth scores for each artefact, based on how difficult it would have been to obtain the raw material and an estimate of the time needed to manufacture the object. From this it was possible to calculate the 'wealth' buried with each individual. If, she argued, wealth was inherited, we would expect to find some rich burials of young people, who would not have had the opportunity to acquire wealth through their own efforts or skill. Similarly, it might be possible to assess the relative wealth of women compared with men. Before considering some of Shennan's conclusions, a note of caution must be expressed about attempting to assess the value of grave goods in this way. This is a particular problem when two more or less mutually exclusive groups are compared, as often occurs between women's and men's sets of grave goods. Several other archaeological studies have made similar attempts to assess the value of artefacts in order to allow a comparison of the wealth of one burial with that of another. Different and often conflicting scales of values have been created by different scholars studying very similar material. Moreover, these reflect our own scales of value. How can we assess the value of a gold bracelet compared with a bronze one, or with a shale bracelet? If a type is rare, this may imply that it was hard to obtain, or, alternatively that it was not very popular. The value allotted to manufacturing time depends on the value placed on human labour: the scarcity of a raw material may have been perceived to be quite different from its actual rarity. How might a society equate the weight of a quantity of raw material with the skill of manufacture of the finished object? And beauty is a particularly subjective value. In most of the Bronze Age graves, women and men have almost totally different ranges of artefacts, so while it may be comparatively easy to compare two women's graves, it is far more difficult to assess the relative wealth of women and men. Such studies, then, can only serve as approximate guides to the balance of resources within a society, rather than as a precise statement of social stratification.

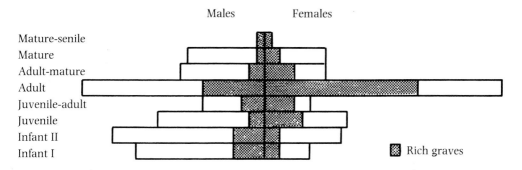

Males   Females

Mature-senile
Mature
Adult-mature
Adult
Juvenile-adult
Juvenile
Infant II
Infant I

▨ Rich graves

34 Distribution by age and sex of the burials at Branč, with rich graves highlighted. From Shennan, 1975.

Returning to the Branč study, the community which was buried in the cemetery was a small one, consisting of about 30–40 people at any one time; half of these were children. It has been argued that the wide range of combinations of grave goods suggests a quite complex society with a number of different status positions or classes. Some graves had a particularly large number of artefacts, and gave a high wealth score. Certain types of artefact were only found in the richest graves, and rich women tended to have very similar sets of artefacts. This suggests that the objects were being used as symbols of status, or sumptuary goods, a term used in anthropology to define possessions which only a certain group of individuals are allowed to wear or carry, and which make their position immediately obvious to everyone in the society. Typical examples from our own society would be the regalia of a monarch, or a nurse's uniform. The richest women were all in the juvenile-adult age group or older, and there were proportionately few rich female infants. These data can be interpreted in a number of different ways. The most traditional would be that the rich graves reflect wealth achieved at marriage: some children may have had marriages arranged at birth, but then died young. The greater proportion of rich females than males could be taken to suggest that polygyny – where men may have more than one wife – was practised. On the other hand, the evidence could just as well indicate a society in which women held high status.

A higher proportion of young girls (presumably defined either on the basis of grave goods, or by which side they were buried on, as the sex of children is not apparent from their bones) than boys were 'rich' (Fig. 34), and this could be used to argue that female wealth was ascribed at birth, that is that these girls were born into rich families with the expectation of inheritance in later life. If male wealth was also ascribed in this way, more wealth may have been given to girls than boys. Alternatively, the lower ratio of rich females who died in childhood compared with the child mortality rate of rich males could suggest that rich girls were more carefully looked after, perhaps through better nutrition or living conditions, than rich boys (though some imbalance would be expected in any society, since male infants are always more prone to illness and death than female babies). If Shennan's relative scaling of female and male grave goods is correct, it seems that rich women were considerably richer than rich men, and were particularly marked out by a clear-cut group of possessions, whereas the rich men's grave goods were far less uniform or distinctive. This suggests that the high status of these women was marked in a way obvious to the whole society. If this position was hereditary, it would explain why greater care might have been taken in nurturing rich female infants, especially if descent was matrilineal so that the future of the group depended on the survival of young women. The same statistics could, however, also be used to come to quite different conclusions: that the society was patrilineal and polygynous; that rich artefacts were given to women on marriage; and that wealth was owned by men but displayed on women, such as has been usual in more recent Western society. This problem merely emphasises the ambiguity of much of the archaeological record. However, if the former interpretation is accepted, the Branč material, and that from other cemeteries in the surrounding area which offer the same picture, may suggest that in south-west Slovakia in the Early Bronze Age women had high status, were nurtured more carefully than boys as children, and owned distinctive 'sumptuary' objects which defined the position of some leading women in a way which did not apply to men.

Work on other cemeteries in the surrounding area[19] has suggested that the appearance of rich women with distinctive costume was a feature which built up gradually in the area. In all but the earliest cemetery women have more grave goods than men, and a small number of 'rich' women have a special but standard costume shown in the archaeological record by elaborate necklaces, metal pins and leg garters. Only adult women wear this special dress, and men have no equivalent uniform attire. The recurrence of the pattern at several cemeteries suggests that the same symbolism was used to unite women over a wide area, although probably only one or two women living within each community at any one time would have worn the costume. It also seems that the difference between rich and poor women decreased over time, though male burials continued to be marked by wealth distinctions. Could this be a sign of female solidarity in contrast to continuing male competition? Furthermore, it is noteworthy that wealth distinctions in south-west Slovakia are nothing like as marked as those in many other parts of Europe at the time. Although these are not Shennan's conclusions, I would like to suggest that the women in sumptuary costume could, perhaps, have been part of an area-wide council of women, or similar women-led grouping, the effect of which might have been to discourage, rather than encourage, the development of extremes of wealth, and perhaps power, found in other regions.

Southern Britain in the Early Bronze Age

Studies of British Early Bronze Age burials have also shown significant differences between the sexes, though, as elsewhere in Europe, too much discussion has been based solely on grave goods, without independent skeletal studies. The usual practice involves burying the body under a round earth or stone mound (barrow or cairn). These are usually very carefully built, concealing internal structural features: in some cases their external shape is more complex than a simple hemisphere, especially in the area of southern England known as Wessex, where some of the barrows cover a group of very rich burials which have been given the name 'Wessex culture'.[20] Two of these barrow forms are particularly relevant here. The 'disc barrow' is characterised by an annular raised mound around a shallow ditch; a small mound in the centre covers the burial or burials. This type is usually found only within major groups or cemeteries of barrows of varied forms. The 'bell barrow' has bell- or S-shaped curved sides created by a flat area or 'berm' between the mound and a surrounding ditch. These disc and bell barrows are invariably associated with female and male burials respectively. The grave goods found in them also show interesting differences (Fig. 35):[21] they include a variety of rich artefacts made of gold, bronze and other materials, but the range of grave goods found with the men seems to be about five times as great as those with women. The objects found with women typically include gold, amber, shale and faience bead necklaces and other ornaments, small bronze knives and small pottery cups. Men are buried with bronze daggers, stone battle axes and other weapons, a variety of bronze and bone pins, and bone tweezers.

These Wessex culture burials contrast with another group also found in southern England, broadly contemporary or slightly later in date, and known as the Deverel-Rimbury tradition or culture. It is characterised by small farming settlements with associated fields (see Chapter 5) near which a cemetery of small round barrows is often found.[22] The Deverel-Rimbury cemeteries are mainly situated on the fringes of the Wessex upland area, away from the chalk. Each barrow typically covered a number of burials, few of which contained any grave goods, and which included the cremated remains of both women and men, of all ages, in an apparently natural balance.

The reason for the contrast between the Wessex culture and the Deverel-

Rimbury burials is worth considering here, as it is possible to interpret it as indirect evidence that Deverel-Rimbury women had higher status than those of the Wessex culture. The Deverel-Rimbury settlements and barrows are located on soils which are very productive for agriculture, and especially for arable farming.[23] As we have seen, women were often involved in crop growing, and if this was the case here, Deverel-Rimbury women would probably have played a greater part in food production than the women of the Wessex culture, which, situated on chalk downlands, probably concentrated on sheep farming.[24] Ethnographic evidence indicates that in pastoral societies wealth is usually displayed in a much more showy fashion, in the form of portable objects such as jewellery, than in agricultural groups. The apparent wealth of the Wessex culture may, therefore, perhaps in part at least, be illusory. In pastoral societies the status of women is often low,[25] so that Deverel-Rimbury women would probably have been more

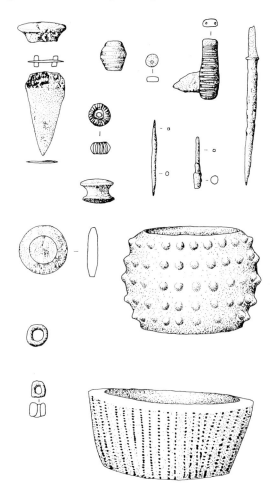

35 Grave goods from two typical rich Wessex culture burials.
(*Right*) From the Manton barrow, Wiltshire, found with one of the only skeletons in the group which have been independently identified as female: a knife-dagger (length 4.6 cm); shale, amber and chalk beads; a halberd pendant with sheet gold; bronze awls; and two small pottery vessels.
(*Facing page*) Found with a presumed male burial from Wilsford (G23), Wiltshire: a dagger (length 20 cm); a knife-dagger; a whetstone-pendant; a bronze pin, and a bone tube, perhaps a flute. After Gerloff, 1975.

highly valued members of their community than their Wessex counterparts. It has also been argued that these differences in status were reflected in differences in marriage patterns. Within the Wessex culture, the theory goes, women, who played only a small active part within the community and had few rights, were exchanged as marriage partners exogamously – that is, outside their own community – almost as part of a trade deal. Upon marriage they would thus have been lost to their own community as a labour force, and deemed to have little value other than as objects of exchange. In the Deverel-Rimbury culture, by contrast, endogamous custom, in which the population married within the local group, is thought more likely to have prevailed, as a means by which a valuable part of the work force remained within the community: this is possible in villages made up of a number of families. Land or property may have been inherited by either sex, again giving greater equality between women and men.[26]

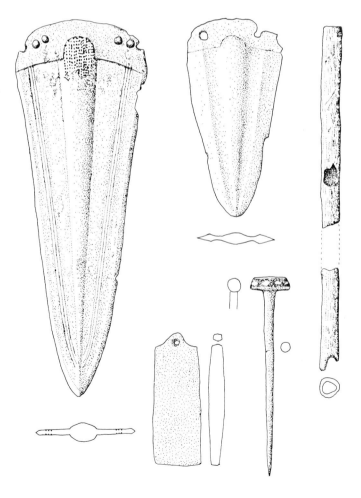

Burials and hoards in southern Scandinavia

Our third area of interest is Denmark and southern Sweden, where a number of key studies of Bronze Age burials have been carried out, highlighting a pattern which may be mirrored throughout Europe. Hardly any of the burials in these areas have been examined to ascertain the sex of the individual from the skeletal remains. As elsewhere, most of them have been assumed to be either female or male on the basis of any artefacts found with the body, although many burials (presumably those of poorer members of society) had few or no grave goods. Men are typically buried with weapons, razors or tweezers, while women have arm-rings, belt plates, pins and a particular type of brooch. Knives, fibula brooches and 'double studs' are found with both women and men, and small daggers sometimes accompany female burials, although they are more usually associated with male ones.[27]

One of the earliest studies to attempt to assess the wealth of Early Bronze Age burials was that by Klaus Randsborg[28] in Denmark. His initial observations concluded that twice as many men were buried with grave goods as women, and a similar pattern has recently been reported from southern Sweden.[29] Randsborg's method of assessing wealth differs from that of Shennan, discussed above. As raw metals are not found in Denmark and would therefore have had to be imported, Randsborg thought that the total weights of bronze and gold used in the grave goods would give a reasonable estimate of the status of the individual. It is noteworthy that twice as many men's graves contained gold objects as did those of women. Moreover, many male graves contained over 200 grammes of bronze, whereas this was true of only very few women's graves. If the weight of gold in the graves is also taken into account, the difference between female and male graves becomes very marked indeed.

From this Randsborg argued that women must have had considerably lower status than men. However, an obvious problem with this analysis is that men were usually buried with weapons, which are bound to be heavier than the jewellery normally found with women. He also subdivided the material into chronological phases, which showed that as the Early Bronze Age progressed, more bronze and gold was used in burials and that the relative proportion found in the graves of women increased over time. If these artefacts are a true reflection of all the grave goods deposited, this suggests that, from a low point at the beginning of the Early Bronze Age, the status of women gradually improved.

In the later part of the Bronze Age in Scandinavia, as in other parts of northern and western Europe, there was a change in burial patterns and the number of richly equipped burials decreases. Funerary rituals which

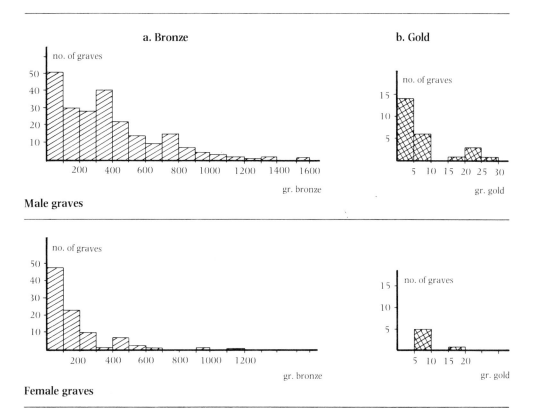

36 The total weight of **a.** bronze and **b.** gold objects found in male and female graves of the Danish Early Bronze Age. After Randsborg 1974.

have left archaeological traces become less common. In some areas the inhumations which in the Early Bronze Age were often accompanied by a range of bronze ornaments and equipment were replaced in the later Bronze Age by cremations which had either no grave goods at all, or usually only small items such as pins or tweezers.

As well as in graves, bronze objects are frequently found in hoards, where anything from two to several dozen or more bronze artefacts seem to have been deliberately buried together. Such hoards, which have been found all over Europe, date from all periods of the Bronze Age, but particularly from the later phases, when in some areas they seem to take the place of the elaborate burial depositions of the Early Bronze Age. The objects have usually been found in good condition, and the range of artefacts in each hoard is often similar to the assemblage accompanying an inhumation burial in the early period. In some areas of Europe 'female' and 'male' hoards can thus be distinguished. In Scandinavia, groups of artefacts which regularly recur, and are characteristic either of female or of male burials of the Early Bronze Age, are also found together as a group in contemporary hoards. This makes it seem likely that the hoards also represent the possessions of an individual, and that female and male hoards may be distinguished. In the late Bronze Age the hoards, but not the burials, occur, and the suggestion that they too represent either women or men rests on analogy with the types of tools, ornaments and weapons buried with each sex in the Early Bronze Age and depicted on a small number of contemporary human figurines. The hoards can therefore be analysed in a similar way to the burials, and studied either alone or in conjunction with them to suggest differences in the possessions and status of women and men, through the phases of the Nordic or Scandinavian Bronze Age. Six periods, I to VI, are traditionally recognised in the area, and a number of studies have demonstrated that grave goods and hoards show a similar pattern of increasing 'wealth' in the complexity and quantity of female-related artefacts, while the quantity and quality of male goods remains constant or even declines.

A study of Danish hoards by Janet Levy[30] showed that, except in Period II, when the number of female and male hoards was equal, female hoards outnumbered male ones. In Period II, the later part of the Early Bronze Age, male hoards contained a wide range of artefacts; this range then declined gradually until Period VI, the final phase of the Bronze Age, when the decline was steep. Female depositions, on the other hand, became more numerous from Periods II to V, and then matched the decline in male depositions in Period VI. The design of ornaments worn by women also seems to have increased in complexity, until, in Period V, they appear to have been completely impractical to wear, while male swords became less varied in style and showed less artistic skill in their manufacture as the Bronze Age progressed.

Another key study focuses on the contents of depositions – graves, hoards and single finds – from Bronze Age Denmark, but concentrates on changes in the numbers of swords, associated with men, and of ornaments, associated with women.[31] Kristian Kristiansen shows that during the course of the Bronze Age the number of swords declined, while female ornaments increased (Fig. 38a). In Period I, the earliest phase of the Bronze Age, hardly any female ornaments were produced; after an increase in Period II, the number of female depositions remained approximately constant throughout the remainder of the Bronze Age. The pattern of male depositions was rather different. The number of male burials and hoards which included swords decreased, although the overall number of male depositions remained constant. We therefore find in Bronze Age Denmark a similar pattern to that already discussed: from a situation in the Early Bronze Age

37 A typical rich female ritual hoard of the Late Bronze Age, Period V, from Simested, central Jutland, Denmark, including (*listed clockwise*) spiral armrings, a fibula, an armband, a sickle, a belt ornament, a twisted neck-ring (diameter 19.5 cm; other objects at same scale) and a hanging vessel or belt box. Copenhagen, National Museum.

where women were scarcely represented either in the hoards or the burials, the difference in 'wealth' between female and male depositions became less marked during the course of the Bronze Age.

The recurring pattern shown in all these studies can be interpreted in either of two ways. It may signify a shift in the way in which men chose to display prestige goods, from demonstrating their wealth through their own possessions to using women as a vehicle for such display; alternatively the pattern may be demonstrating an actual shift in the balance of status between the sexes.

Kristiansen[32] himself prefers the former interpretation, emphasising a possible change in attitude to the demonstration of male status, in which the man dresses his female kin in rich ornaments rather than displaying status objects himself. He argues that at around the middle of the Bronze

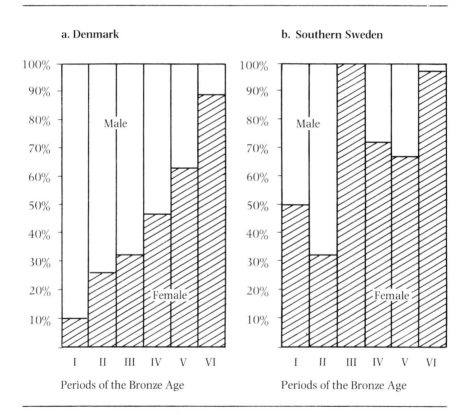

38 The proportion of female (*shaded area*) and male hoards and burials in southern Scandinavia in successive phases of the Bronze Age: **a.** Denmark, shown by swords (male) and ornaments (female) in burials and hoards (data after Kristiansen, 1984); **b.** southern Sweden, shown by the relative number of hoards with weapons and with ornaments (data after Larson, 1986).

Age the need to display male wealth and status in burials decreased, as the hierarchic social structure which had evolved in the early Bronze Age stabilised. Therefore, the apparent decline in male wealth does not reflect a real decline but rather an ideological change in the manifestation of wealth and status, and thus mainly mirrors male attitudes and behaviour. This is related to the increased importance given to female ornaments, and shows that male wealth was being invested increasingly in wives and daughters. Kristiansen argues that an important role of women was to act as pawns in long-distance alliance networks (to be considered in the next section), which were necessary for the continued flow of bronze into Scandinavia.

Alternatively, it may be argued that the same changes demonstrate a real shift towards greater equality between women and men at a time when society as a whole became more stable and competition between groups diminished, so that a fixed ladder of rank within society had become established.

If the status of women was improving at this time, this may be related to a shift away from pastoralism and towards arable agriculture, for which there is some evidence in Scandinavia during the later Bronze Age. The explanation for this, relating the status of women to the display of wealth and the subsistence pattern, is similar to the argument we have already seen for southern England. Evidence for this change is provided in Scandinavia by the increase in cereals found in pollen analyses, and the apparent abandonment of some grassland, which reverted to woodland.[33] If the change in the apparent quantity of wealth associated with women were merely due to men's choice of how to demonstrate their own wealth, we might expect the exact opposite of the pattern displayed, as men far more frequently use women to parade their status in pastoral than in agricultural societies. Although the role of women in agricultural production may never have been as significant in the Bronze Age or later periods as it was in the early Neolithic, it was probably considerably greater than in pastoralist societies, where women typically play very little part in production. Randsborg[34] points out that settlement in Denmark appears to have expanded from land best suited to an agricultural economy based primarily on animal breeding into areas more suitable for arable. Regional differences in the status of women within Denmark, measured on the same basis, have also been examined, and again the relative status of women appears to have been higher in areas of Denmark where the soils are better suited to arable farming. There is also evidence to suggest that women may have been responsible for harvesting cereals.[35] Small bronze sickles are found in hoards and burials associated with women. These may actually have been used for cutting crops, or may merely be symbolic expressions of ritual activity,[36] but either explanation could imply that women were involved in harvesting. The trend away from a concentration on animal breeding at the beginning of the Bronze Age may have taken place in a number of parts of Europe, and may have had the same effect on women's status in all these areas.

The significance of the burials and hoards as aspects of religious behaviour in Bronze Age Scandinavia, and particularly the role which women may have played in ritual, is another possible perspective on the same material. It has often been argued that most of the Late Bronze Age hoards from this area were deposited as part of a ritual; as women's goods predominate, it would be argued that women controlled or performed some of these rituals themselves, and may have gained status from this activity.[37] This may be linked with the small bronze figurines of late Bronze Age date, which are usually interpreted as connected with ritual in some way: of those whose sex is identifiable, most are women,[38] some of whom are dressed in the short corded skirts also found in early Bronze Age burials. They are sometimes described as statuettes of mythical beings;[39] some are in postures, such as bent over backwards, which have been well described as 'ritual acrobatics',[40] and may be seen as votaries, rather than the deities themselves. While the relationship between female deities and the roles of women in religious practice and their roles and status in real life is not necessarily clear-cut, as has already been considered, these figurines and the prominent place of female ornaments in Late Bronze Age Scandinavian hoards might suggest that this was an area in which women (though on this evidence not women alone) played a significant part.

The burials with grave goods and the hoards of metalwork thus provide a rich source of data on which to base a discussion of the position of women in the Bronze Age. However, it is important to reiterate here the point with which I began. Of necessity this discussion has focused on burials with grave goods, which are assumed to be those of the richer or at least reasonably well-off members of society. Most Bronze Age burials, however, contain no grave goods at all, and these are thought to be the burials of the poorer people. We cannot even begin to discuss the relative status of these less affluent women and men, and if we consider almost any present-day society it will be clear that it would not be justifiable to extrapolate this information from the theories put forward for wealthier people.

A trade in women?

The evidence provided by burials with grave goods, hoards, and stray finds of metal objects has also been used to show patterns of trade in Bronze Age Europe. The most usual method of study is to look at the stylistic features of artefacts which are typical of one particular area, and then to examine whether a type appears in smaller numbers in another area. If so, it can usually be argued that the object must have been traded or exchanged, or perhaps carried to the other area by a migrant. As well as trade in finished objects, trading in raw materials can often also be demonstrated.

Many raw materials, including stone, metals – especially copper – and the clay from which pottery is made, have distinctive patterns of trace elements (minerals found in minute quantities). These do not in general affect the quality or properties of the raw material, but the exact content of different minerals may be characteristic of the material's provenance. It is thus possible, by analysing these trace elements, to establish that a particular sample of copper probably came, for example, from Austria or Ireland. If that object is found, say, in Sweden, then either the raw material or the finished artefact must have been brought there from the area of origin.

Large numbers of often very fine bronze objects are found in Scandinavia, yet the area itself possesses no source of the raw materials (copper and tin) necessary to produce them. Analyses of Scandinavian bronze objects have shown that most of the raw materials come from the ore-rich areas of central, eastern and south-east Europe, but the distinctive design of Scandinavian Bronze Age metalwork makes it clear that the artefacts were actually manufactured in Scandinavia. This raises a perennial archaeological problem. What was given in exchange for the raw materials? Many, if not most, of the materials used in prehistory have not been preserved. Most items of food, clothes, timber, skins and all other organic materials have only survived in exceptional circumstances, but would have been just as important a part of life and trade as the metal and stone objects and pottery that form such a large part of the archaeological record. So it often happens that we can see one side of a trade link but not the other, and the case of Bronze Age Scandinavia is very typical. The problem of what was traded for the raw bronze has long exercised the minds of prehistorians in the area. Most have pointed to amber, which is native to Scandinavia but widely found in graves and other archaeological contexts throughout much of Bronze Age Europe. The Danish archaeologist Kristiansen has, however, put forward an intriguing alternative suggestion.[41]

In the Early Bronze Age, burials with complete sets of ornaments provide important evidence for trade and inter-regional connections. If someone is found buried with one or two foreign items, which were made at different times and in different workshops, or a 'matching set' which was probably acquired at one time, the objects may have been traded or acquired piecemeal. If, however, a body is accompanied by a series of ornaments, perhaps made over a length of time but all from the one area, which is far from that in which they were found, then it is reasonable to suggest that the individual moved from the first area, bringing them all with her or him. A number of instances of this kind occur in Early Bronze Age contexts in northern Europe. A woman wearing a set of jewellery from the Lüneberg area of north Germany was found on the Danish island of Zeeland, and female outfits typical of the Nordic or Scandinavian areas have been found in north Germany, both in Pomerania and south of the Elbe. Male burials with Scandinavian costume have not, it seems, been found there. Similarly, in the Late Bronze Age, Nordic ornaments are commonly found in neighbouring cultural areas of northern Europe in contexts which suggest the

39 (*right*) and 40 (*facing page*) Bronze Age rock engravings from Bohuslan and Scania, southern Sweden. While some figures are clearly phallic, others engaged in similar activities are not. Are these women? What interpretation should be placed on the apparently different costumes worn by some of the figures? After Gelling and Davidson, 1969.

exchange of people rather than just of goods. Both the position of ornaments on bodies in graves and wear patterns on ornaments found in hoards show that they were worn in a manner traditional in Scandinavia, but unusual in the area in which they were found. The reverse pattern – northern European outfits in Scandinavia – is much rarer than the occurrence of Scandinavian goods in north Germany. It has also been observed that the distribution of Nordic female ornaments extends much further south than the distribution of male objects. On the other hand, foreign objects associated with men are more common in Scandinavia itself than foreign objects associated with women. Kristiansen's interpretation of this pattern is that there was an extensive trade network throughout northern Europe: bronze objects and raw materials may have been the main items of trade, but the system was backed up by important social contacts and alliances. Often, perhaps, these were secured by intermarriage between groups, with the woman moving to her husband's home. These marriage alliances would ensure continued kinship obligations and regular contacts between the groups, stimulating continued trading.

Rock art in the Alps and Scandinavia

Another potentially rich source of evidence for the role of women in the Bronze Age is the rock art found in several locations in Europe. The two major zones where this art is found are southern Sweden and the southern

41 Naquane rock, Val Camonica, Italy: engraved scenes including houses, domestic animals, hunting and various other activities. After Anati, 1961.

Alps. In both these areas rocks are engraved with detailed designs including scenes showing people involved in various activities. Usually, though often without clear justification, these engravings are considered to have some religious function, so there is uncertainty about how far they should be used as evidence for daily activities.

In Scandinavia, boats, often depicted with people rowing them, are a favourite scene; other carvings show weapons, sometimes in the hands of combatants, or scenes of people playing the huge Scandinavian curved trumpets or *lurer*. The human figures are of necessity rather crudely drawn, usually as stick-figures, because pecking the hard granite could have been no easy task. Deciding whether the artist intended to depict a woman or a man would be difficult, were it not for the fact that a large number of the figures have very obvious, erect penises. Is this a convention for representing males, and if so are all the figures shown without penises women, or is some other meaning intended? People brandishing swords or daggers include figures with and without penises, yet it is usually assumed that all burials with these weapons are male; on the other hand, as has already been pointed out, much of the work on burials has been done without independent osteological studies of the bones themselves. Another feature which might define women is 'long hair', a sort of curved pigtail sitting on the head of some figures and extending down the back.[42] If these are the only women represented, women are very rare; if, on the other hand, all non-phallic representations are women, they are as common as representations of men, and are shown involved in a wide range of activities.

The most impressive Alpine rock art comes from two locations, Val Camonica in northern Italy and Monte Bego in south-east France.[43] Scenes here also show combat, but hunting and farming are depicted too. As in Scandinavia, some of the figures have obvious penises: warfare and hunting scenes include figures both with and without them. Emmanuel Anati, who has carried out most of the recent work at Val Camonica, has calculated that six out of ten human figures are phallic, and four out of ten are of indeterminate sex. He also suggests that only about four per cent of the figures are women, shown praying or dancing, though he does not make it clear how he identifies them. One scene shows two people guiding a plough drawn by two animals. Behind them is a figure with a hoe, apparently carrying another figure on its back. This has been interpreted as a women with a child. If this is indeed a woman, it is important to note that she has no other features which might identify her as such: this raises the possibility that many of the other figures may also be women. Also, assuming that the interpretation of the scene is correct, it is obviously very significant in that it shows women taking part in agriculture alongside men.

42 Farming scene from Seradina, Val Camonica. The figures on the right seem to be a woman with a hoe, carrying a child on her back. They are following a plough drawn by two animals. After Anati, 1961.

5 The Celtic Iron Age

With the Iron Age we at last enter the era of written records in Europe. Most of our information about the period still relies on the archaeology of settlement sites, burials and other excavated sites, and the archaeology of women is as difficult to disentangle. But while the inhabitants of north-west Europe were themselves technically 'prehistoric', in that they did not keep written records, the peoples of the Mediterranean, and especially the Greeks and the Romans, were already producing an extensive body of literature, including geographies or travel writings and histories which contained descriptions of the peoples of other parts of Europe. As we shall see, there exist quite a number of written accounts of the lives of women in Iron Age Europe. These accounts of course vary considerably in quality and detail, and their accuracy or otherwise must be carefully weighed up.

The evaluation of these documentary sources and the way in which they can be used alongside archaeological evidence is more controversial than might be supposed. A good example of this is the name which is to be given to the period in question, the last few centuries before the Roman conquest. In earlier chapters I have referred to the 'women of Neolithic Europe', or the 'people of the Bronze Age': because we possess no records written either by people of the societies themselves or by literate neighbouring societies, we do not know what the various peoples of prehistoric Europe called themselves; we have to make do with terms invented by nineteenth-century archaeologists, based on the materials from which some tools were made at the time. But for the Iron Age we can do better. The classical civilisations called the people of Europe to the north and west of their own homelands 'Celts', which is presumably a version of the name some of them called themselves. The earliest references to the Celts occur in the mid-fifth century BC, and the word is of course still in use today, referring to the peoples of some areas of western or Atlantic Europe. Geographically it is clear that by 'Celts' the classical world meant people living in an area stretching at least from the Pyrenees to the Danube. But how much before the fifth century people called themselves Celts, and over how wide an area, is a controversial topic and not directly relevant to the present subject. Suffice it to say that I will follow conventional practice and use the terms Celt and German (much the same argument applies to the Germanic peoples east of the Rhine) to describe the inhabitants of north-west Europe.[1]

Domestic organisation in Iron Age Britain

Settlements of the first millennium BC, especially in Britain, often provide considerably more evidence, both of structural features and of the material remains of artefacts and the economy, than those of earlier periods. At a number of carefully excavated sites these have allowed more discussion of the use of different buildings and areas within houses. In a few cases suggestions have been made about the amount of domestic space used by women and men, and which roles were assigned to each, which in turn have a bearing on the social roles of women and the status accorded to them.

As we have already seen, houses, farms and villages provide archaeologists with a wealth of evidence about the society which occupied them. How archaeologists work out the use of a particular room or space on a settlement site has been discussed briefly in earlier chapters. In some cases, as we have seen, it is easy to assign debris to a particular activity or craft, while in other cases it may be very difficult. And even if the activity can be determined it will rarely, if ever, be directly apparent whether it was carried out by a woman or a man. All but the most sceptical of archaeologists would agree that the regular association of specific tools with one or other sex in burials suggests that the relevant activity was carried out by people of that sex. The discovery of the same tools in a particular area of a settlement site would probably indicate that people of that sex also used that particular space. In the later prehistoric period we may also find literary references to specific activities. Unfortunately, in Britain at least, there are comparatively few known Iron Age burials, and those there are do not include craft tools among the grave goods; apart from a few documentary references which will be discussed later, we have little direct evidence for gender roles. The pioneering archaeological study by the late David Clarke of the Iron Age settlement at Glastonbury, Somerset, is of particular relevance, even though many of his interpretations are very controversial: he gives detailed consideration to the probable use of space, based on the deposition of artefacts, and goes on to discuss the implications for the respective roles of women and men.

Clarke's study of the settlement at Glastonbury is based on a reanalysis of the results of excavations carried out in the first decade of this century.[2] The exceptionally precise recording of the position of each object found during the excavations allowed him to study the relationship between the distribution of each category of artefact and the buildings on a large village site of around the second to first centuries BC. Because the site was located in very marshy ground in the Somerset Levels, the preservation of wood and other organic materials was unusually good, so a particularly wide range of artefacts was available for study.

Clarke suggests that the site was made up of a number of clusters or units of buildings, each of which comprised a similar pattern of different building types. Each cluster consisted of two main houses, a minor house and a variety of ancillary structures such as workshops, stables, bake-houses and granaries. The attribution of these building types to different functions is based on the occurrence within them of artefacts which would have been used there. The suggested use of the major and minor houses is of particular interest. Artefacts found in the major houses, which were substantially built timber structures, included horse- and chariot-gear and weaponry, tools for various activities, needles and combs, and sherds of pottery, a high proportion of which were decorated fine wares. The minor houses, by contrast, were somewhat smaller and set in the opposite side of the compound. No weapons, metalworking evidence or workshop tools were found in them, but there was evidence of spinning, weaving, fur- and leather-working and grinding corn. There were also beads and bracelets, and bronze tweezers. A higher proportion of the pottery in the minor houses was undecorated. Clarke makes the assumption, without further discussion, that the artefacts missing from these minor houses are male-associated, while those present are female-associated. While the attribution of some of the artefacts is justified on the grounds of associations elsewhere with burials of the respective sexes, he suggests that the basis of distinction between the types of house is that the major houses were male-owned or

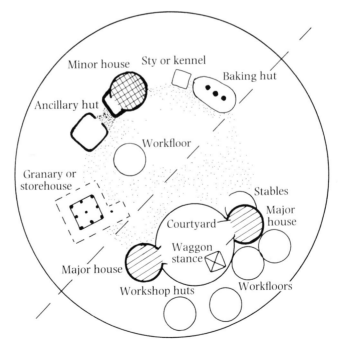

43 Schematic plan of the presumed function of various elements of the settlement clusters at the Iron Age site of Glastonbury, Somerset, according to Clarke, 1972.

predominantly used by men, though women were sometimes present in them, while the minor ones were the 'especial centres of female residence'. The implied assumption, then, is that the activities listed above were women's tasks. The presence of harnesses is explained as evidence that women were responsible for the production and maintenance of all leather gear, rather than the alternative possibility (assuming Clarke's rigid separation of the houses on sex grounds is correct) that the harness gear might be evidence that women rode or drove horses!

A category of buildings which Clarke calls 'ancillary huts' is also characterised by female-associated artefacts, such as beads, spindle whorls and bone combs, while artefacts which he defines as male are rarely found in them. Flint artefacts are more common in these structures than elsewhere on the site. The location and nature of these artefacts led Clarke to suggest that the huts might have served as animal pens, storage or milking parlours, used by women, though the evidence for this seems to be far from conclusive. 'Workshops' are distinguished by the presence of an assortment of tools and unfinished wooden articles turned on a lathe, and 'an absence of a significant level of female artefacts'. The crafts represented in these huts are therefore assumed to have been carried out by men.

Clarke thus made a number of unfounded assumptions about which artefacts were associated with which sex, and gave a great deal of weight to the absence of certain artefacts, although there may have been many other social reasons for this. For example, would anyone be likely to wear, and lose, their best beads while engaged in a manual craft activity? Other problems relate to the location of artefacts on the site. The buildings are divided into a number of chronological phases, and the use of a particular area does not remain constant throughout. It is not always certain to which phase, and therefore to which type of building, a particular artefact belongs, though this relationship is crucial to Clarke's argument. Other authors have pointed out specific problems in this connection. It has been noted, for instance,[3] that although some of Clarke's categories of structure type fit the evidence well, others do not. For example, only one of the 'baking huts' had an oven, and one had several hearths while others had none. Despite new work at Glastonbury, the current excavators, Bryony and John Coles, deny that any clear gender differences in the use of particular structures are apparent, or that the society was necessarily male-dominated.

Although we may question Clarke's actual interpretations, his methods and the detailed way in which he studied the data must point the way to future studies of gender roles on settlement sites. His work has stimulated other archaeologists to think about this issue, in relation both to Glastonbury and to other sites. A number of other studies have attempted to use

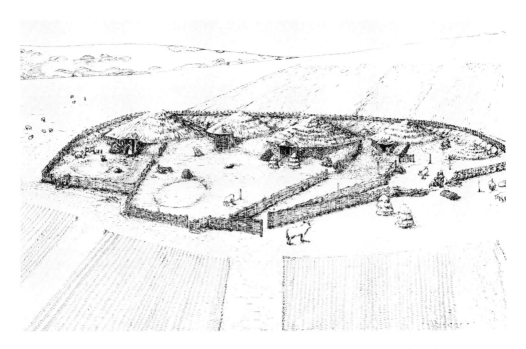

44 Reconstruction of part of the Late Bronze Age agricultural settlement at Blackpatch, Sussex. Drawing by L. Drewett.

similar methodology in connection with other settlement sites. Two of these focus on the slightly earlier period of the later Bronze Age in southern England. At Blackpatch in Sussex, for example, a site belonging to the period *c.*1400–900 BC,[4] several huts were recently excavated. In each of these, evidence of different activities was found. One hut, which appeared to have been used for grain storage and craft activities, was interpreted as the head person's hut, but the excavator was rightly cautious in assigning a sex to this head person, although a bronze razor, usually assumed to have been used by men for shaving, was found in it. In another large hut, which was used for food preparation, two bronze finger rings led him to suggest that the occupier had 'some status' and, tentatively, that this was the wife's hut, where food was prepared and children reared, away from the craft activities practised in the other large hut.

The settlements of the later Bronze Age in southern England, already discussed in the last chapter, form a close-knit group, and are often known as Deverel-Rimbury sites. In an analysis of all the excavated examples Ann Ellison discusses evidence which might reflect different female and male roles.[5] Again, as at Blackpatch, a pattern of different-sized houses was discerned, and different artefacts were found in them. A similar pattern recurred on all the sites. Each site had some large huts in which food was eaten, where various craft activities such as leather working were carried out, and where bone, metal and stone tools were made and maintained. These activities, she suggests, may have been male-associated, though the huts also contain evidence for 'those [activities] more often associated with females (notably weaving)'. The other main category of house was somewhat smaller, and was mainly used for food storage and preparation, 'which were probably the major tasks for the females'. Each site comprises a number of units, each made up of one or two large residential structures, one or two of the smaller houses and sometimes a special weaving hut.

The recurring evidence that different tasks were performed in different areas within settlement sites shows that it is possible to look at social and gender role patterns on these and probably other sites, though the method has not yet reached its full potential. Nevertheless, the studies so far carried out do, for the first time, put forward models which interpret these patterns and suggest the roles played by women in the later prehistoric period in southern Britain.

Decoration on Hallstatt pottery and bronze vessels

Turning to another part of Europe, and a quite different type of archae-ological evidence, we will now look at depictions of women on pottery and bronze vessels from the earliest phase of the European Iron Age, known as the Hallstatt period. Scenes of women engaged in everyday tasks are comparatively rare in prehistoric art, but a notable exception is a series of delightful designs engraved on pottery from Sopron in north-west Hungary, and probably made in the sixth century BC (Fig. 45).[6] The pottery was probably funerary ware, made especially to contain cremated human ashes, and the pots themselves are unique in the detail and clarity of their decoration, though other vessels from the surrounding area fall within the same general tradition.

The figures which seem to be women are wearing flared skirts and appear to have curls or ringlets in their hair – or are possibly wearing earrings – while most or all of the men have long trousers. The women are engaged in weaving and spinning, and one is dancing or praying. A figure which may be a woman is playing a lyre, and another figure often taken to be female is shown riding an apparently rather too small horse. The men, by contrast, are shown also riding horses, herding or chasing animals and leading horse-drawn wagons. Figures are also seen in pairs: two women, two men, and a woman and a man. These couples have been interpreted as fighting, though they may just as easily be dancing. Even in these seemingly clear representations, however, the identification of the sex of individuals is not entirely straightforward. Are the triangular forms really dresses, or rather some form of cloak? Some of the figures are wearing a garment represented by a wide-based triangle, while others have a narrow-based triangular one, and some scholars have argued that this may in fact be the distinction between women and men. Some of the figures have a little 'beak' protruding from the front of their face: is this supposed to represent the nose, or a beard? If it is the latter, the figure with a large triangular body riding a horse would be a man rather than a woman. However, the clearest distinction in the figures is between those wearing trousers and those wearing skirts. But we cannot assume that at this early date this traditional Western distinction necessarily applied, and a number of scholars have questioned this, presumably because they were unhappy about the idea of women engaged in the various activities described. There is ample documentary evidence that later in the Iron Age, at least, Celtic men did indeed wear trousers (see below), though the provenance of these finds may be outside the geographic limits of true Celtic culture. Moreover,

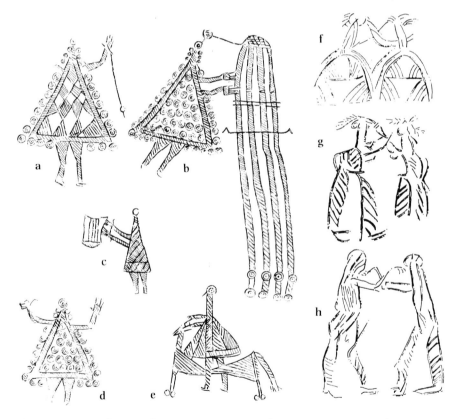

45 Designs incised on pots from Sopron, Hungary, showing women engaged in various activities: **a.** spinning; **b.** weaving on an upright loom; **c.** playing the lyre; **d.** dancing; **e.** riding on horseback; **f-h.** women and men fighting or dancing? From Piggott, 1965.

46 The Certosa situla. The second zone seems to show a funeral procession, with women carrying pots on their heads. Bologna, Museo Civico.

47 Detail of the Certosa situla, depicting women carrying various large objects on their heads. Bologna, Museo Civico.

we have no evidence to suggest that women at this time and in this area did not play instruments or ride horses, or fight.

Other scenes appear on a group of sheet-bronze buckets or *situlae*, as well as on other sheet-bronze items such as belt ornaments, also from the so-called Hallstatt Iron Age (sixth to fifth century BC) and from a small area at the head of the Adriatic in present-day Yugoslavia and northern Italy.[7] The artistic style on these vessels, known as Situla Art, shows Greek, Etruscan and, indirectly, oriental influence, though by 500 BC it was becoming increasingly local. The scenes themselves seem to represent a similar progression from stylised imported scenes to local activities and behaviour. The sheet bronze was beaten out or embossed with complex scenes featuring humans and animals. Many of the scenes are stylised and repetitive, showing a variety of social gatherings, presumably of the high-class élites which would have used the vessels at just the occasions represented. Scenes of warriors and depictions of wild beasts are also typical. Others, however, are more individualistic, and show everyday and farming activities. Men seem to be portrayed far more frequently than women, and the few women that do appear are usually waiting on men. A belt-plate from northern Italy shows a woman pouring out wine from an Etruscan beaked flagon for a man reclining on a couch in Etruscan fashion, and a similar scene appears on a situla from Bologna. A belt-fitting from Brezje in Yugoslavia, however, shows women sitting on chairs, with men kneeling before them. A scene interpreted as a funeral procession, on a situla from Certosa in Italy, depicts both women and men laden with various objects, the women with large vessels and other goods on their heads.

Literary sources

In the discussion of European prehistory from the Old Stone Age to the Bronze Age the evidence was purely archaeological, but for the Iron Age we have an additional source – the written testimony of Greeks and Romans who described the people and events to the north of their own lands. Some of these writers, like the Greek historian and geographer Herodotus, were interested in documenting the lives of all the 'barbarians', which to the Greeks meant all the non-Greek speaking peoples known at the time. For an author like Julius Caesar, on the other hand, descriptions of the lifestyles of the Gallic tribes, the Germans and the Britons, were incidental to his accounts of his battles against them. But we must appreciate that, just as in modern histories and ethnographies, what these authors include and what they leave out of their texts reflects as much on their own society and its interests as those of the society on which they are commenting.

In all these accounts, references to women, though fairly few and far between, are probably more numerous than has generally been acknowledged by ancient historians and archaeologists.[8] However, the number of authors who say much about women in Iron Age Europe is quite small, and includes the Romans Caesar and Tacitus and the Greek Dio Cassius. Some authors make only one or two comments of any relevance to this discussion. Nor must we forget that these authorities undoubtedly drew upon the accounts of other writers and travellers whose own work is no longer extant.

The subjects covered in these literary sources are varied. There are numerous references to the role played by women in war, which reflect not so much the European or Celtic attitudes to war but rather those of the Romans, and particularly the context in which the Romans, in attempting to conquer their territory, chose to encounter them. We also find a number of important references to social organisation, marriage and descent patterns. And, thirdly, a number of passages deal with the everyday lives of women in various parts of Europe. Several statements suggest that women were responsible for some religious functions such as making prophecies, while others attest their role as healers. Other brief references mention the sexual division of labour in daily tasks.

Archaeologists have often been reluctant to place too much reliance or belief in these literary sources.[9] Few of the authors would have had first-hand knowledge of the people or customs they were describing. Quite clearly, too, habits which seemed curious to the narrator are liable to have become exaggerated in the telling, especially as many of the authors were deliberately setting out to make the Celts seem as 'uncivilised' or 'barbarous' as possible. Some authors almost certainly drew upon the same original sources for their information, and will therefore have repeated the same stories. However, in the case of many customs enough independent versions exist to make it unlikely that they could have been a Roman or Greek invention. Furthermore, although much of the behaviour seemed exotic and curious to the classical authors, most has close parallels with patterns found in present-day traditional societies described by anthropologists. Traditional archaeological theory holds that social patterns, such as those relating to marriage restrictions, for example, are not capable of being tested against archaeological data. Therefore, either documentary accounts have to be taken at face value or this rich source of evidence has to be completely ignored, which is what many archaeologists have done. Current archaeological theoretical method, on the other hand, is ideally suited to testing ideas or information put forward by classical authors, and as far as possible this is how the various categories of information relating to women's lives will be treated here.

A further question concerns how far some of the statements about women, and indeed other matters, apply solely to the part of Europe under discussion, or whether they were also relevant to other areas. Sometimes an author specifically refers to one tribe or group, and it may be that he is picking out idiosyncrasies of these individual groups. In other cases the customs of one population probably reflect those practised over a wider area: archaeological evidence shows that there was a great deal of unity in Europe at this time. The classical author himself may not have been clear about this, but even if he was, a custom which was widespread will be of more interest to us. The timespan during which a custom prevailed may also be uncertain. Some authors based their work on earlier information, which may or may not have still been correct at the time of writing. But it would also interest us to know how far back in time a particular tradition went.

Another rich source of information about prehistoric Europe is the Irish sagas, the most important of which is the *Cattle Raid of Cúailnge* or *Táin Bo Cúailnge* (often abbreviated simply as the *Táin*). Like the early medieval Welsh sources, for example the *Mabinogion*, and Continental sources of the same period, these were written down around the ninth to twelfth centuries AD but are thought to embody elements based on life in the Roman and indeed pre-Roman Iron Age. This tradition, however, is seen through the eyes of the early medieval Christian storytellers, and the interpretation of the pagan tribal society depicted is therefore beset with problems.

So what do the classical sources tell us about women in Iron Age Europe? Firstly, they give descriptions of their appearance and dress. Women are described as being tall and strong. 'Gallic women are not only equal to their husbands in stature, but they rival them in strength [or courage] as well.'[10] 'In a fight [a man may] call in his wife, stronger by far than he, with flashing eyes; most of all when she swells her neck and gnashes her teeth and poising her huge white arms begins to rain blows mingled with kicks like shots discharged from the twisted cord of a catapult.'[11] Even if these descriptions need to be taken with a pinch of salt, they must surely reflect a significant contrast between Roman women and those of north-west Europe in the Iron Age. Archaeological evidence suggests that in the Iron Age the difference between the heights of women and men was similar to that today, though the data available is limited. For example, where statistics have been produced, as at Danebury, an Iron Age hillfort in Hampshire, fifteen men were between 157 and 175 cm tall (5 ft 2 in–5 ft 9 in), while seven women were between 150 and 160 cm (4 ft 11 in and 5 ft 3 in).[12] Another, larger, sample, from the early La Tène phase (c. 500–400 BC) in the Champagne area of northern France, gives similar figures, suggesting that men were on average 165 cm (5 ft 5 in) tall while women were 155 cm (5 ft 1 in).[13] These figures compare with the average heights of present-day British men and women of 174 cm (5 ft 8½ in) and 162 cm (5 ft 3½ in) respectively.[14] By modern standards, therefore, these Celts were not particularly tall; there was perhaps marginally less difference between the heights of women and men than today, though scarcely enough to justify the classical author's comments objectively.

It seems that Celtic women, like their men, typically had long fair hair, which they wore either plaited or curled. They wore long tunics, held in place with a brooch, while Iron Age men are represented in classical literature and art wearing trousers, perhaps for the first time in history. Over the tunic a woollen, tartan-like cloak could be worn, a garment frequently mentioned with admiration in the classical literature. Archaeological evidence supports the literature in attesting a wide range of jewellery, including necklaces, brooches and bracelets.[15]

A few classical references to Iron Age Europe speak of daily tasks and everyday life, and a few of these mention which tasks are performed by women and which by men. These confirm the picture of gender roles suggested in earlier chapters.

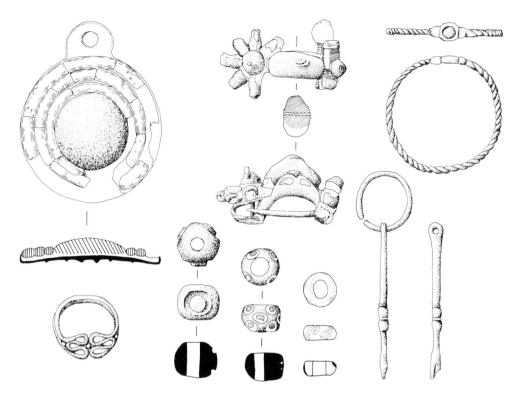

48 The jewellery worn by a rich Iron Age woman of the Arras culture, from the 'Queen's Barrow', East Yorkshire, including a pendant of bronze, sandstone and coral, a brooch of bronze and iron with coral inlay, a bronze bracelet, a finger-ring, blue and white glass beads, and a bronze nail-cleaner (?) (various scales). After Stead, 1979.

Strabo,[16] a geographer writing under the emperor Tiberius in about AD 20, and the author of a lengthy account of much of the then known world, makes the significant comment that feminine roles in Gaul 'in common with many barbarian peoples' were the reverse of those in Rome. It is unfortunately not really clear what sort of roles he means. He may be thinking of agricultural tasks, or perhaps implying that specific crafts were practised by women rather than men. Nevertheless it brought, even to the Romans, the notion that gender roles are not universal or 'natural' throughout the world, or through time.

The *Germania* of Tacitus is one of the most informative sources on many aspects of life in late Iron Age Europe, and what it tells us about women adds considerably to the knowledge we can gain from archaeology. Tacitus was a Roman author, writing in the AD 90s. At this time Britain, Gaul (France) and much of Europe had already been incorporated into the Roman Empire, but Germany, to the east of the river Rhine, had not, and was to remain independent throughout the Roman period. The *Germania* is an account of the character, customs and geography of the people of this area. Tacitus' report on everyday tasks contrasts the easy life of men with the onerous and time-consuming duties of women:

...[men] when not engaged in warfare, spend a certain amount of time hunting, but more in idleness thinking of nothing else but sleeping and eating.... The care of house, home and fields is left to the women, old men and weaklings of the family. (*Germania*, 15)

Caesar, in his famous history of his invasion of Gaul in the 50s BC, mentions land use amongst the same peoples:

...the Germans ... men and women bathe together in rivers ... no one possesses a definite portion of land. Chiefs allot land to clans and groups of people living together ... and in the following year compel them to move to another piece of land. (*De Bello Gallico*, VI, 21)

These descriptions are very reminiscent of horticultural societies, such as those in New Guinea, Africa or South America, where women are wholly or mainly responsible for crop-growing and domestic chores, while the men hunt or, as in this description, sit around doing very little! The women produce the vast bulk of the food, and also many of the items which can be exchanged with other people either within or outside the society. As a result, they have considerably more prestige and status, both within the family and outside, than in societies where men are the chief providers. This higher status of women seems to be implied by most of Tacitus' other comments. It is also typical of many horticultural societies that land is not deemed to be owned by any individual, but rather, as is suggested here, by the clan, lineage or tribe as a whole. The likelihood that statements such as these are true must add to our confidence that other comments by Caesar and Tacitus, such as those about gender roles, are also valid.

Tacitus also describes the peoples surrounding the main group of Germanic tribes. He concentrates on the aspects of their culture which differ from those of the other Germans, and makes important references to the women of two tribes, the Sitones and the Fenni. The Sitones seem to have lived approximately in the area that is now Lithuania, perhaps on the Baltic coast or in Finland. Tacitus says of them:

...[the Sitones] resemble [the Suiones] in all respects but one – woman is the ruling sex. (*Germania*, 45)

Much literary criticism[17] tends to dismiss this statement as fable, while other scholars see it as fitting into Engels' model of matriarchy as the most primitive form of society, and have argued that the Sitones must have been a last surviving remnant. Tacitus' subsequent comment, 'that is a measure of their decline, I will not say below freedom, but even below decent slavery', mirrors general Roman attitudes to women, and clearly implies how much he disapproves and derides the idea. While it is certainly true that his account of the Sitones may easily be unreliable, since these people lived as far from his first-hand or even second-hand experience as any society he describes, the statement does follow on from a reasonably accurate description of how amber is formed and collected around the Baltic Sea. But Tacitus' view and the interpretations put on his statement by the more recent critics are also typical of almost all early ethnographic writing in that they assume either that women's status will be lower than men's, or where the evidence for the higher status of women seems undeniable, that the society is in some way anomalous or peripheral.

The Fenni, who also lived somewhere in north-east Europe, perhaps on the eastern shores of the Baltic,

...are astonishingly savage and disgustingly poor. They have no proper weapons, no horses, no homes. They eat wild herbs.... The women support themselves by hunting, exactly like the men.... Yet they count their lot happier than that of others who groan over field labour. (*Germania*, 46)

The Fenni sound like a classic hunter-gatherer society. As we saw in Chapter 1, in most surviving hunter-gatherer societies women mainly gather plant food or are involved in processing animal products, as in Arctic regions where little plant food is available. This may also have been the case here. However, there are a few anthropologically attested examples where women hunt alongside the men, such as the Agta of the Philippines.[18]

A second hunter-gatherer group is the Scrithifinni, who are probably to be identified with the later Lapps. They are mentioned in the sixth century AD by Procopius in his *History of the Gothic War*.[19] He says that the Scrithifinni 'neither till the land themselves, nor do their women work it for them, but the women regularly join the men in hunting, which is their only pursuit.'

Although the descriptions of societies such as the Fenni and the Scrithifinni are often dismissed as the product of classical imagination and as mythological inversions of Roman values, it seems just as plausible that they were hunter-gatherers, since archaeological evidence shows that hunter-gatherer societies continued to exist in northern Scandinavia well into this period. There does not therefore seem any good reason to doubt the suggestion that women hunted, and shared other tasks equally with men.

Prophets and priestesses

Both Tacitus and Càesar mention that among the Germans women acted as prophets. Caesar[20] tells us that it was apparently customary that the *matres familiae*, the senior women of the household (more usually, but perhaps rather negatively, translated as 'matrons') drew lots and used other sorts of divination to decide whether it was advisable to engage in battle. Tacitus reinforces this idea:

They believe that there resides in women an element of holiness and a gift of prophecy; and so they do not scorn to ask advice or lightly disregard their replies. ... Veleda [was] long honoured by many Germans as a divinity; and even earlier they showed similar reverence for Aurinia and a number of others – a reverence untainted by servile flattery or any pretence of turning women into goddesses. (*Germania*, 8)

Veleda was clearly a force in politics, and represented her tribe in political arbitrations.[21]

The best known of the Celtic religious leaders are undoubtedly the Druids, mentioned by several of the classical authors as the priests, teachers and judges of the community. It has been argued that they may have included women.[22] The women described by Tacitus[23] as 'dressed in black with hair dishevelled waving firebrands' on Anglesey, when the Roman governor Suetonius Paulinus attempted to attack the island in AD 61, were clearly in league with the Druidic cult though there is no suggestion that these women were themselves Druids. Other references also hint that women were involved in activities similar to those of the Druids, though not described as such. Late Roman authors are more specific, and refer to a class of women known as *dryades*, a word closely related to Druids. Vopiscus, writing at the end of the fourth century AD but not regarded as a particularly trustworthy source, twice refers to these women in the role of prophetess.

In the Irish saga the *Táin*, a woman named Fedelm is credited with prophetic powers, and other early Irish sagas speak of druidesses and prophetesses.[24] Both these and the late Roman sources may lead us to suggest, with caution, that the origins of this female role may go back several centuries earlier into the prehistoric period, and be one of the roots of an overall higher status and greater power (though by no means domination) enjoyed by women in the Celtic world.

Descent and marriage patterns

The marriage patterns of the Celts and the way they viewed descent and inheritance seem to have had the same fascination for the classical world as variations in these practices have had for eighteenth and nineteenth-century explorers and more recent anthropologists. Although only a few of these classical references explicitly mention the status of women, numerous anthropological studies have shown a close correlation between descent patterns and their situation. In particular, in societies where descent is reckoned through the mother (matrilineal), women are respected and valued more highly and their status is much greater than in societies where descent is reckoned through the father (patrilineal). However, the anthropological evidence of present-day societies suggests that even where matrilineal descent is the rule, men invariably act as leaders and have political power.

From the classical sources it seems that there were very significant differences in marriage and descent patterns between one part of Europe and another. Tacitus, in *Germania*, suggests that the Iron Age people of Germany were mainly monogamous and marriages patrilocal, with the wife moving to her husband's home:

> [The people of Germany have] ... one wife apiece – all of them except a very few who take more than one not to satisfy their desires, but because their exalted rank brings many pressing offers of matrimonial alliances. The dowry is brought by husband to wife ... gifts [such as] oxen, a horse and bridle, or a shield, spear and sword.... She in her turn brings a present of arms to her husband.... The woman must not think that she is excluded from aspirations to manly virtues or exempt from the hazards of warfare.... She enters her husband's home to be the partner of his toils and perils, that both in peace and war she is to share his sufferings and adventures....
>
> Clandestine love-letters are unknown to men and women alike. Adultery is extremely rare....
>
> Girls too are not hurried into marriage. As old and full-grown as the men they match their mates in age and strength.... The sons of sisters are as highly honoured by their uncles as by their own fathers. Some tribes even consider the former tie the closer and more sacred of the two. However a man's heirs are his own children. (*Germania*, 18–20).

Apart from this last statement, the implications are that descent is reckoned matrilineally, though residence is patrilocal – 'she enters her husband's home' – or more likely what is described in anthropological literature as avunculocal, where a young man moves to his mother's brother's residence when he is old enough to leave home, and his wife then moves to live with him. This is one of the few possible arrangements whereby matrilineal descent and the wife moving to the husband's residence can be combined. Many other references support this suggestion. For example, Livy[25] records that Ambigatus, the ruler of the Bituriges, a Gallic tribe, sent two of his sister's sons to lead emigrations to find more land in the late fourth century BC. Thus a man's children are considered to belong to their mother's descent group, and his own descendants will be his sister's children. It is also typical of non-patrilineal systems that women marry men of about their own age, as suggested here, whereas in patrilineal systems it is common for young girls to be married to much older men. This pattern of descent is quite common in many horticultural societies, and is usually linked with relatively high status for women. However, despite this, it is not unknown for material possessions to be inherited from father to son or children, as is said to be the case in Iron Age Germany, though other property or rights, such as land rights or political rights, would probably follow the matrilineage, a pattern sometimes known as 'double-descent'.

Burials in a late Hallstatt cemetery at Mühlacker in north Württemberg have been claimed to provide evidence for matrilineal descent. Although the cemetery dates from several centuries before Tacitus' description, it is geographically within the area of which he speaks.[26] There is a clear contrast in dress between girls and women, which Ludwig Pauli interprets as a distinction between unmarried and married women. The central or primary burials under the mounds or tumuli in the cemetery were those of married women. In one case a woman was accompanied by the bodies presumably of her husband and unmarried children. It seems, then, that on the death of a married daughter, a new mound was built, in which all the dead members of the next generation were buried. From this Pauli concludes that the people using this cemetery practised matrilineal descent.

The Gauls, on the other hand, according to the documentary sources, seem to have had a different pattern of inheritance, but one which also implies that women had high status, particularly with respect to the interesting and balanced dowry system:

When a man marries he contributes from his own property an amount calculated to match whatever he has received from his wife as dowry. A joint account is kept of all this property, and the profits from it are set aside. Whichever of the two outlives the other gets both shares, together with the profits that have accumulated over the years. Husbands have power of life and death over their wives and children.... (Caesar, *De Bello Gallico*, VI, 19)

A similar system of joint ownership of property is implied in the *Táin*. Queen Medb and her consort Ailill have quarrelled, and all their possessions are brought before them so that they may determine who owned what. Among other things Medb owned a fine ram, a splendid horse and bulls. She had bestowed a chariot on Ailill as part of her bride-price, worth twenty-one female slaves. The implication is that in the first centuries AD, in Ireland, at least, high-ranking women could own possessions equal to men's, though the *Táin* also makes it clear that social stratification was a very important feature of early Irish society; that there were female, as well as male, slaves, and that precious possessions were valued in terms of these female slaves.

Returning to marriage customs, monogamy was the rule among the

Gauls and Iberians, as it was in Germany,[27] but this contradicts what Caesar says about Iron Age Britain:

Wives are shared between groups of ten or twelve men, especially brothers, and between fathers and sons, but the offspring of these unions are counted as the children of the man with whom a particular woman cohabited first. (*De Bello Gallico*, v, 14)

Although this sentence is often dismissed as at least highly improbable by most archaeologists, it is in fact a pattern well recognised by anthropologists. Polyandry, where one woman marries more than one man, is much less common than polygyny (one man having several wives), but the Toda of the Nilgiri hills of southern India practise this same form of polyandry in which, when a woman marries, she marries all the man's brothers as well.[28] In order to give a child a socially recognised father in situations where the natural or genetic father is not necessarily known, rules have to be made, such as that the eldest brother is always counted as the 'father' – as is usually the rule amongst the Toda – or as suggested by Caesar, that the father is the 'man with whom a particular woman cohabited first'.

Is there any archaeological evidence to back up Caesar's assertion? Many features of the archaeology of Britain on the one hand, and Continental Europe on the other, provide contrasts which indicate that there were significant differences between Iron Age society in the two areas. One feature which has puzzled generations of archaeologists is the difference in shape between houses in these two areas. In Britain nearly all Iron Age houses are circular and extremely large, whereas on the Continent they are usually small and rectangular. Many of the classic British round houses have diameters of 10–15 metres and are over 100 square metres in floor area, though smaller round houses of only about 33 square metres also exist.[29] The rectangular houses on the Continent vary considerably in size, though most seem to have a considerably smaller floor area than British round houses. Examples from the Hallstatt phases include the Goldberg, a hillfort in southern Germany, where the average house size was 8×8 metres, Aulnay-la-Planche, a small settlement site in France, 4×2 metres, Kornwestheim 3×2.5 metres, and the Heuneberg, a rich hillfort on the Danube, 12×5 metres.[30]

Why is there this significant difference in size between British and Continental Iron Age houses? Although archaeologists have frequently pointed it out, few have attempted an explanation. However, as was discussed in Chapter 3, when the Linear Pottery Culture was considered, the sizes and shapes of houses are bound to reflect the social and domestic arrangements of any society. This has been demonstrated in a number of anthropological studies, which have looked at different aspects of house form. Perhaps most obviously, a polygamous extended family would usually be more suited to a large round house (unless, as is often the case in Africa, all the wives or husbands have separate dwellings, or each household's domestic space comprises more than one building), just as a much smaller house would be more appropriate to a monogamous couple with a small nuclear family. An ethnographic survey of house shapes[31] also showed an interesting difference in the types of house built by particular societies. Societies with curvilinear house shapes tend to be polygamous, while those with rectilinear house shapes tend to be monogamous. A sample of 136 societies from all over the world and representing all forms of agricultural subsistence base was studied. There was of course a link between the shape of the house and other architectural features such as the building materials and type of roof used, but these factors were not considered to be the primary determinants of house shape. Other aspects, such as preferences in art forms, were also considered, but the most significant correlation discovered was between house shape and marriage patterns. Polyandrous societies are comparatively rare, so the study actually compared polygynous societies and house forms. As polygyny and polyandry have significant social and economic differences, the house forms resulting from polygyny may be different from those resulting from the polyandrous marriage pattern described in Iron Age Britain. Nevertheless, the correlation between British and Continental Iron Age houses and the contrasting marriage customs suggested in the two areas would fit well with the anthropological patterning.

In recent years several articles have pointed out that the dichotomy between Continental and British houses is not in fact as great as was formerly thought. Regional variations and exceptions have been found in both areas.[32] The contrast which was noted both in the classical sources and in the earlier archaeological studies was in fact between inland Iron Age Britain, as described by Caesar, and central Europe, to which Tacitus was referring. However, the fact that round houses are also found in coastal mainland Europe merely opens up a discussion as to whether a social or political boundary existed at the English Channel or within Continental Europe: differences in marriage patterns could accompany this boundary, and need not invalidate the argument put forward in the previous paragraph, that Caesar's claim that the Iron Age Britons were polyandrous is quite likely to have been true, and that this explains the differences in house form between the two areas. Nor is our contention upset by the possibility that both our classical sources and the archaeological dichotomy may be gross generalisations, and that there were local or individual exceptions to both the house shape and the marriage pattern rules.

The description of the British Celts as polygamous has often been dismissed on various grounds: for instance, that it cannot be substantiated archaeologically; that Caesar could not have known, or that Caesar is merely repeating a rumour; or, worse still, that he was indulging in the literary device of imitation and repeating all the possible bad or 'un-Roman' practices attributed to the 'barbarians'. It has even been dismissed as 'a bad rumour'[33] because Herodotus[34] describes similar practices elsewhere. But polygamy is very common throughout the world, and, as Tim Champion points out,[35] there is a limit to literary imitation. The custom is therefore more likely to have been a geographically widespread phenomenon which struck the classical mind as unusual.

Another important question is whether marriages were arranged, and, if so, by whom. How much say did the women, or even the couple, have in the choice of partners? As in many societies around the world today and in the past, we have substantial documentary evidence that in Iron Age Europe marriage was used as a means of securing alliances between families or tribes. The references are to ruling families, and invariably it is the woman, usually a chief's sister, who is married into a neighbouring tribe. How widely through the social spectrum marriages were arranged is not clear, nor whether arranged marriages were the general rule. Nevertheless, as we shall see, they did not prevent women from becoming leaders and possessing considerable power.

Women in war

We probably know more about the military techniques of the Celts than any other aspect of their lives. This is not surprising, since it was in battle that the Romans, from whom most of our written sources stem, most frequently came face to face with the native populations of north-west Europe. Archaeological evidence shows that dense populations were living in settlements predominantly devoted to farming activities, accompanied by craft industries, and were engaging in exchange with other settlements throughout Europe. There is little evidence to suggest that warfare or hostilities played a significant role in everyday life during most of the Iron Age period. The bias in the classical sources is without doubt a reflection of the nature of Roman intervention in north-west Europe, necessitating defensive action on the part of the native populations and providing the context for the descriptions and discussions of most of the classical writers concerned with the area.

Our information comes from a number of authors. Caesar, in particular, writing in his *De Bello Gallico*, knew more about this aspect of his enemy than any other, and Tacitus in his *Germania* and *Annales* also provides us with informative insights. Women, it seems, were nearly always present on the battlefield, though in most cases probably not actually fighting; they usually watched from the sidelines, shouting encouragement, rather like a crowd at a sports match today. But they did sometimes get injured or killed, or captured by the enemy, either as bystanders or perhaps because they were playing a rather greater role:

Close by them too, are their nearest and dearest, so that they can hear the shrieks of their womenfolk, and the wailing of their children. These are the witnesses whom each man reverences most highly, whose praise he most desires. It is to their mothers that they go to have their wounds treated, and the women are not afraid to count and compare the gashes. They also carry supplies of food to the combatants and encourage them.... It stands on record that armies wavering and on the point of collapse have been rallied by the women. (Tacitus, *Germania*, 7 and 8)

A similar picture also emerges from a number of other sources, referring to different parts of Europe. These also suggest that, as well as tending the wounded and supplying provisions, women also bound and guarded prisoners.[36]

The presence of women on the battlefield is mentioned a number of times, in connection with different tribes. For example, Caesar[37] says that 'behind their line' the Gauls 'arranged the carts and waggons...; on this barrier they placed their women'. Tacitus describes the tactics of Civilis, who with the help of other Germanic tribes led the Batavians, a tribe living in the Rhine delta, to a victory against the Romans in AD 69–70, thus:

In the rear, he placed his own mother and sisters, together with all the wives and little children of his men, to incite them to victory or to shame them if they gave way. And when the battle-cry of the men and the yells of the women rang out from their line it was responded to by but a feeble cheer from the [Roman] legions and cohorts.[38]

The Thracians, too, 'were spurred on by the wailing of their mothers and wives nearby',[39] and the Britons 'brought their wives with them to see the victory, installing them in carts stationed at the edge of the battlefield'.[40] This picture of all the population going off to battle together is in sharp contrast to the modern, or even the Roman, pattern of fighting men going alone to the battlefield, often far from home.

Iron Age women were not only observers and supporters in battle, but may also sometimes have been involved in disputes as arbiters, or even in actual fighting. Plutarch, a Greek philosopher writing in the early second century AD,[41] described the influence Celtic women had as negotiators and arbiters between armed forces in the period before the Celts had crossed the Alps and settled in northern Italy, around 400 BC:

[The Celtic women] arbitrated with such irreproachable fairness that a wondrous friendship of all towards all was brought about. As a result of this they continued to consult with women in regard to war and peace.

When the Romans were about to invade Anglesey, in AD 60, they faced 'black-robed women with dishevelled hair like Furies brandishing torches..., the Roman soldiers ... then urged each other, and were urged by the general, not to fear a horde of fanatical women'.[42] At the same time, Suetonius Paulinus, the Roman general facing Boudica, tried to bolster his men's morale with the information that in her army there were more women than fighting men. This presumably reflects the Roman assumption of male superiority in warfare, which was not subscribed to by the Celts, who accepted that women could play a significant part in military affairs.

The women of the Ambrones, a Teutonic tribe, were also directly involved in fighting. When the Roman general Marius was engaging in warfare with the tribe in the late second century BC, the women, brandishing swords and axes, met their own men as they retreated, as well as the pursuing Romans, and attempted to slay both, the former as traitors, the latter as foe.[43] This does, however, imply that they were not in the front line of attack, but were certainly nearby and not unwilling to use force themselves.

On the other hand, further evidence suggests that it was not universal practice throughout Iron Age Europe for women to take part in battles or to be present on the battlefield. Caesar[44] says that the Suebi ordered their wives and children and belongings to be placed in forests for safety. But the fact that the women had to be ordered by the men to go into the forest may imply that this was not normal practice in times of crisis.

Tribal chiefs and commanders in battle

As well as being present on the battlefield and actually taking part in battles, a few Iron Age women are known to have been commanders and tribal chiefs, though it is not clear whether it was exceptional or quite common for women to hold these positions. By far the most famous of these was Boudica (or more popularly, though incorrectly, Boadicea), who was leader of the Iceni, a tribe which lived in East Anglia, and who led the British in revolt against the Romans in AD 60.[45] Her name is derived from the Celtic word *bouda*, meaning victory. Boudica's exploits were recorded by two classical historians, Tacitus, in his *Annals of Imperial Rome*,[46] and the Greek writer Dio Cassius, who wrote his *History of Rome*[47] at the beginning of the third century, over 150 years after Boudica's death; this history must have been based on some more contemporary acount, now lost. Neither of these sources is totally reliable, and the attributes, actions and words ascribed to Boudica must be treated with caution; equally, however, they cannot be disregarded as pure fabrication, and both authors would have had access to sources no longer extant.

Boudica's two daughters had inherited the position of tribal co-chiefs from her dead husband. After Boudica had been brutally treated and her daughters raped by the Roman officials who had been sent in to seize her tribe's assets, she came forward and was accepted in the role of commander-in-chief of all the British troops:

The person who was chiefly instrumental in rousing the natives and persuading them to fight the Romans, the person who was thought worthy to be their leader and who directed the conduct of the entire war was Boudica, a British woman of the royal family and possessed of greater intelligence than is usually found among women. (Dio Cassius, *History*, LXII, 2, 2)

Dio Cassius also provides us with a physical description of Boudica. While it is presumably based on rumour, and perhaps on the Roman stereotype

49 Statue of Boudica on the Thames embankment, London. Although there are no contemporary depictions of Boudica, over the last century she has been the subject of many often fanciful portrayals, such as this well-known statue by T. Thornycroft, cast in bronze in 1902 from an earlier mould.

of a fierce but successful Celtic woman, it nevertheless must contain some semblance of truth and is worth repeating:

She was of great stature, most terrifying in appearance with piercing gaze and a strident voice. She had very fair hair which fell to her hips, and she wore a big gold torc around her neck and a brooch to hold her outer cloak and a tunic of many colours.[48]

Initially Boudica enjoyed considerable success in leading the people of her tribe and their allies in an uprising and the subsequent destruction of the newly established colony of retired Roman soldiers at Camulodunum (Colchester). She then proceeded to the Roman capital at London, and then to Verulamium (St Albans) where an estimated 80,000 of the Roman oppressors and their allies were killed and most of these new towns burnt to the ground. To the patriarchal Romans the worst of this disaster seems to have been that it was led by a woman. 'All this, moreover, was brought upon the Romans by a woman, a fact which caused them the greatest shame.'[49] Boudica then exhorted and led the British troops in what was probably the largest and most unified, albeit disastrous, uprising by the British against their Roman conquerors. From the content of Boudica's address to the troops before the battle, Dio Cassius leads us to believe that the British, and particularly Boudica herself, thought the Romans to be as weak and wimpish – for instance, needing to be encased in heavy armour, eating leavened bread, drinking wine, bathing in warm water and sleeping on soft beds – as the Romans obviously thought the British uncivilised and foolhardy. The total strength of the British fighting force in Boudica's final

50 Gold torc from Snettisham, Norfolk, 1st century BC (diameter 19.5 cm). Perhaps it is similar to the gold torc which Boudica is described as wearing around her neck. British Museum.

battle has been estimated[50] at over 100,000, of whom 80,000 may have perished. After the defeat, according to Tacitus, Boudica felt obliged to take her own life. Alternatively, according to Dio, she fell ill and died. Her death, combined with the heavy losses suffered by the British, marked the end of the rebellion, so it is clear that there was no other leader of similar stature to take her place.

Although Boudica is the best-known female leader of the period, the accounts of her exploits provide indirect evidence that she was not unique among the Celts. It is common for Roman historians to include speeches as though recorded verbatim. Particularly when made by enemies of the Romans, such speeches clearly could not have been reported first-hand but were literary devices invented and used by the historians. Their texts are therefore usually dismissed as not to be taken literally. Nevertheless, they must contain at least an element of the Romans' idea of the enemy's position and thinking. In a speech before her final battle, Boudica is said to have exhorted the troops with the words, 'We British are used to women commanders in war'[51] and this is repeated by Tacitus in his *Agricola*,[52] where he says that Britons 'make no distinction of sex in their appointment of commanders'. It is important to appreciate that we know the names or other details of very few leaders of either sex in Britain during the late Iron Age, so the fact that few women are mentioned personally cannot be seen as an indication that it was unusual for them to hold positions of power. One of the key sources of names of late Iron Age tribal leaders comes from inscriptions on some of the earliest coins. These inscriptions usually give the name in abbreviated form, and the ending which would often indicate the sex of the individual is unknown; conventional scholarship attributes male names to these leaders, some of whom could in fact be women. Indeed, a second female chief of a British tribe is mentioned by Tacitus. Named Cartimandua, she ruled at about the same time as Boudica, in the late AD 50s. She is described as queen of the Brigantes,[53] the huge tribe spread over much of northern England. She must have been in power before AD 57, reigned throughout the Boudican episode in the south of England and was still leader of the Brigantes in AD 69, a rule of over twelve years. Twice during this period, when she had problems with her anti-Roman consort, Venutius, the Romans backed her, so they were obviously not opposed to a female leader at all costs. The length of her reign and the huge area of her kingdom must give justification to the claim that Cartimandua was in her own right a much more powerful figure than Boudica.

Tacitus also 'quotes' a speech by another British leader, Calgacus, who speaks of a woman leader of the Brigantes who had burned a Roman colony and stormed a camp, at a date which probably would have been between AD 71 and 83.[54] Cartimandua was certainly pro- rather than anti-Roman, and the incident can hardly have taken place before her time, as it is unlikely that Rome would then have considered leaving the area as a client kingdom. It has been argued that this is merely a confusion on Tacitus' part between Cartimandua and the Brigantes and Boudica and the Iceni, and that he is in fact referring to the Boudican rebellion.[55] However, the Brigantes were a large and divided tribe which the Romans found difficult to control, and little is known about their detailed history in the third quarter of the first century, so it is possible that another female leader and separate incident are at issue.

The literary sources are supported by archaeological data which can be interpreted as evidence that there were women of extremely high status, possibly tribal rulers. In mainland Europe in the early Iron Age (sixth and fifth centuries BC), and the early La Tène phase (fourth century) a small number of extremely rich burials stand out. Funerary wagons, very rich jewellery, imported goods from the Greek world and other artefacts which can only be described as luxury items were buried with the dead person beneath an often huge mound. In the earliest phase, known as Hallstatt D, these burials are particularly rare, adding up to only about twenty of the richest burials from a wide area of southern Germany and eastern France. They are located near hilltop settlements in which imported goods have also been found and which are interpreted as the former seats of these rich dead. The relevance of these burials to the present argument is that several of them are of women.

The richest, and most celebrated of these burials is that at Vix, on the Saône, at the foot of the hilltop settlement of Mont Lassois. This burial was probably that of a woman, though some doubt has been expressed over the sex of the skeleton found in the grave. Originally it was identified as female, but some skeletons will always fall between the extremes of certain measurements typical of each sex, for example in the hips and skull. Unfortunately, the Vix burial is one such skeleton, and to add to the problem it is poorly preserved. There has therefore been considerable debate as to its sex, though the most recent studies argue that the body is indeed that of a woman.[56] The grave goods found with the body, while also not providing a clear-cut answer, favour a female interpretation. They include the remains of a chariot and a number of unique artefacts, including a huge Greek bronze vessel, or *krater*, 1.64 metres high, which would have been used for mixing wine, and a variety of personal ornaments, the most notable of which is a gold torc. There were no weapons, though these are often found in male graves of this period. This was originally taken as confirmation of the sex of the body, but no objects were found which are regularly associated with either sex among the Hallstatt D burials. If the person was indeed female, what was her status or position? Most debate has either avoided the issue, or argued that she was the wife of the tribal chief, or a priestess. The latter seems least likely in view of the lack of other evidence for Hallstatt religious practices involving priestesses, and no suggestion has been made that rich male burials were of a religious nature. But the wealth of the burial is exceptional, and no matching male burial has been found in the immediate area which could be interpreted as that of her husband, so why should this woman not have been a chief in her own right? As we have just seen, women leaders are attested in literary sources only a few centuries later. René Joffroy,[57] the excavator of the Vix burial, at least admits that it gives the impression of a person of remarkable social rank, and suggests that the burial implies that at the end of the first period of the Iron Age women played a very important social role. Furthermore, he points out that at least one of two other burials excavated

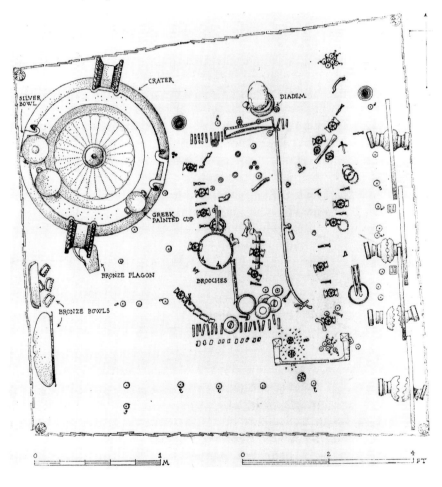

51 Plan of the Vix burial. From Piggott, 1965.

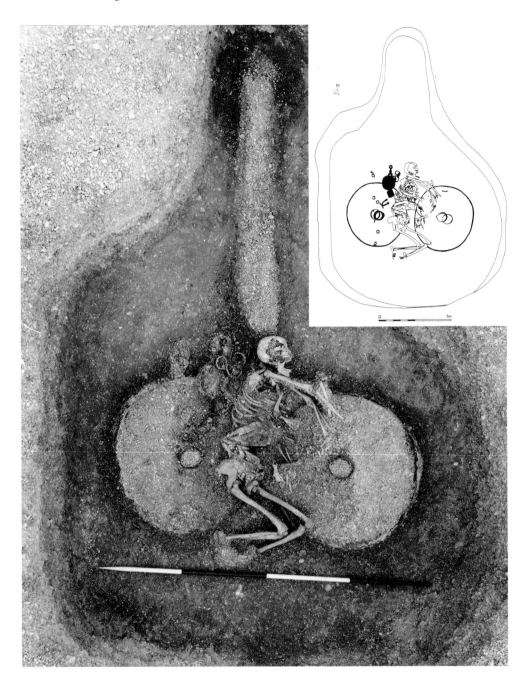

52 Photograph and plan of the burial of a woman in the Iron Age cemetery at Wetwang, Humberside. Her body was laid on a chariot and surrounded with rich grave goods. Photo by Bill Marsden, Humberside County Archaeology Unit; drawing from Dent, 1985.

much earlier at Vix was also female, so 'in this Celtic society women were not only respected but also able to retain their power'.

Another rich grave of the same period, at the Hohmichele, a burial mound near the Heuneberg, another important hilltop settlement of the same period on the Danube, contained the body of a woman in the main chamber, laid to rest on a chariot draped in textiles. Within the mound were two other chambers, one with a male and female body lying side by side, and the third with a male burial.[58] At Klein Aspergle, a third grave of the same group, a woman was buried in a robe ornamented with gold, and with a silver chain, Etruscan vessels and other imports.[59]

These and other examples of very rich female burials show that at the beginning of the Iron Age in central Europe rich women, presumably of high standing, were buried with as much wealth as men. The Vix burial is especially significant, as its wealth is so striking that one would expect the deceased to have held power in her own right, rather than being honoured only for her position as a male ruler's wife.

In the later phases of the European Iron Age, from around 400 BC, burial rites changed, and the difference between women's and men's graves is usually clear from the grave goods present. However, there are few cemeteries where the skeletal evidence has been analysed in sufficient depth to be certain that the distinctive 'male' grave goods are never associated with female skeletons, or vice versa, or whether any 'sumptuary goods' – symbols of office or status – can be identified which could be used as evidence that there were other women leaders like Boudica. However, there are other Iron Age graves in Europe which may be those of important women. For example, a group of three burials, dated between the fourth and second century BC and excavated in the Wetwang cemetery in Yorkshire, England, stand out from most of the other graves in the cemetery by the richness of their grave goods. These included chariots, rarely found in European Iron Age burials, and even where there are clusters of them, such as in east Yorkshire, they are still exceptional among a mass of simpler graves. The three graves formed a line, with the earliest burial, which was also the richest, in the centre; the grave goods buried with the body included an iron mirror, an iron and gold dress-pin and a unique bronze canister. All three burials were covered by earth mounds, and the central one was the largest, a feature which is often taken as an indication of wealth or status. What is significant here is that this richest central burial was that of a young adult woman, while those on either side contained the bodies of men.[60] Could this have been the grave of another woman leader?

6 Conclusions

We have looked at a number of episodes in European prehistory, from the advent of human populations, through the discovery of agriculture and the social impact of bronze as a medium for display, to the classical world's writings about the last prehistoric peoples of Europe before their conquest by the Romans, and the inevitable social changes this conquest brought about over much of Europe. Although I have followed the chronological sequence of events, I have not attempted to give a continuous account of the changing lives of women. I would rather draw an analogy with snapshots in an album, which pick out episodes and events not always directly related: each photograph tells a different story, yet they are stuck into the album in the sequence in which they were taken; other equally significant episodes have gone unrecorded. So I have picked out themes and developed them as far as present evidence will allow; and, as in the photograph album, I have ordered those chosen themes in chronological sequence. There are undoubtedly many other topics which could have been pursued. I therefore will not summarise or pretend to tell a coherent story: to do so would require the study of far more evidence, in far more detail, than has been possible here; indeed, coherence and comprehensiveness may not be possible at the present time, before specialists have considered and discussed the evidence for the lives of women in their own particular periods and areas of Europe. I hope, however, that I have shown that it is possible to study women in prehistory, and some of the ways this may be done.

The relationship between the role of woman in economic production and distribution and her social status has been a recurrent theme. It has been argued that in the forager societies of the Palaeolithic and Mesolithic, plant foods, gathered by women, would have provided the bulk of the diet. This would have ensured that women and their work were highly valued throughout society, particularly where this food was exchanged within the society. This continued in the first days of horticulture in the early Neolithic, when women discovered the secrets of crop growing, and tended and harvested the new cereal crops. But with the increasing contribution of male-tended herds of animals and the various secondary products they supplied, and the introduction of the plough, men may have become increasingly involved in farming and food production. The lessening of women's role in food production, in itself, may have lowered her status within the family. But clearly the story is not so simple. On the one hand, change would not have been continuous or uniform throughout Europe:

we must expect patterns long abandoned in one area to have continued in another, and not all social changes will be felt in every area. Furthermore, the equation between production and social status is not straightforward, but in reality a very complex issue, which is difficult to determine from archaeological evidence alone. Other factors must also be important.[1] Some writers[2] have considered that of even greater significance than her actual role in production is the extent to which a woman is able to give or exchange goods outside the immediate family, which creates obligations to her. This in turn seems to depend on the way the society is organised: whether a woman is perceived to own any goods she produces, and whether she herself takes them to the place of exchange and receives goods or services in return. Thus, women who do a large proportion of work within the family, producing food and other items, may not invariably be able to acquire high status from it, especially if the produce is used entirely to sustain the immediate family. On the other hand, if a woman plays no part in production, and has no means of creating alliances and obligations, she will certainly not be able to gain status within the society.

In pastoral agricultural communities of the Early Bronze Age, women may have had little role in primary food production, and been regarded as inferior by their men. From the Bronze Age onwards, women may always have been considered 'second-class citizens', but the exact regard with which societies viewed them may have varied from area to area and from time to time, depending partly on their economic balance. We should not expect a unilineal decline or improvement in the status of women.

In later societies particularly, a distinction must be drawn between the lives of ordinary women and the evidence for a small number of wealthy or 'high-class' women reaching individual positions of power, or taking on the role of religious leaders. This may be true of Minoan Crete, and is particularly problematic in the Iron Age, when we have evidence that women such as Boudica did become rulers, but do not really know what influence most women had within their families or villages.

But, although the social status of women has long been inferior to that of men, it must also be remembered that the foraging societies of the Palaeolithic and Mesolithic spanned an immense period, many hundred times longer than the mere 12,000 or so years from the Neolithic to the present, and that many of the world's people continued to be foragers long after farming had been discovered in the Near East. So, throughout human history, the great majority of women who have ever lived had far more status than recently, and probably had equality with men.

I have here merely skimmed the surface of the possibilities of studying the lives of women in prehistory. Many more themes, from various periods and areas of Europe (not to mention the rest of the world), might be addressed using evidence already available. But there is even more scope for fresh primary research: many times throughout my study my conclusions have been limited by the inadequacy of the data. For example, new excavations could and, I am sure, will yield far more evidence of the range of plant foods consumed, and where within the settlements and how they were processed. Tools need to be studied to find out precisely what they were used for, and especially if they can be linked to grave goods we may be able to assess directly which tasks women were engaged in. The scope and potential of the information which could be derived from skeletal material seems endless. Many innovative techniques and studies have been discussed here which so far have only been applied to one or two sets of data. These need to be applied far more widely.

In addition to considering the lives of women in prehistory, more traditional archaeological themes can be reviewed from a feminist perspective. Although there have been a significant number of women archaeologists over the past decades, we have all learnt and worked within male-dominated institutions, and have grown accustomed to considering topics such as weapons, warfare and invasions from traditional male viewpoints of victory, conquest and triumph. Yet many women (and men, too, of course) turn to quite different thoughts and concerns when these subjects are discussed in relation to our own world. What of the social cost to society as a whole of war and battles in prehistory? Was warfare really glorified, and as common in the Iron Age as some writers would have us believe? Or was the greater premium rather placed on peace? Did racism exist between people of different origins in the Bronze Age, or did people of different religious beliefs live harmoniously side by side? These questions are not easily answered from archaeological evidence alone, but within the context of the current scope of archaeological enquiry they are perfectly valid: the evidence which would justify the male colonial interpretations which are habitually offered needs to be just as carefully garnered, rather than assumed unthinkingly.

Throughout the book, I have tried to stress the problems of interpreting the archaeological evidence for the prehistoric period, particularly when addressing an issue such as the lives of women. We have seen that many interpretations are possible for each topic which has been examined. In many cases this depends on which class of evidence is stressed, but it especially depends on the preferred interpretative framework of the individual author or archaeologist. Thus in the past many archaeologists have written accounts of prehistoric men in Europe, ignoring, albeit unconsciously, the prehistoric women with whom they must have shared their lives. But women did exist in prehistory, and can be made visible: this book has shown that it is possible to write a prehistory of women.

Glossary

Absolute dating Dates which can be expressed in calendar years, rather than merely as earlier or later than another date (relative dating).

Agriculture The domestication and cultivation of plants and animals.

Anthropology The study of the human species. Social anthropology is the comparative study of human societies and institutions, and patterns of human social behaviour; in Britain it is usually restricted in definition to present-day and recent societies, but in North America also includes past societies, and hence archaeology. Physical anthropology studies the physical development of the human species.

Archaeology The study of past societies from their material remains.

Artefact An object made, modified or used by humans.

Barrow A mound of earth or rubble covering one or more burials.

Bipedalism The predominant use of two hind legs for walking, rather than moving on all four limbs.

Bronze Age The period of European prehistory during which bronze, an alloy of copper and tin, was the main inorganic material used for making tools such as axes and weapons. It broadly spans the period 2000 BC–700 BC.

Carbon 14 (C^{14}) dating See radiocarbon dating.

Culture Traditionally used in archaeology to describe a recurring assemblage of similar artefacts and sites, confined in time and space and thought to represent a group of people who considered themselves to be a social unit, or society (q.v.). Whether such an assemblage can be interpreted so easily has been the subject of much recent debate. In anthropology the term is used to describe those aspects of life, such as behaviour patterns and modes of thought, which are the product of human creation, rather than of the natural world, and which are transmitted through learning.

Descent patterns The rules or beliefs by which a society recognises kin, birth and inheritance.

In most societies this is perceived to be either through the female (matrilineal) or the male line (patrilineal), rather than through both parents (bilateral). Matrilineal and patrilineal descent patterns result in distinct descent groups, people who share a common ancestor.

Deverel-Rimbury A group of burials and settlements of the Earlier Bronze Age in southern England (c. 1500 BC–1000 BC), forming a fairly complete assemblage and often described as a culture (q.v.).

Ethnoarchaeology The examination of the material aspects of a particular, observed, activity or practice, usually carried out by a traditional society, where the relationship between an activity and the material remains which it leaves can be studied.

Ethnography The first-hand study and description of all aspects of a particular society.

Faience A blue glass-like substance used mainly around the eastern Mediterranean, but also elsewhere in Europe, during the Early Bronze Age period, for making beads and other simple artefacts.

Forager See hunter–gatherer.

Gender The behaviour, roles and other aspects of culture expected of, or usual to, a person of a particular sex within the society in question. In keeping with modern feminist and anthropological practice, a distinction is made between gender and sex, which refers to the inborn and physical distinctions between women and men.

Grave goods Objects placed in a grave with a burial, and presumably associated in a significant way with the individual, or for the well-being of the individual in an after-life.

Hallstatt A cemetery and salt mines in Austria, used as the type-site for the earlier phase of the European Iron Age, c. 700–475 BC.

Hillfort A defended hilltop settlement, principally of Iron Age date.

Hominid A member of the human and closely related species *Hominidae*, including modern humans, *Homo sapiens*, and earlier forms.

Horticulture Used in anthropology to describe plant cultivation using simple technology, without the assistance of the plough, traction animals or irrigation, and allowing the plots of land to remain fallow for long periods to restore soil fertility.

Hunter-gatherers or **foragers** People subsisting without cultivating plants or keeping animals, relying instead on collecting plant foods, insects, eggs and small creatures and hunting animals from the natural environment. This lifestyle was universal in the Palaeolithic and Mesolithic.

Inhumation Burial of a body without cremation.

Iron Age The final phase of European prehistory, when iron was the principal raw material used for the manufacture of tools and weapons: 700 BC till the Roman conquest.

Linear A The written script of the Minoans, which has not yet been deciphered by archaeologists.

Matriarchy A society in which women regularly dominate all aspects of life, hold power and have authority over men (but see Chapter 2).

Matrilineal descent Descent pattern reckoned through the female line only.

Matrilocal residence Post-marital residence arrangement, where the married couple live in the woman's family home or village.

Mesolithic The Middle Stone Age, between the Palaeolithic and the Neolithic in north-west Europe, marked particularly by social and economic adaptations to the post-glacial forest environment, *c.* 13000–6000 BC.

Model A theoretical reconstruction of a set of data or phenomena.

Neolithic The New Stone Age, the period when agriculture was first practised in Europe, from *c.*7000 BC in the Near East to a beginning in the fourth millennium in north-west Europe and ending with the advent of bronze technology and the Bronze Age around 2000 BC; also characterised by the earliest use of pottery and ground stone tools, and a sedentary lifestyle.

Palaeobotany The study of plant remains from archaeological or other early contexts.

Palaeolithic The Old Stone Age, the earliest phase of human history, including the development of the species from the earliest use of tools, and characterised by a hunter-gatherer subsistence economy.

Palaeopathology The study of early health and disease from bones from archaeological and other contexts.

Patriarchy A society in which men dominate and hold most or all key positions of power.

Prehistory The period in the past before written records. In north-west Europe this is usually taken as the period up to the Roman conquest, but it varies from area to area, particularly when other areas of the world are considered.

Radiocarbon dating An absolute or chronometric dating technique based on the measurement of radioactivity surviving in organic materials; by far the most widely used absolute dating method used in European prehistory. Dates directly quoted from the analysis are expressed as bp (before present), bc, or ad, with a standard deviation, expressed as ± years either side of that date, e.g. 2300 ± 50 bc. To express these dates in calendar years they must be calibrated to allow for known, but unavoidable, scientific errors; for the prehistoric period this makes these absolute dates between 100 and 1000 years before the radiocarbon date. *All dates quoted in this book are corrected dates.*

Role The duties and behaviour which a society expects of an individual of a particular status.

Sedentism Settlement and economic pattern based on living year-round in one location.

Settlement site A convenient term used to describe any archaeological site where people have lived, from a hunter–gatherer camp to a farmstead to a town.

Society A group of people distinguishable from another group by their way of life, behaviour, ideology and often geographical location.

Status The social position occupied by an individual in relation to other people within the society, carrying with it a series of rights, duties and behavioural expectations (roles).

Theoretical archaeology A recent trend within archaeology where the emphasis is placed on interpretation of the material remains, rather than solely on their description and dating, and on the construction and testing of theoretical models (q.v.) of past societies.

Tumulus Burial mound, usually built of earth, also known as a barrow.

Notes

Introduction

1 Archaeology and anthropology are by no means unique in this. The position of women and women's perspectives have been discussed in almost every academic field in recent years. For a comprehensive account see Spender, 1981.

Chapter 1
The Search for Prehistoric Woman

1 Numerous examples from almost all spheres of endeavour could be cited, and have been brought to light by recent research. For example, in literature and in art many women, such as the playwright Aphra Behn, had become virtually forgotten. Others such as George Eliot only achieved fame by writing under a male pseudonym. See for example Spender, 1981; Spender, 1982.

2 Piggott, 1959, 14. Some archaeologists in recent years, notably Ian Hodder, have questioned how far this is true, and argue that every human action is governed by subconscious or learnt behaviour. Messages transmitted within a social or ethnic group in this way still seem very different from the conscious, deliberate act of writing.

3 The processes which go to make up the archaeological record are discussed in detail in Schiffer, 1976.

4 This wider view of the potential of archaeology was first put forward in Britain by David Clarke and was dubbed the 'new archaeology', and in the United States by Lewis Binford; now the approach is often termed theoretical archaeology.

5 Randsborg, 1984, is one of the very few articles to discuss the topic of women in prehistory and makes the same point, concentrating on a brief review of the Danish evidence.

6 For more discussion of the use and misuse of anthropology by archaeologists, see Hodder, 1982; Binford, 1983.

7 For a recent and light-hearted account of anthropological fieldwork the reader is recommended Barley, 1983; however, although this is a very recent account, the critical reader will not fail to notice the almost total male bias of both the observations and the interpretations made by the author.

8 The literature within the field of the anthropology of women is now extensive: references to specific works are made throughout the present volume. Key texts include, for example, Rosaldo and Lamphere, 1974; Reiter, 1975; Martin and Voorheis, 1975; Freidl, 1975; Dahlberg, 1981.

9 See for example Binford, 1983.

10 Spector, 1982; Conkey and Spector, 1984.

11 Goodall, 1971; Goodall, 1986; Fossey, 1983.

12 Examples of these sources include the *Táin* and the *Mabinogion*.

13 Ross, 1986, 124.

14 Brothwell, 1981; Manchester, 1983.

15 Merbs, 1983.

16 Dutour, 1986.

17 For example articles in Gilbert and Mielke, 1985.

18 Wing and Brown, 1979, ch. 5; Sillen and Kavanagh, 1982.

19 Wing and Brown, 1979, 76.

20 McHenry, 1968.

21 Molnar, 1971.

22 The classic article warning of such pitfalls is Ucko, 1969.

23 Conkey and Spector, 1984, 11; Winters, 1968, 206 quoting earlier accounts. Winters himself acknowledges as one possibility that 'some women were hunters of one type of game or another'.

24 E.g. Shennan, 1975; see also Chapter 4.

25 Discussed, for example, by Binford 1972, 60 ff; Hodder, 1982, 128.

26 Whiting and Ayres, 1968.

27 Ember, 1973.

28 Krzywinski, Fjelldal and Soltvedt, 1983, 156.

Chapter 2
The Earliest Communities

1 For more detail the reader is recommended Wymer, 1982; Leakey, 1981; Dennell, 1983; Gamble, 1986.

2 Zihlman, 1981.

3 Slocum, 1975.

4 For example Tanner, 1981; Martin and Voorheis, 1975.

5 Zihlman, 1981; Isaac and Crader, 1981.

6 Zihlman, 1978; the same arguments are used by Friedl, 1975 and 1978, who explains in more detail than here why present-day foragers divide food collecting tasks along gender lines.

7 Dennell, 1983, 55.

8 McGrew, 1981; Goodall, 1986.

9 Tanner and Zihlman, 1976.

10 McGrew, 1981, 47.

11 Lee, 1968.

12 Martin and Voorheis, 1975, 181.

13 Rohrlich-Leavitt, Sykes and Weatherford, 1975.

14 Goodale, 1971.

15 Estioko-Griffin and Bion Griffin, 1981.

16 Goodale, 1971, 55.

17 Clarke, 1952, 86; Clarke, 1948.

18 Clarke, 1952, 34, though the location of the site does not agree with Obermaier, 1925, fig 116; Beltran, 1982.

19 Gamble, 1984; Isaac, 1971.

20 Péquart *et al.*, 1937.

21 Keeley and Toth, 1981.

22 Clarke, 1976.

23 Lee, 1984.

24 Lumley, 1969.

25 Harrold, 1980; Gamble, 1984, 108.

26 Sahlins, 1972.

27 Childe, 1951.

28 Bachofen, 1861.

29 Morgan, 1877; Engels, 1884.

30 Sanday, 1981, argues that females are dominant in the mythology of those societies where women have higher than average status.

31 E.g. Leacock, 1978; Fluehr-Lobban, 1979; Rohrlich-Leavitt, Sykes and Weatherford, 1975.

32 See for example Friedl, 1975.

33 There are numerous references to these figurines, both in the feminist and the scholarly archaeological literature. It is important to distinguish between most of these. For archaeological accounts see Wymer, 1982, 246–7, 261–2; Champion *et al.*, 1984; Ucko and Rosenfeld, 1967; Powell, 1966; Sandars, 1985.

34 Gamble, 1986.

35 Leakey, 1981.

36 Ucko, 1962; Ucko, 1968.

37 Mellaart, 1967.

38 Mellaart, 1975, 111–19.

39 Ucko, 1962.

40 Doumas, 1968; Renfrew, 1972.

41 Ucko, 1962; Ucko, 1968.

42 Leakey, 1981, 180.

43 Cf. Ucko, 1968.

44 Sandars, 1985, 69.

45 Leacock, 1977, 24.

46 Ucko, 1962; Ucko, 1968, ch. 16.

47 Gamble, 1986.

Chapter 3
The First Farmers

1 Recent discussions on the origins of agriculture include Mellaart, 1975; Be 1975.

2 Jarman, 1972; Bender, 1975, 94 ff.

3 Mellaart, 1975, 42–8.

4 Hillman, 1975; Moore, 1979, 54.

5 Martin and Voorheis, 1975; Friedl, 1975; Boserup, 1970.

6 Martin and Voorheis, 1975, ch. 8.

7 Moore, 1979, 54.

8 Stanley, 1981.

9 Cf. for example Mellaart, 1975; Moore, 1979.

10 Flannery and Winter, 1976, discuss and use this approach, including an attempt to look for 'male' and 'female' work areas, in a classic study of a prehistoric Mesoamerican site. It is also the basis of Janet Spector's task-differentiation method, discussed in Chapter 1.

11 Flannery, 1969, 80.

12 Some archaeologists argue that sedentism or population growth may have triggered the transition to agriculture, rather than the other way around; see Bender, 1978; Binford, 1968.

13 Mellaart, 1975, 44–7.

14 Stanley, 1981, 291–3.

15 Binford, 1972, argues the case that population growth is closely linked to the advent of agriculture and to sedentism.

16 Also known by its German name Linearbandkeramik, and formerly as the Danubian Culture.

17 Sherratt, 1981.

18 Milisauskas, 1978, 71.

19 Whittle, 1985, 90.

20 Milisauskas, 1978, 71.

21 Whittle, 1985, 88.

22 Ember, 1973; Whiting and Ayres, 1968.

23 Milisauskas, 1978, 99–105.

24 Soudsky, 1964.

25 Divale, 1974.

26 Hodder, 1984.

27 Brown, 1970.

28 Sherratt, 1981.

29 See for example Boserup, 1970.

30 Stanley, 1981.

31 Sherratt, 1983.

32 Sherratt, 1981.

33 Sherratt, 1981, 280.

34 E.g. Boserup, 1970, 24 ff; Martin and Voorheis, 1975.

35 Sherratt, 1983, 100.

36 Cf. for example Champion et al., 1984, 160.

37 This argument has been put forward in relation to the development of megalithic tombs in western Europe, and to the spread of settlement onto poorer soils in the later Neolithic, by Renfrew, 1973, and others.

38 The origins of social stratification, and its relationship with the status and subordination of women, are key questions in both Marxist and feminist anthropological literature; the balance of importance of different contributing factors is obviously complex, and a matter of much debate, e.g. Engels, 1884; Sacks, 1974; Leacock, 1978, 255; Reiter, 1978. Quinn, 1977, provides a summary of various views up to that date.

Chapter 4
The Bronze Age

1 For a detailed discussion of the archaeology of Bronze Age Europe, see Coles and Harding, 1979.

2 Evans, 1921–4.

3 General discussions of the Minoans include Cadogan, 1976; Hood, 1971.

4 Thomas, 1973; Immewahr, 1983.

5 Evans, 1921–4.

6 Pomeroy, 1984.

7 E.g. Willetts, 1977, 78.

8 Thomas, 1973.

9 Immewahr, 1983.

10 Graham, 1962.

11 Pomeroy, 1984, 348.

12 Gesell, 1983.

13 There are some contrasts in more or less contemporary burial rites which have not been satisfactorily explained, such as the coexistence of various types of burial urns in the British Early Bronze Age.

14 Glob, 1974.

15 Coles and Harding, 1979, 329, n. 84.

16 Quoted by Glob, 1974, 64.

17 Broholm and Hald, 1940, 150.

18 Shennan, 1975.

19 Shennan, 1982.

20 Piggott, 1938; for discussion of recent work on the Wessex culture, see for example Burgess, 1980, 98–111.

21 Bradley, 1981, 97.

22 See for example Burgess, 1980, 199–209; Ellison, 1981.

23 Bradley, 1981; Bradley, 1978, especially ch. 3 and p. 116 ff.

24 As above and Fleming, 1971.

25 E.g. Martin and Voorheis, 1975, ch. 10

26 Bradley, 1981, 103, following Goody, 1976.

27 Larsson, 1986.

28 Randsborg, 1974.

29 Larsson, 1986.

30 Levy, 1982.

31 Kristiansen, 1984.

32 Kristiansen, 1984.

33 Kristiansen, 1984; Larsson, 1986.

34 Randsborg, 1974.

35 Kristiansen, 1984, 94.

36 Larsson, 1986, 65.

37 Levy, 1982, and pers. comm; Kristiansen, 1984, 86.

38 Gibbs, 1987, 86; Coles and Harding, 1979, 519.

39 Randsborg, 1984, 150.

40 Kristiansen, 1984.

41 Kristiansen, 1981.

42 Gelling and Davidson, 1969, 76.

43 Anati, 1961.

Chapter 5
The Celtic Iron Age

1 The reader is referred to Powell, 1980, or Ross, 1986, for more discussion of this topic.

2 Clarke, 1972, based on Bullied and Gray, 1911 and 1917.

3 Coles and Coles, 1986, 169.

4 Drewett, 1982.

5 Ellison, 1981.

6 Piggott, 1965, 198–9; Gallus, 1934; Dobiat, 1982.

7 Collis, 1984, 69–73; Kastelic, 1965.

8 But see Rankin, 1987, ch. 13.

9 For a recent discussion of the problems and possibilities of using these sources see Champion, 1985.

10 Diodorus Siculus, v, 28; this and other quotations from classical sources are from the edition quoted in the bibliography, with modifications by the author.

11 Ammianus Marcellinus, xv, 12.1. Ammianus was a late Roman historian writing in the fourth century AD.

12 Hooper, 1984, 465.

13 Rozoy, 1987. Two slightly different methods of estimating the height of individuals from the surviving bones were used, the second method giving average heights of both men and women 4 cm taller than the first method quoted in the text.

14 Data from *The New Encyclopedia Britannica*, 15th ed. 1986, vol. 20, p. 446, for 18-year-old (after growth has ceased) British men and women, in 1965.

15 Ross, 1986, 32–9.

16 Strabo, *Geographia*, IV, 4, 3.

17 E.g. Anderson, 1938, 215.

18 Estioko-Griffin and Bion Griffin, 1981.

19 Procopius, *History of the Wars: the Gothic War*, VI, xv, 16–17.

20 Caesar, *De Bello Gallico*, I, 50, 4.

21 Chadwick, 1966, 80.

22 Chadwick, 1966, 78–83; Ross, 1986.

23 Tacitus, *Annales*, xIV, 30.

24 Rankin, 1987, 253.

25 Livy, *Histories*, v, 34.

26 Pauli, 1985, 37.

27 Anderson, 1938, 109.

28 Rivers, 1906, 515.

29 Guilbert, 1981.

30 Harke, 1979.

31 Whiting and Ayres, 1968.

32 Harding, 1973; Champion, 1975.

33 Thomson, 1948, 193.

34 Herodotus, iv, 104; iv, 172; iv, 180. Each of these cases is different in detail, and perfectly feasible given the broad range of practices known in the ethnographic record.

35 Champion, 1985, 17.

36 Anderson, 1938, 70.

37 Caesar, *De Bello Gallico*, i, 51, 3.

38 Tacitus, *Histories*, iv, 18.

39 Tacitus, *Annales*, iv, 51, 2.

40 Tacitus, *Annales*, xiv, 34, 2.

41 Plutarch, *De virtute mulierum*, 6.

42 Tacitus, *Annales*, xiv, 30.

43 Plutarch, *Marius*, 19.

44 Caesar, *De Bello Gallico*, iv, 1.

45 Webster, 1978.

46 Tacitus, *Annales*, xiv, 30–5.

47 Dio Cassius, *History of Rome*, lxii, 1 ff.

48 Dio Cassius, *History of Rome*, lxii, 2, 4.

49 Dio Cassius, *History of Rome*, lxii, 1, 1.

50 Webster, 1978, 99.

51 Tacitus, *Annales*, xiv, 34.

52 Tacitus, *Agricola*, 16.

53 Tacitus, *Annales*, xii, 35 and 40; Richmond, 1954, 53.

54 Tacitus, *Agricola*, 31.

55 Hanson, 1987, 21; Burn, 1969, 40.

56 Sauter, 1980; Langlois, 1987.

57 Joffroy, 1962, 126.

58 Filip, 1977, 43.

59 Filip, 1977, 45.

60 Dent, 1985.

Chapter 6
Conclusions

1 For a survey of various ideas which have been suggested, see Quinn, 1977.

2 E.g. Friedl, 1975 and 1978.

Bibliography

AMMIANUS MARCELLINUS, *Rerum gestarum libri*, trans J. C. Rolfe, Loeb Classical Library, Heinemann, London, 1935–9.

ANATI, E., 1961. *Val Camonica*, Knopf, New York.

ANDERSON, J. (ed. and trans.), 1938. *Tacitus' Germania*, Oxford UP, Oxford.

BACHOFEN, J., 1861. *Das Mutterrecht*, Benno Schwabe, Basel.

BARLEY, N., 1983. *The Innocent Anthropologist*, British Museum Publications, London.

BELTRAN, A., 1982. *Rock Art of the Spanish Levant*, Cambridge UP, Cambridge.

BENDER, B., 1975. *Farming in Prehistory*, John Baker, London.

BENDER, B., 1978. 'Gatherer-hunter to farmer: a social perspective', *World Archaeology* 10, 204–22.

BINFORD, L. R., 1968. 'Post-pleistocene adaptations', in Binford, S. R. and Binford, L. R. (eds), *New Perspectives in Archaeology*, Aldine, Chicago.

BINFORD, L., 1972. *An Archaeological Perspective*, Seminar Press, New York.

BINFORD, L., 1983. *In Pursuit of the Past*, Thames and Hudson, London.

BOSERUP, E., 1970. *Women's Role in Economic Development*, Allen and Unwin, London.

BRADLEY, R., 1978. *The Prehistoric Settlement of Britain*, Routledge and Kegan Paul, London.

BRADLEY, R., 1981. 'Various styles of urn', in Chapman, R., Kinnes, I. and Randsborg, K. (eds), *The Archaeology of Death*, Cambridge UP, Cambridge.

BRAIDWOOD, R. J., 1967. *Prehistoric Men*, Scott, Foresman and Co., Glenview, Ill.

BROHOLM, H. C. and HALD, M., 1940. *Costumes of the Bronze Age in Denmark*, Nyt Nordisk Forlag, Copenhagen.

BROTHWELL, D., 1981. *Digging up Bones*, Oxford UP, Oxford.

BROWN, J., 1970. 'Economic organization and the position of women among the Iroquois', *Ethnohistory* 17, 151–67.

BULLIED, A. H. and GRAY, H. St G., 1911 and 1917. *The Glastonbury Lake Village*, Glastonbury Antiquarian Society, Wessex Press, Taunton.

BURGESS, C., 1980. *The Age of Stonehenge*, Dent, London.

BURN, A. R., 1969. 'Tacitus on Britain' in Dorey, T. A. (ed.), *Tacitus*, Routledge and Kegan Paul, London.

CADOGAN, G., 1976. *Palaces of Minoan Crete*, Barrie and Jenkins, London.

CAESAR. *De Bello Gallico*, trans H. J. Edwards, Loeb Classical Library, Heinemann, London, 1919.

CHADWICK, N., 1966. *The Druids*, University of Wales Press, Cardiff.

CHAMPION, T. C., 1975. 'Britain in the European Iron Age', *Archaeologica Atlantica* 1, 127–45.

CHAMPION, T. C., 1985. 'Written sources and the study of the European Iron Age', in Champion, T. C. and Megaw, J. V. S. (eds), *Settlement and Society: Aspects of West European Prehistory in the First Millennium BC*, Leicester UP, Leicester.

CHAMPION, T. C., GAMBLE, C., SHENNAN, S. and WHITTLE, A. 1984. *Prehistoric Europe*, Academic Press, London.

CHILDE, V. G., 1951. *Social Organization*, Watts, London.

CLARKE, D. L., 1972. 'A provisional model of Iron Age society and its settlement system' in Clarke D. L. (ed.), *Models in Archaeology*, Methuen, London.

CLARKE, D. L., 1976. 'Mesolithic Europe, the economic basis', in Sieveking, G. *et al.* (eds), *Problems in Economic and Social Archaeology*, Duckworth, London.

CLARKE, G. 1948. 'The development of fishing in prehistoric Europe', *Antiquaries Journal* 28, 45–84.

CLARKE, G., 1952. *Prehistoric Europe, The Economic Basis*, Methuen, London.

CLARKE, G., 1977. *World Prehistory in New Perspective*, Cambridge UP, Cambridge.

COLE, S., 1963. *The Neolithic Revolution*, British Museum (Natural History), London.

COLES, J. M. and COLES, B., 1986. *Sweet Track to Glastonbury*, Thames and Hudson, London.

COLES, J. M. and HARDING, A. F., 1979. *The Bronze Age in Europe*, Methuen, London.

COLLIS, J., 1984. *The European Iron Age*, Batsford, London.

CONKEY, M. and SPECTOR, J., 1984. 'Archaeology and the study of gender', *Advances in Archaeological Method and Theory* 7, 1–38.

DAHLBERG, F. (ed.), 1981. *Woman the Gatherer*, Yale UP, New Haven.

DENNELL, R., 1983. *European Economic Prehistory*, Academic Press, London.

DENT, J., 1985. 'Three cart burials from Wetwang, Yorkshire', *Antiquity* 59, 85–92.

DIO CASSIUS. *History of Rome*, trans. E. Cary, Loeb Classical Library, Heinemann, London, 1914.

DIODORUS SICULUS, trans. C. H. Oldfather *et al.*, Loeb Classical Library, Heinemann, London, 1933–67.

DIVALE, W., 1974. 'Migration, external warfare and matrilocal residence', *Behaviour Science Research* 9, 173–203.

DOBIAT, C., 1982. 'Menschendarstellungen auf Ostalpiner Hallstattkeramik', *Acta Archaeologica* 34, 279–322.

DOUMAS, C., 1968. *Early Cycladic Art*, Praeger, New York.

DREWETT, P., 1982. 'Later Bronze Age downland economy and excavations at Black Patch, East Sussex', *Proceedings of the Prehistoric Society* 48, 321–400.

DUTOUR, O., 1986. 'Enthesopathies (lesions of muscular insertions) as indicators of the activities of Neolithic Saharan populations', *American Journal of Physical Anthropology* 71, 221–4.

ELLISON, A., 1981. 'Towards a socioeconomic model for the Middle Bronze Age in southern England', in Hodder, I. *et al.* (eds), *Pattern of the Past*, Cambridge UP, Cambridge.

EMBER, M. 1973. 'An archaeological indicator of matrilocal versus patrilocal residence', *American Antiquity* 38, 177–82.

ENGELS, F., 1884. *The Origins of the Family, Private Property and the State*, ed. E. Leacock, International, New York, 1972.

ESTIOKO-GRIFFIN, A. and BION GRIFFIN, P., 1981. 'Woman the hunter: the Agta', in Dahlberg, 1981.

EVANS, A., 1921–4. *The Palace of Minos*, Macmillan, London.

FILIP, J., 1977. *Celtic Civilization and its Heritage*, Acedemia, Prague.

FLANNERY, K., 1969. 'Origins and ecological effects of early domestication in Iran and the near East', in Ucko, P. J. and Dimbleby, G. W. (eds), *The Domestication and Exploitation of Plants and Animals*, Duckworth, London.

FLANNERY, K. and WINTER, M., 1976. 'Analysing household activities', in Flannery, K. (ed.), *The Early Mesoamerican Village*, Academic Press, New York.

FLEMING, A., 1971. 'Territorial patterns in Bronze Age Wessex', *Proceedings of the Prehistoric Society* 37, 138–66.

FLUEHR-LOBBAN, C., 1979. 'A Marxist reappraisal of the matriarchate', *Current Anthropology* 20, 341–53.

FOSSEY, D., 1983. *Gorillas in the Mist*, Houghton Mifflin, Boston.

FRIEDL, E., 1975. *Women and Men: An Anthropologist's View*, Holt, Rinehart and Winston, New York.

FRIEDL, E., 1978. 'Society and sex roles', *Human Nature* 1, 68–75.

GALLUS, S., 1934. 'Die figuralverzierten Urnen von Soproner Burgstall', *Archaeologica Hungarica* 13.

GAMBLE, C., 1984, 'Subsistence and society in Palaeolithic Europe', in Champion *et al.*, 1984.

GAMBLE, C., 1986. *The Palaeolithic Settlement of Europe*, Cambridge UP, Cambridge.

GELLING, P. and DAVIDSON, H., 1969. *The Chariot of the Sun*, Dent, London.

GERLOFF, S., 1975. *The Early Bronze Age Daggers in Great Britain with a Reconsideration of the Wessex Culture*, Prähistorische Bronzefunde 6, 2, C. H. Beck, Munich.

GESELL, G. 1983. 'The place of the goddess in Minoan society', in Krzyskowska, O. and Nixon, L. (eds), *Minoan Society*, Bristol Classical Press, Bristol.

GIBBS, L., 1987. 'Identifying gender representations in the archaeological record: a contextual study', in Hodder, I. (ed.), *The Archaeology of Contextual Meaning*, Cambridge UP, Cambridge.

GILBERT, R. and MIELKE, J. (eds) 1985. *The Analysis of Prehistoric Diets*, Academic Press, London.

GLOB, P., 1974. *The Mound People*, Faber, London.

GOODALE, J., 1971. *Tiwi Wives*, University of Washington Press, Seattle,

GOODALL, J. VAN LAWICK, 1971. *In the Shadow of Man*, Houghton Mifflin, Boston.

GOODALL, J., 1986. *The Chimpanzees of Gombe: Patterns of Behaviour*, Harvard UP, Cambridge, Mass.

GOODY, J., 1976. *Production and Reproduction*, Cambridge UP, Cambridge.

GRAHAM, J. W., 1962. *The Palaces of Crete*, Princeton UP, Princeton, New Jersey.

GUILBERT, G., 1981. 'Double-ring roundhouses probable and possible in prehistoric Britain', *Proceedings of the Prehistoric Society* 47, 299–317.

HANSON, W. S., 1987. *Agricola and the Conquest of the North*, Batsford, London.

HARDING, D. W., 1973. 'Round and rectangular: Iron Age houses, British and foreign' in Hawkes, C. F. C. and Hawkes, S. C. (eds), *Greeks, Celts and Romans: studies in venture and resistance*, Dent, London.

HARKE, H., 1979. *Settlement Types and Patterns in the West Hallstatt Province*, British Archaeological Reports S57, Oxford.

HARROLD, F. B., 1980. 'A comparative analysis of Eurasian Palaeolithic burials', *World Archaeology* 12, 195–211.

HERODOTUS. *Histories*, trans. A. D. Godley, Loeb Classical Library, Heinemann, London, 1921.

HILLMAN, G., 1975. 'The plant remains', in Moore A. *et al.*, 'The excavation of Tell Abu Hureya in Syria: a preliminary report', *Proceedings of the Prehistoric Society* 41, 50–77.

HODDER, I., 1982. *The Present Past*, Batsford, London.

HODDER, I., 1984. 'Burials, houses, women and men in the European Neolithic', in Miller, D. and Tilley, C. (eds), *Ideology, Power and Prehistory*, Cambridge UP, Cambridge.

HOOD, S., 1971. *The Minoans*, Thames and Hudson, London.

HOOPER, B., 1984. 'Anatomical considerations', in Cunliffe, B. (ed.), *Danebury: The Excavations 1969–78*, Council for British Archaeology, London.

IMMEWAHR, S., 1983. 'The people in the frescoes', in Krzyszkowska, O. and Nixon, L. (eds), *Minoan Society*, Bristol Classical Press, Bristol.

ISAAC, G., 1971. 'The diet of early man: aspects of archaeological evidence from lower and middle Pleistocene sites in Africa', *World Archaeology* 1, 1–28.

ISAAC, G. and CRADER, D., 1981. 'To what extent were early hominids carnivorous?', in Teleki, G. (ed.), *Omnivorous Primates: Gathering and Hunting in Human Evolution*, Columbia UP, New York.

JARMAN, H., 1972. 'The origins of wheat and barley cultivation', in Higgs, E. (ed.), *Papers in Economic Prehistory*, Cambridge UP, Cambridge.

JOFFROY, R., 1962. *Le Trésor de Vix*, Fayard, Paris.

KASTELIC, J., 1965. *Situla Art*, Thames and Hudson, London.

KEELEY, L. H. and TOTH, N., 1981. 'Microwear polishes on early stone tools from Koobi Fora, Kenya', *Nature* 293, 464–5.

KRISTIANSEN, K., 1981. 'Economic models for Bronze Age Scandinavia – towards an integrated approach', in Sheridan, A. and Bailey, G. (eds), *Economic Archaeology*, British Archaeological Reports 96, Oxford.

KRISTIANSEN, K., 1984. 'Ideology and material culture: an archaeological perspective' in Spriggs, M. (ed.), *Marxist Perspectives in Archaeology*, Cambridge UP, Cambridge.

KRZYWINSKI, K., FJELLDAL, S. and SOLTVEDT, E., 1983. Recent palaeobotanical work at the medieval excavations at Bryggen, Bergen Norway', in Proudfoot, B. (ed.), *Site, Environment and Economy*, British Archaeological Reports S173, Oxford.

LANGLOIS, R., 1987. 'Le visage de la dame de Vix', *Trésors de Princes Celtes*, Editions de la Réunion des musées nationaux, Paris.

LARSSON, T., 1986. *The Bronze Age Metalwork in Southern Sweden*, University of Umeå, Umeå.

LEACOCK, E., 1977. 'Women in egalitarian societies', in Bridenthal, R. and Koonz, E. (eds), *Becoming Visible: Women in European History*, Houghton Mifflin, Boston.

LEACOCK, E., 1978. 'Women's status in egalitarian society: implications for social evolution', *Current Anthropology* 19, 247–75.

LEAKEY, R. 1981. *The Making of Mankind*, Michael Joseph, London.

LEE, R. 1968. 'What hunters do for a living or how to make out on scarce resources', in Lee, R. and DeVore, I. (eds), *Man the Hunter*, Aldine, New York.

LEE, R., 1984. *The Dobe !Kung*, Holt, Rinehart and Winston, New York.

LEVY, J., 1982. *Social and Religious Organization in Bronze Age Denmark: An Analysis of Ritual Hoard Finds*, British Archaeological Reports S124, Oxford.

LIVY. Histories, trans. B. O. Foster *et el.*, Loeb Classical Library, Heinemann, London, 1922–69.

LUMLEY, H. DE, 1969. 'A Palaeolithic camp at Nice', *Scientific American* 220, 42–50.

Mabinogion, trans. G. and T. Jones, Dent, London, 1976.

MANCHESTER, K. 1983. *The Archaeology of Disease*, University of Bradford, Bradford.

MARTIN, M. K. and VOORHEIS, B. 1975. *Female of the Species*, Columbia UP, New York.

McGREW, W., 1981, 'The female chimpanzee as a human evolutionary prototype', in Dahlberg, 1981.

McHENRY, H., 1968. 'Transverse lines in long bones of prehistoric Californian Indians', *American Journal of Physical Anthropology* 29, 1–17.

MELLAART, J., 1967. *Çatal Hüyük, a Neolithic town in Anatolia*, Thames and Hudson, London.

MELLAART, J., 1975. *The Neolithic of the Near East*, Thames and Hudson, London.

MERBS, C.F., 1983. *Patterns of Activity Induced Pathology in a Canadian Inuit Population*, National Museum of Canada, Ontario.

MILISAUSKAS, S., 1978. *European Prehistory*, Academic Press, London.

MOLNAR, S., 1971. 'Human tooth wear, tooth function and cultural variability', *American Journal of Physical Anthropology* 34, 175–90.

MOORE, A., 1979. 'A pre-Neolithic farmers' village on the Euphrates', *Scientific American* 241, 50–8.

MORGAN, L. H. 1877. *Ancient Society*, World Publishing, New York.

OBERMAIER, H., 1925. *Fossil Man in Spain*, Yale UP, New Haven.

PAULI, L., 1985. 'Early Celtic society: two centuries of wealth and turmoil in central Europe', in Champion, T. and Megaw, V. (eds), *Settlement and Society: Aspects of West European Prehistory in the First Millennium BC*, Leicester UP, Leicester.

PÉQUART, M., ST-J., BOULE, M. and VALLOIS, H., 1937. *Téviec – Station-Nécropole Mésolithique du Morbihan*, Archives de l'Institut de paléontologie humaine, mémoire 18, Paris.

PIGGOTT, S., 1938. 'The early Bronze Age in Wessex', *Proceedings of the Prehistoric Society* 4, 52–106.

PIGGOTT, S., 1959. *Approach to Archaeology*, A. and C. Black, London.

PIGGOTT, S., 1965. *Ancient Europe*, Edinburgh UP, Edinburgh.

PLUTARCH. 'De virtute mulierum', in *Moralia* III, trans F. C. Babbitt, Loeb Classical Library, Heinemann, London 1931.

PLUTARCH. 'Marius', in *Lives* IV, trans. B. Perrin, Loeb Classical Library, Heinemann, London, 1920.

POMEROY, S., 1984. 'Selected bibliography on women in classical antiquity' in Peradotto, J. and Sullivan, J. P. (eds), *Women in the Ancient World – The Arethusa Papers*, State University of New York Press, Albany.

POWELL, T. G. E., 1966. *Prehistoric Art*, Thames and Hudson, London.

POWELL, T. G. E., 1980. *The Celts*, Thames and Hudson, London.

PROCOPIUS. *History of the Wars: the Gothic War*, trans. H. B. Dewing, Loeb Classical Library, Heinemann, London, 1914–40.

QUINN, N., 1977. 'Anthropological studies on women's status', *Annual Review of Anthropology* 6, 181–225.

RANDSBORG, K., 1974. 'Social stratification in early Bronze Age Denmark: a study in the regulation of cultural systems', *Praehistorische Zeitschrift* 49, 38–61.

RANDSBORG, K., 1984. 'Women in prehistory: the Danish example', *Acta Archaeologica* 55, 143–54.

RANKIN, H. D., 1987. *Celts and the Classical World*, Croom Helm, London.

REITER, R. (ed.), 1975. *Towards an Anthropology of Women*, Monthly Review Press, New York.

REITER, R., 1978. 'The search for origins: unraveling the threads of gender hierarchy', *Critique of Anthropology* 3, 5–24.

RENFREW, C., 1972. *The Emergence of Civilization*, Methuen, London.

RENFREW, C., 1973. *Before Civilization*, Jonathan Cape, London.

RICHMOND, I., 1954. 'Queen Cartimandua', *Journal of Roman Studies* 44, 43–52.

RIVERS, W. H. R., 1906. *The Toda*, Macmillan, London.

ROHRLICH-LEAVITT, R., SYKES, B. and WEATHERFORD, E., 1975. 'Aboriginal women: male-female anthropological perspectives', in Reiter, 1975.

ROSALDO, M. and LAMPHERE, L. (eds), 1974. *Women, Culture and Society*, Stanford UP, Stanford.

ROSS, A., 1986. *The Pagan Celts*, Batsford, London.

ROZOY, J.-G., 1987. *Les Celtes en Champagne: Les Ardennes en Second Age du Fer, le Mont Troté, les Railier*, Société Archéologique Champenoise 4, Charleville-Mézières.

SACKS, K., 1974. 'Engels revisited: women, the organization of production and private property', in Rosaldo and Lamphere, 1974.

SAHLINS, M., 1972. *Stone Age Economics*, Aldine, Chicago.

SANDARS, N. K., 1985. *Prehistoric Art in Europe*, Penguin, Harmondsworth.

SANDAY, P., 1981. *Female Power and Male Dominance*, Cambridge UP, Cambridge.

SAUTER, M. R., 1980. 'Sur le sexe de la dame de Vix', *L'Anthropologie* 84, 89–103.

SCHIFFER, M. J., 1976. *Behavioural Archaeology*, Academic Press, New York.

SELLEVOLD, B. J., HANSEN, V. L. and JØRGENSEN, J. B., 1984. *Iron Age Man in Denmark*, Det kongelige Nordiske Oldskriftselskab, Copenhagen.

SHENNAN, S. E., 1975. 'The social organization at Brančč', *Antiquity* 49, 279–88.

SHENNAN, S. E., 1982. 'From minimal to moderate ranking', in Renfrew, C. and Shennan, S.J. (eds), *Ranking, Resource and Exchange*, Cambridge UP, Cambridge.

SHERRATT, A. (ed.), 1980. *Cambridge Encyclopedia of Archaeology*, Cambridge UP, Cambridge.

SHERRATT, A., 1981. 'Plough and pastoralism: aspects of the secondary products revolution', in Hodder, I., Isaac, G. and Hammond, N. (eds), *Pattern of the Past*, Cambridge UP, Cambridge.

SHERRATT, A., 1983. 'The secondary exploitation of animals in the Old World', *World Archaeology*, 15, 90–104.

SILLEN, A. and KAVANAGH, M., 1982. 'Strontium and paleodietary research: a review', *Yearbook of Physical Anthropology* 25, 67–90.

SLOCUM, S., 1975. 'Woman the gatherer: male bias in anthropolgy', in Reiter, 1975.

SOUDSKY, B., 1964. 'Sozialökonomische Geschichte des alteren Neolithikums in Mitteleuropa', *Aus de Ur- und Frühgeschichte 2*, 62–81.

SPECTOR, J. 1982. 'Male/female task differentiation among the Hidatsa: toward the development of an archaeological approach to gender', in Albers, P. and Medicine, B. (eds), *The Hidden Half: Studies of Plains Indian Women*, University Press of America, Washington.

SPENDER, D. (ed.), 1981. *Men's Studies Modified*, Pergamon, Oxford.

SPENDER, D., 1982. *Women of Ideas*, Ark, London.

STANLEY, A., 1981. 'Daughters of Isis, daughters of Demeter: when women sowed and reaped'. *Women's Studies International Quarterly* 4, 3, 289–304.

STEAD, I. M., 1979. *The Arras Culture*, Yorkshire Philosophical Society, York.

STRABO. *Geographia*, trans. H. L. Jones, Loeb Classical Library, Heinemann, London, 1917.

TACITUS. *The Agricola and The Germania*, trans. H. M. Mattingly, Penguin, Harmondsworth, 1970.

TACITUS. *The Annals of Imperial Rome*, trans. M. Grant, Penguin, Harmondsworth, 1971.

TACITUS. *Histories*, trans. C. H. Moore, Loeb Classical Library, Heinemann, London, 1962.

Táin bó Cuailnge, ed. and trans. C. O'Rahilly, Dublin Institute for Advanced Studies, Dublin, 1976.

TANNER, N., 1981. *On Becoming Human*, Cambridge UP, Cambridge.

TANNER, N. and ZIHLMAN, A. 1976. 'Women in evolution. Part I: Innovation and selection in human origins', *Signs* 1, 3, 585–608.

THOMAS, C. G., 1973. 'Matriarchy in early Greece: The Bronze Age and Dark Ages', *Arethusa* 6, 2, 173–96.

THOMSON, J. O., 1948. *History of Ancient Geography*, Cambridge UP, Cambridge.

UCKO, P. J., 1962. 'The interpretation of prehistoric anthropomorphic figurines', *Journal of the Royal Anthropological Institute of Great Britain and Ireland* 92, 38–54.

UCKO, P. J., 1968. *Anthropomorphic Figurines*, Andrew Szmidla, London.

UCKO, P. J., 1969. 'Ethnography and archaeological interpretation of funerary remains', *World Archaeology* 1, 262–77.

UCKO, P. J. and ROSENFELD, A., 1967. *Palaeolithic Cave Art*, Weidenfeld and Nicolson, London.

WEBSTER, G., 1978. *Boudica: The British Revolt Against Rome AD 60*, Batsford, London.

WHITING, J. and AYRES, B., 1968. 'Inferences from the shape of dwellings', in Chang, K. (ed.), *Settlement Archaeology*, National Press, Palo Alto.

WHITTLE, A. W. R., 1985. *Neolithic Europe: A Survey*, Cambridge UP, Cambridge.

WILLETTS, R., 1977. *The Civilization of Ancient Crete*, University of California Press, Berkeley.

WING, E. S. and BROWN, A. B., 1969. *Paleonutrition*, Academic Press, New York.

WINTERS, H. D., 1968. 'Value systems and trade cycles of the late Archaic in the Midwest', in Binford S. R. and Binford L. R. (eds), *New Perspectives in Archaeology*, Aldine, Chicago.

WYMER, J., 1982. *The Palaeolithic Age*, Croom Helm, London.

ZIHLMAN, A., 1978. 'Women in evolution. Part II: Subsistence and social organization among early hominids'. *Signs* 4, 4–20.

ZIHLMAN, A., 1981. 'Woman as shapers of human adaptation', in Dahlberg, 1981.

Index

Aborigines, Australian 51, 53, 59
Abri Pataud, France 68
Abu Huyera, Syria 80, 82
Africa 38, 73, 74, 80, 104, 155, 161;
 central 51, 81; east 33, 38, 43, 57;
 southern 47, 51–3; west 75
aggression 49–50
agricultural societies 19, 59, 60, 76,
 77–107
agriculture 28, 30, 38, 64, 77–107,
 108, 113, 128, 140–1, 150, 154,
 161, 172, 173, 175, 179; intensive/
 plough 81, 99, 103–5; origins of 9,
 77–90, 99, 178
Agta 53, 156
Akrotiri, Greece 113
Ali Kosh, Iran 79
alliances 135, 139, 162, 173
Alps 109, 139–41, 163
amber 108, 127, 137, 156
Ambigatus 158
Ambrones 164
America, North 64, 75, 175; South 81,
 91, 155
American Indians see Indians
Anati, E. 141
Anatolia 70, 73, 78
ancestors 72
Anglesey, Wales 157, 164
animal behaviour 20, 44, 46, 48
animal food 19, 38, 39, 41, 43–4, 49,
 51–5, 60, 80–1, 84, 93–4, 98
animal husbandry 64, 77–8, 81–3, 95,
 99–105, 135, 145, 147, 172
animals 44, 116, 141; models of/in
 art 56, 66, 69, 76, 89, 139–41, 150
anthropological analogues 14–17, 32–
 5, 38, 50–1, 73–5, 80–1, 94–9, 103,
 108, 128, 152, 156, 158, 160,
 177
anthropologists 19
anthropology: early 12, 18–19, 51, 63–
 5, 98, 157; physical 20, 25–9, 175;
 social 9, 14–20, 99, 175–9
apes 41
archaeological evidence: decay of 12,
 13, 21, 46, 109; interpretation of 13,
 19, 115, 145; nature of 10, 23–37,
 57, 104, 177; recovery of 13, 35, 54,
 82; see also preservation
archaeological excavation see
 excavation
archaeology 7; American 9; early 14,
 114–15, 120, 142, 174; limitations
 of 7, 10; methods 7–8, 12; theory 7,
 8, 13–14, 152, 176–7
architecture 109, 110, 114–15, 160
Arctic 51, 57, 156
art 14, 36, 66, 76, 101, 103, 109–14,
 139–41, 147–51, 153, 161;
 conventions in 36, 110, 113;
 depictions of women in 36, 55–6, 63,
 66–76, 110–14, 140–1, 147–51;
 function of 37, 76, 110–11, 115,
 140–1

artefacts 15, 175
Asia 81, 104
 south-west see Near East
atatls 29–30
Aulnay-la-Planche, France 160
Australia 51, 53, 55, 59
Austria 137, 175
Ayia Triada, Crete 110
Ayres, B. 94
axes 109, 115, 164; hand 39;
 stone 39, 127

Bachofen, J. 12, 63–4
bags, skin 43, 46–7, 52–3, 85, 87
Baltic Sea 155–6
bands, forager 59, 65
barbarians 151, 152, 154, 162
barley 57, 78, 80, 85–6
barrows, burial see tumuli
baskets 12, 29, 43, 46, 52, 54
Batavians 163
battles 21, 151, 157, 162–4, 167, 174
beliefs 32, 66, 72–4
Bergen, Norway 35
bias, male in archaeology see male bias
Bicorp, Spain 55–6
bipedalism 41–2, 46, 48, 175
births, spacing of 61, 88–9
Biturges 158
Blackpatch, England 146
Black Sea 95
blood 35
blood groups 32
boats 138, 140
Bologna, Italy 151
bones: animal 39, 54, 61, 79, 82, 90,
 93, 102, 103; human 25–9, 61, 122–
 3, 125, 168, 180
Borum Eshøj, Denmark 119–22
Boudica (Boadicea) 164–7, 171, 173
bracelets 119, 124, 144, 153
Brančc, Czechoslovakia 123–7
breast feeding 60, 89
Brezje, Yugoslavia 151
Brigantes 167–8
Britain 100, 143–7, 160, 164–8;
 northern 57, 167; southern 127–9
Britons 151, 163
Bronze Age 31, 66, 72–3, 104, 108–
 41, 142, 151, 173, 174–5, 179
bronze: artefacts 108–9, 122, 127–39,
 147, 149–51, 154, 168, 171, 172;
 discovery of 108
brooches 31, 120, 153, 166
buildings 10, 21, 86, 160–1; use of 34–
 5, 86, 95, 114–15, 143–7
bull leaping 112–13
burial 11, 12, 13, 25–32, 34, 55, 61,
 69, 72, 76, 83, 93, 97, 99, 108, 118–
 39, 140, 142, 143–4, 159, 168–71
burial rites 27, 29, 179

Caesar, Julius 21, 151, 155, 157, 160–2
Calgacus 167

Californian Indians 28–9
Camulodunum see Colchester
Canada 26, 51
carbon 14 dating 78, 108, 175
carbon isotope analysis 28
Cartimandua 167–8
carts 100, 163
Çatal Hüyük, Turkey 70
cattle 93–5, 98, 100–3, 106
caves 39, 59, 60, 66, 76, 116
Çayönü, Turkey 78
Celts 22, 142, 148, 151–3, 157, 162–
 7, 171
cemeteries 11, 26–7, 31–2, 123–7,
 159, 171
cereals 57, 60, 79–82, 85, 89, 93, 114,
 135, 172
ceremonial 30, 74, 122
Certosa, Italy 149–51
Champagne, France 153
Champion, T. 162
chariots 168, 169, 171
chiefs 155, 164–71
childbirth 23, 26, 60–1, 65, 72, 75, 89
child rearing 11, 20, 41–3, 48–9, 65,
 103, 105, 146
Childe, V.G. 63
children 26, 31, 48, 52, 60–2, 70, 75,
 83, 85, 88, 96, 98, 103, 105, 107,
 120, 124–6, 141, 158–9, 160, 163–4
chimpanzees 20, 41–2, 44, 46, 49
Christianity 22, 37, 74, 152
Civilis 163
civilisation 23, 90, 109
Clarke, D. 58–9, 143–5
classical mythology 12, 22–3, 63–4, 74
classical sources 21–2, 142, 151–9,
 161–8, 172, 180; reliability of 151–2,
 162, 164–5, 167
climate 38, 50–1, 54, 57, 81–2
cloaks 148, 153, 166
cloth 12
clothing 10, 26, 31, 54, 62, 119–22,
 137, 145
coffins 31, 116, 119
coins 21, 35, 167
Colchester, England 166
Coles, B. and J. 145
communication 76
containers 48
copper 108, 124, 137
costume see dress
crafts 28, 30, 32–4, 105, 114, 143,
 145–7, 154, 162
craft specialisation 26, 74, 106
cremation 25, 109, 120, 127, 131, 147
Crete 69–70, 72, 74, 109–18
crop growing 23, 60, 77–90, 91, 99,
 100, 128, 135, 155, 172
Cuevas de la Araña, Spain 55–6
cultivation see plants
customs 29, 152
Cycladic Islands, Greece 69–72
cylinder seals 100–1
Czechoslovakia 40, 67, 123–7

daggers 119, 127–30, 140
dairy products 27, 60, 100–3, 145
dancing 141, 147–8
Danebury, England 153
Danube, R. 57, 90, 142, 160, 171
Danubian culture 90–9
dating methods 78, 108, 175, 176
death: age of 25–6, 32, 119, 123, 125; causes of 26–32
debt 107
decay 12, 13, 21, 46, 109
deities 23, 37, 63–4, 69, 72, 74–5, 112–13, 122, 116–18, 136
Demeter 23
Denmark 31, 57, 100, 119–23, 130–6, 138
descent patterns 31–2, 64, 97, 106, 126, 151, 157–9, 175
Deverel-Rimbury culture 127–9, 146–7, 175
diet 8, 27–9, 35, 39, 43, 51–9, 60, 76, 80, 84, 100, 126, 172
dimorphism, sexual 42, 49
Dio Cassius 151, 164–7
diseases 8, 25–7, 59
division of labour *see* labour
documentary sources 10, 21–3, 102, 142, 148, 151–9, 162–8
dolls 72, 75–6
Dolni Vestonice, Czechoslovakia 40, 67–8
domestic space 34, 94–5, 114–16, 143–7, 160–1, 179
Don, R. 67
dowry 158–9
dress 31, 36, 110, 113, 116–22, 126, 144–5, 148, 153, 159, 166
Druids 157
dryades 157

earth goddesses *see* goddesses
East Anglia 164
economy 11, 51, 143, 172
egalitarian societies 11, 63–6, 75
Egtved, Denmark 119–22
Egypt 21, 63, 100, 101, 110
Elbe, R. 138
elderly people 52, 62, 85, 98, 155
élites 108, 118, 150
Ellison, A. 146–7
Ember, M. 94, 96
endogamy 129
Engels, F. 12, 64, 155
England: northern 57, 167; southern 123, 127–9, 135, 143–7, 153
environment, natural 38, 41, 43, 46, 48, 50, 54, 57, 60, 62, 76, 82, 98
equality, social and sexual 38, 52, 61–6, 74, 106, 119, 129, 173
Eskimos (Inuit) 15, 26, 51
enthnoarchaeology 19, 175
ethnographic parallels 14–17, 29, 31–2, 35, 40, 50–1, 58, 73–5, 80–1, 91, 94, 97–9, 103–6, 123, 128, 161, 181
ethnography 15, 19, 26, 151, 156, 175
Etruscans 150–1, 171
Euphrates, R. 79–80
Europe: central 90–1, 104, 137, 161, 171; eastern 66, 137; northern 23, 55, 130–9; north-east 156; north-west 38, 91, 102, 104–5, 118, 127–9, 142, 153, 162; south-east 77–91, 101, 104–5, 137; western 142, 179

Evans, A. 110–11, 115–16
evidence, archaeological *see* archaeological evidence
evolution, human 9, 20, 38–9, 41–51, 175
excavation 11–13, 54, 83, 114, 143, 174; methods 54, 83, 143
exchange 8, 53, 106–8, 155, 172–3; of women 107–8, 129, 135–9
exogamy 129
explorers, early 18, 98, 157

faeces 35, 57, 60
faience 116, 127, 175
family 32, 64, 94–5, 99, 107, 125, 129, 155, 160–2, 173
farming *see* agriculture
farms 143
Fedelm 157
feminist literature 9, 22, 177–9
feminist theories 7, 11, 12, 41–2, 63–4, 98, 118, 174, 175
Fenni 155–6
Fertile Crescent 79
fertility magic 37, 66, 73–6, 113
fighting 147, 163
figurines: animal 76; female 23, 36–7, 63, 66–76, 116–18, 126, 132, 136, 178; male 69–70, 72, 76
fingerprints on pottery 32
Finland 155
fish and fishing 54–5, 93–4
flint 45, 57–9, 83, 88, 145
flotation of soils 54, 57
food 11, 27–9, 38–42, 48, 51–9, 62, 65, 76, 80, 84, 85, 103, 123, 128, 137, 156, 163; preparation 19, 26, 39, 57, 60, 62, 81, 83, 93, 105–6, 114–15, 146–7; preservation and recovery 12, 82; providers, women as *see* women; sharing 43, 49, 98, 172; storage 52, 54, 65, 83, 85–7, 95, 114, 146–7
forager societies 14, 26, 29, 38–43, 46, 50–62, 64–5, 76–8, 80, 82–6, 88, 90, 106, 156, 172–3, 175, 176, 178
Fossey, D. 20
France 21, 57, 60–1, 66, 68, 141, 153–4, 160, 168–9
Franchthi Cave, Greece 57
frescoes 110–18
funerary rituals 130, 147, 149–51

Gamble, C. 76
gathering 38, 42–3, 47–9, 51–9, 62, 83–5, 156, 172
Gaul 21, 151, 153–5, 159, 163
gender roles 8, 14, 17–20, 26, 29, 37, 42, 77, 80–2, 100, 102, 104–5, 123, 143, 147, 151–6, 175, 176, 178; assessment of 143; assumptions about 8, 17–18, 148, 154
Germans 142, 151, 155, 157–8, 163
Germany 138, 154, 158–60, 168
girls 31, 74–5, 120, 125–6, 158–9
glaciations 38, 44, 51, 57, 76
Glastonbury, England 143–5
goddesses 23, 37, 63, 66–76, 112–13, 116–18, 122
gold 108, 124, 127, 130–1, 166, 168, 171
Goldberg, Germany 160
Goodall, J. 20

gorillas 20
grain 85–7, 146; *see also* cereals
grasses 28, 57–8, 79–80, 82, 85
grave goods 11, 28–31, 61, 72, 76, 97, 108–9, 118–39, 143, 154, 168–71, 175
Great Rift Valley, Africa 38
Greece 57, 74, 102, 112, 150
Greek literature 21, 63, 102, 142, 151–2, 163–4

Hacilar, Turkey 70
hairstyles 55, 110–11, 113, 116, 119, 141, 147, 153, 157, 164, 166
Hallstatt phase 147, 150, 159–60, 168–9, 175
Hanseatic league 35
Harris lines 28
harvesting 81, 85–6, 103, 135, 172
healing 151, 163
health 119
hearths 60, 74, 87, 95, 98, 114
Helen 63
Herodotus 151, 162
Heuneberg, Germany 160, 171
Hidatsa 19
hierarchies 106, 135
hillforts 153, 160, 168, 171, 175
historical sources *see* written records
history 21–2; women's 7, 8, 10
hoards, bronze 131–4, 139
hoe agriculture 19, 80–1, 91–3, 98, 104, 106
Hohmichele, Germany 171
Holmegaard, Denmark 57
homebases 19, 38, 40, 43, 48, 59–62, 67, 75, 86, 89
Homer 63, 102, 114
hominids 38–9, 41–3, 46, 48–9, 175
Homo sapiens sapiens 39, 41, 175
honey 55–6
horses 145, 147–8, 156, 158
horticultural societies 29, 53, 80–99, 155, 159
horticulture 80, 98, 103–4, 172, 176
houses 11, 12, 14, 34, 39, 40, 59–62, 67, 70, 74–5, 80, 83–4, 86–7, 89, 94–8, 105, 118, 144–7, 155–6, 160–1; shape of 34, 94, 160–1; function of 34–5, 86, 95, 114–15, 143–7
human evolution *see* evolution
Hungary 100, 147–8
hunter-gatherer societies *see* forager societies
hunting 20, 26, 29, 38–9, 41–4, 46, 49, 65–6, 82, 84, 90, 94, 98, 100, 102–3, 105, 141, 147, 155–6, 176; by women 14, 29–30, 43, 53, 55, 156, 177
huts 59–60, 74, 86, 145–7

Iberians 160
Ice Age 15, 38, 44, 51, 76
Iceni 164, 168
Icoana, Romania 57
ideology 76
idols 66
India 160
Indians, American 28; Hidatsa 19; Iroquois 64, 97–9; Knoll 29–30; Navaho 16; Zuni 75
infanticide 27, 60
infant mortality 26–7, 89, 125–6

infants 31, 42–3, 46, 48–9, 105, 125, 141
inheritance 30–1, 106, 124–6, 129, 159
inhumation 118, 120, 131, 176
initiation ceremonies 74
interpretation, archaeological 13
Inuit 15, 26, 51, 53
invention, tool 41–2, 48, 87
Iran 79
Iraq 54, 58, 79, 88–9
Ireland 22, 57, 137, 159
Irish sagas 22, 152–3, 157, 159
iron 108, 171
Iron Age 21, 31, 35, 142–71, 173, 175, 176
Iroquois 64, 97–9
irrigation 80, 100
Israel 79
Italy 139–41, 149–51, 164

Jericho, Israel 79, 89
jewellery 31, 108–9, 111, 119, 127–8, 130, 132–9, 153, 168
Jocasta 63
Joffroy, R. 169
Jordan 79

Kalahari desert 47, 51–3, 59, 84
Kalambo Falls, Tanzania 57
Kenya 57
kinship 50, 96–7
kinship patterns 106, 116, 139, 157–62
Klein Aspergle, Germany 171
Knossos, Crete 110–12, 114–18
Kombe, Tanzania 20, 44
Koobi Fora, Kenya 57
Kornwestheim, Germany 160
Kostienki-Borchevo, Russia 67
krater 168
Kristiansen, K. 132–5, 137–9
!Kung 47, 51–3, 59, 84

labour, division of 32, 41, 43, 53, 65, 80–1, 83, 91, 100, 102, 104–5, 143–7, 151–6
labour force 97, 105, 129
land ownership 98, 99, 104, 106, 129, 155, 159
language, development of 50
Lapps 156
La Tène phase 153, 168
latrines 35
Laussel, France 68
laws 22
leaders 11, 146, 162, 164–71
leadership 63, 113, 158, 173
learning 49, 106
leather working 26, 144–5, 147
legends 22–3, 111
Lengyel Culture 95
Levant 86
Levy, J. 132
Linear A 110, 176
Linear Pottery Culture 90–9, 103, 160, 179
literary sources 10, 21–3, 63–4, 142–3, 148, 151–6
Lithuania 155
Livy 158
London, England 166
longhouses 92–9

loomweights 102
Lüneberg, Germany 138
luxury goods 168
lyre 147

Mabinogion 152
magic 73–5
Majorca 69
male bias in archaeology and anthropology 8, 17–18, 41, 51, 65, 120, 156, 174, 177
male dominance 10, 12, 50, 63, 99, 135, 145, 173
male-female bonding 49–50
male figurines 66–70, 72, 76
Mallia, Crete 110, 114
malnutrition 27
Malta 69
Man the Hunter 41, 51
Marius 164
marriage 31, 49, 120, 125–6, 139, 152, 169; residence after 32–4, 94–8
marriage patterns 34, 94, 96, 129, 151, 157–62
Marxist theories 14, 179
material culture 14, 105
material possessions 11, 62, 86, 90, 106–7, 143, 159
matriarchies 11–12, 22–3, 63–6, 109–10, 155, 176
matrifocal groups 49–50
matrilineal descent 63–4, 97–8, 106, 116, 126, 158–9, 175, 176
matrilocal residence 32, 64, 94–8, 106, 175, 176
matrons 98, 157
Mbuti 51
Medb 159
meat 27–8, 39, 42, 46, 51–5, 57, 76, 82, 100, 102–3
medieval period 21, 35; early 22, 152–3
Mediterranean 23, 57–8, 60, 66, 69, 73, 109, 142
megalithic tombs 179
Mellaart, J. 70
Melville I., Australia 55
men, depicted with penises 55, 70, 149–51
Menelaus 63
menstruation 35
merchants 35, 108
Mesoamerica 179
Mesolithic 38, 54–9, 62, 176
Mesopotamia 21, 79, 100–2
metal analysis 131
metals, raw 130, 137
metalworking 30, 108, 147
microliths 58–9
microwear analysis 45, 57
migration 96–7, 158
milk and milk products 27, 60, 100–3, 145
Minerva 23
Minoans 37, 69, 101, 109–18, 173
missionaries 18, 81, 98
models: animal 66, 69, 76; human 23, 66–76; theoretical 176
monogamy 34, 41, 49, 94, 158–9, 161
Mont Lassois, France 168
Monte Bego, France 141
Morgan, L. H. 12, 64
Mórrígan 23

mortality patterns 25–32, 125–6
mother goddess 22–3, 66–76
mounds, burial 32, 127, 159, 168, 171, 175
Mühlacker, Germany 159
Mureybet, Syria 80, 86–7
Mycenaean period 102
mythology 12, 22, 23, 63–4, 74, 111, 114, 136, 152–3, 156, 178

Natufian phase 86
Near East 34, 63, 69, 70, 77–90, 93, 99, 101, 104–5, 173
necklaces 119, 126, 127, 153
Neolithic 26, 29, 34, 54, 55, 60, 66, 69–74, 76, 77–107, 116, 135, 142, 172, 173, 176
Newferry, Ireland 57
New Guinea 80, 81–2, 91, 155
New York, USA 98
nomads 38–40, 59–60, 65, 77, 84–5, 88
Nordic area 132–9
Norway 35
nutrition 26–7, 126
nuts 46, 48, 52–3, 56–7, 62, 84, 98

obligations 88, 173
Odyssey 114
Oedipus 63
offspring 42, 46, 48–9
open-air sites 39, 60, 76
organic materials 12, 21, 31, 46, 58, 59, 62, 114, 119, 123, 137, 143
ornaments 31, 62, 97, 108–9, 119–20, 124, 128–39, 144–5, 153–4, 168
osteo-arthritis 26

Pacific Islands 81, 82
palaces 110, 114–16, 118
Palaeolithic 9, 37, 38–76, 77–8, 80, 86, 151, 172–3
paleopathology 119, 123, 176
pastoral societies 102, 128, 135, 173
patriarchy 10, 12, 63–6, 166, 176
patrilineal descent 64, 97, 99, 106, 116, 126, 158
patrilocal residence 32, 94–8, 106, 139, 158
Pauli, L. 159
Paulinus, S. 157, 164
peace 164, 174
Penelope 114
Phaestos, Crete 110
phallic representations 55, 70, 140–1
Philippines 53, 156
phosphate analysis 95
physical anthropology 20, 25–9, 41, 175
pigs 82, 93–4, 98, 103
pins 30, 119, 126, 127, 130
plant food 27, 38–9, 42–3, 48, 51–9, 62, 93, 156, 172, 174
plants, cultivation of 77–90, 91, 175
plough agriculture 81–2, 99, 103–5
plough marks 100
ploughs 64, 80, 93, 100–2, 104, 106, 141, 172, 176
Plutarch 163
Poland 100
political organisation 13, 74, 105
political power 11, 64, 157, 158
pollen analysis 60, 135

polyandry 160–1
polygamy 34, 94, 160–2
polygyny 125–6, 160
Pomerania 138
population: growth 77, 85, 89, 90, 97, 104, 105, 179; size 66, 119, 162; statistics 26
Posidonius 21
possessions, personal 62, 64–5, 84, 86, 88, 107, 108–9, 118–19, 126, 132, 159, 168, 173
post-excavation analysis 13
post-marital residence 33, 34–5, 94–8, 106, 129, 139, 158–62, 175, 176
pottery 32–4, 46, 69, 77, 87, 90, 93, 100, 101, 114, 137, 144, 147–8, 179
poverty 11, 107, 118, 130, 136, 156, 171
power 14, 63, 98, 158, 171, 176; women with 11, 118, 157, 162, 164–71, 173
praying 141, 147
pregnancy 26, 28, 37, 43, 60, 70, 72, 73, 74–5, 105
prehistory, definition of 21, 176
preservation of archaeological material 12, 31, 35, 39, 46, 54, 58, 59, 82, 95, 100, 109, 113, 114, 119, 143, 168
prestige 53, 155
prestige goods 134–5
priestesses 74, 112, 116–18, 157, 169
primates 20, 38, 41–4, 46, 48–9
Procopius 156
property *see* possessions
protein 100
puberty 74–5
pygmies 51
Pyrenees 67, 142

queens 11, 63, 114–16, 159
quernstones 87–8, 93, 97

racism 174
radiocarbon dating 78, 108, 175, 176
radiographic analysis 28
Randsborg, K. 130, 135
raw materials 124, 130, 137
religion 15, 51, 72–3, 111, 136, 140, 151, 157, 169, 173, 174
residence patterns 94–8, 106
Rhine, R. 90, 142, 154, 163
riding 139, 145, 147–8
ritual 18, 35, 64, 72, 73, 109, 111, 113–18, 122, 136, 151
rock art 55, 109, 138–41
roles, gender *see* gender roles
Roman conquest 142, 172, 176
Roman empire 10, 21, 74, 154, 162
Roman literature 21, 142, 151–9, 172
Romania 57
rooms, function of 95, 110, 114–16, 143
roots (as food) 46, 48, 52, 58, 62, 81, 98
Rossen culture 95
rulers, women 63, 168
Russia 66
Rwanda 20

sagas, Celtic 22, 152–3, 157
Sahara 26
sanitary protection 35

Santorini, Greece 113
Scandinavia 55, 109, 118–23, 130–40, 156
scavenging 39, 43, 86
scientific analysis 13, 35
Scrithfinni 156
secondary products revolution 99–107
sedentary lifestyles 77, 85–7, 176, 179
seeds as food 58, 79, 81, 83–7; archaeological recovery of 13, 54, 57, 82
Senufo 75
settlement patterns 77
settlement sites 11, 12, 34–5, 72, 83, 91–9, 105, 118, 127–8, 142–7, 162, 174, 176
sex roles *see* gender roles
sexist bias in archaeology *see* male bias
sexual differences, natural 20, 24–5, 41–2, 123
Shanidar cave, Iraq 54, 58
sharing food 48–9, 98, 172
sheep 82, 98, 102, 103, 128
shellfish 55
shells 97
shelters 39, 59, 60, 62, 76, 86
Shennan, S. 123, 126, 130
Sherratt, A. 100–2, 104
shrines 70, 119
sickles 133, 135
Sitones 155–6
situla art 149–51
skeletal evidence 25–34, 38, 41, 57, 61, 83, 109, 122–3, 141, 153, 171, 174, 180
skeletons, sex of 24–5, 61, 109, 122–4, 127, 130, 168
skins 57–8, 59
skirts 110, 113, 116, 119–22, 136, 147–8
slaves 113, 120, 156, 159
Slocum, S. 42
Slovakia 123–7
snake goddesses 110, 116–18
snakes 110, 116
social anthropology 9, 14, 15–20, 99, 175, 177, 179
social change 105
social equality 38, 61–2, 63–6, 74, 106, 119, 129, 135
social gatherings 150
social status 12, 29, 62, 74, 77, 105, 109, 116–18, 128–30, 136, 143, 155–9, 168, 172, 176, 179
social stratification 11, 74, 104, 106, 108, 119, 124–5, 135, 159, 179; origin of 11, 88, 106
social structure 13, 15, 61–5, 94, 105, 115, 151–2, 160, 173
societies: classless/egalitarian 11, 63–6, 75; present-day/traditional 14–15, 17, 20, 38–9, 43, 65, 81–2, 84, 99, 118, 136, 152, 175; Western, effect on traditional 18, 50, 81, 82; Western, expectations of 15, 17, 18, 50, 62, 119, 120, 144–7, 148; *see also* agricultural, forager, horticultural, pastoral
soils 13, 54, 81, 90, 104–5, 135
Sopron, Hungary 147–8
sorcery 75
Spain 55–6, 66
spears 29, 119

specialisation 26, 74, 106
Spector, J. 19–20
speeches 167
spindle whorls 102, 145
spinning 30, 34, 102–3, 144, 147–8
Stanley, A. 99
Star Carr, England 57
statuettes *see* figurines
status, assessment of 31, 125–6, 130, 132
status of women 11, 12, 17–18, 23, 26, 31, 34, 37, 52, 54–6, 59, 65, 74, 77, 81, 96, 98–9, 105–7, 109–13, 116–18, 125–6, 128–9, 132, 134–6, 143, 146, 155–9, 168, 171–2, 176, 178, 179
status symbols 18, 125–6
Stone Age, Old *see* Palaeolithic New *see* Neolithic
stone artefacts 62, 77, 124, 137
storage of food 52, 54, 65, 83, 85–7, 95, 114, 145–7
storage vessels 106, 114
Strabo 21, 154
strontium/calcium analysis 27–8
subsistence patterns 14, 38
Suebi 164
Suiones 155–6
sumptuary goods 123, 125–6, 171
surpluses 88, 107
Sweden 55, 123, 130–40
Switzerland 102
swords 119, 132, 134, 140, 164
sympathetic magic 73, 75
Syria 79, 80, 82, 86

Tacitus 21, 151, 154–65, 167–8
Táin 152, 159
Tanzania 20, 57
'Task Differentiation, Male/Female' 19–20, 179
teacher, mother as 49, 106
teeth 26, 28–9, 49, 57, 123
temples 116
Terra Amata, France 60–1
Téviec, France 57
textiles 35, 102–3, 105, 109, 114, 122–3, 171
theoretical archaeology 7, 8, 13–14, 152, 176, 177
theories, formation of 13–14, 177
Thera, Greece 113
Thracians 163
throne room 115
Tigris, R. 79
Tiwi 53, 55
Toda 160
tools 11, 14, 29, 31, 32, 62, 64, 86–9, 99, 106, 114, 124, 142–5, 147, 176; bronze 108–9, 132; flint 57–9, 83; invention of 41–2, 48, 87; iron 143–4; stone 38–9, 45, 55, 57–9, 60, 77, 88–9, 93
tool using, origins of 20, 39, 41, 43, 46
torcs 166, 168
towns 70, 89, 109, 113
toys 72, 75
trace elements 137
trade 108, 137–9; in women 108, 129, 135, 136–9
tribes 152
Tripolye culture 95

trousers 147–8, 153
tumuli 32, 127, 159, 171, 175–6
Turkey 70, 73, 78, 79

Ucko, P. 69–70

Val Camonica, Italy 140–1
Vaphio, Crete 113
Västerbjers, Sweden 55
vegetation, natural 38, 44, 50–1, 60,
   81–2
Veleda 157
Venus figurines 66–76
Venutius 167
Verulamium, England 166
vessels: bronze 147, 149–51, 168, 171;
   wooden 87
villages 19, 70, 92, 94, 96, 98, 127–9,
   143–4, 146, 173
Virgin Mary 37, 63
Vix, France 168–9
Vopiscus 157
votaries 74, 116, 122, 136

wagons 147, 163, 168
walking upright 41–2, 46, 48, 175
wall paintings 110–18
war 23, 96, 98, 162–4
warfare 22, 29, 65, 105, 141, 155,
   157, 158, 174; women in 151, 162–
   4
warriors 150

waterlogged deposits 31, 35, 100, 119
wealth 10, 11, 14, 88, 99, 104, 106–8,
   123, 125–6, 128, 134–5, 171, 173;
   assessment of 29, 109, 124–5, 130–1,
   134; display of 108–9, 135
weapons 29, 41–2, 58, 108, 119, 123–
   4, 127, 130, 132, 134, 138–40, 143–
   4, 156, 158, 164, 168, 174
wear patterns 28–9, 139
weaving 16–17, 30, 34, 102–3, 144,
   147–8
Wessex Culture 127–9
Western societies *see* societies
Wetwang, England 170–1
wheat 78–80, 85–6, 91, 98
wheel 100
Whiting, J. 94
Willendorf, Venus of 36, 68
women as:
   arbiters and negotiators 163
   farmers 81, 83, 91, 99, 113, 135,
      141, 154
   foragers 156, 172
   gatherers 47, 51–9, 172
   healers 151, 163
   honey gatherers 55–6
   house builders 62
   hunters 14, 29–30, 43, 53, 55, 156,
      177
   leaders 11, 63, 113, 126, 164–71,
      173
   potters 32–4

priestesses 112, 157, 173
prophets 151, 157
providers of food 11, 51–9, 61, 76,
   90, 93, 103, 155, 163, 172
ritual specialists 11, 113, 135, 151,
   173
spinners and weavers 16, 102–3,
   148
teachers 49, 106
tool inventors 48, 99
tool-makers 55
warriors 151, 162–4
women: exchange of 129, 135, 136–9;
   high-status 10, 11, 118; low-
   status 10, 11, 118, 136, 173;
   powerful 11, 98, 113, 118, 157; role
   of in evolution 9, 41–50
women's history 7, 8, 10
wood, preservation of 12, 58, 62, 114,
   143
wood: tools 62; vessels 87, 145
wool 102, 119, 153
workshops 34, 114, 144–5
written records 10–12, 21–3, 63–4, 73,
   99, 110, 142, 148, 151–9, 162–8,
   172, 176

Yugoslavia 150–1

Zeeland 138
Zihlman, A. 41
Zuni 75